NATIONAL BROADCASTING UNDER SIEGE

By the same author

THE KNOWLEDGE ELITE AND THE FAILURE OF PROPHECY
BUREAUCRACY AND DEMOCRACY
SOCIAL CHANGE
POLITICAL MANIPULATION AND ADMINISTRATIVE POWER
POLITICAL CULTURE IN ISRAEL (*with Rina Shapira*)

National Broadcasting Under Siege

A Comparative Study of Australia, Britain, Israel and West Germany

Eva Etzioni-Halevy
Reader and Senior Research Fellow in Sociology
The Australian National University, Canberra

St. Martin's Press   New York

© Eva Etzioni-Halevy 1987

All rights reserved. For information, write:
Scholarly & Reference Division,
St. Martin's Press, Inc., 175 Fifth Avenue, New York, NY 10010

First published in the United States of America in 1987

Printed in Hong Kong

ISBN 0-312-00772-8

Library of Congress Cataloging-in-Publication Data
Etzioni-Halevy, Eva
National broadcasting under siege:
Bibliography: p.
Includes index.
1. Public broadcasting—Australia. 2. Public broadcasting—Great Britain. 3. Public broadcasting—Israel. 4. Public broadcasting—Germany (West) I. Title
HE8689.6.E89 1987   384.54   87-4702
ISBN 0-312-00772-8

Contents

Preface vii
Abbreviations and Translations xi

PART I   INTRODUCTION

1 Framework of the Analysis — 3
2 Historical Setting — 11
3 Ambiguities in Legal Status, Rules and Norms — 24

PART II   EXTERNAL POLITICAL PRESSURES

4 External Pressures through Direct Intervention — 41
5 External Pressures through Funding — 58
6 External Pressures through Privatisation — 71
7 External Pressures through Appointments — 89

PART III   INTERNAL POLITICAL PRESSURES

8 Internal Pressures from the Board, from Management and from Peers — 109
9 Internal Pressures through Appointments and Promotions — 127
10 Internal Pressures through Dismissal, Demotion and Displacement — 143

PART IV   RESISTANCE TO PRESSURES, FRICTION AND CONFLICT

11 Resistance to Pressures (I) — 163
12 Resistance to Pressures (II) — 175
13 Friction and Conflict – Some Case studies — 188

Conclusion 204
References 213
Index 219

Preface

This comparative study of national, public broadcasting corporations in Western-style democracies casts its net both narrowly and widely. Narrowly – in that it is not concerned with broadcasting corporations in their totality but only with their relationships with political structures: the political pressures exerted on them, their reactions to those pressures and the resulting tensions and conflicts. Widely – in that national broadcasting corporations are both instruments of mass media and bureaucratic-type organisations. Hence a study of their relations with politics in a democracy should hold a message for students of mass media and for students of bureaucracy, as well as for all those concerned with the problems and dilemmas connected with the exercise of power in Western democracy. As a four-country study it should afford observers an insight into these problems in countries other than their own; in the countries under study it should also afford observers an additional vantage-point on what is happening in their own backyards by presenting it in a comparative perspective.

As a study of political pressures on broadcasting it is confined to Western-style democracies because only in these countries do such pressures create practically insoluble dilemmas for politicians, broadcasters, and thus for the political system. This analysis does not purport to answer the question of whether such pressures are legitimate or illegitimate; its purpose is neither to praise nor to condemn them. Rather, its task is to document these pressures and the problems and dilemmas that surround them.

Since this study is confined to Western-style democracies the first problem that had to be faced was: which countries could or could not be selected for study. By the definition of democracy adopted here (and presented in Chapter 1) only a small number of countries could be included.

As the study is concerned with national public (rather than with commercial, or voluntarily funded) broadcasting, one major Western democracy which has no such broadcasting system – namely the USA – had to be excluded. Budgetary and time constraints made it necessary to limit the study to four countries only, and of those, it was thought best to choose two countries with relatively large, and two with relatively small populations. Also, for reasons that will become clear later, the choice had to fall on two countries with party-politicised bureaucracies and on two countries with non-partisan bureaucracies. Language and personal constraints narrowed the choice even further and the final selection was as follows:

Size of population	*Type of bureaucracy*	
	Non-partisan	Party-political
Relatively large	Britain	Federal Republic of Germany
Relatively small	Australia	Israel

This choice raises the question whether West German democratic processes, having been disrupted by twelve years of Nazi rule, may still be considered democratic. According to some views, democracy is like virginity: once disrupted, it is rather difficult to reinstate. The fact is, nonetheless, that in the postwar period, West German political processes have borne a marked resemblance to political processes in other Western countries; during this time-span they may be seen to fit the criteria of Western democracy as set out in the definition below – no less than do the other countries included in the study. Ultimately, of course, the appropriateness of the selection must be left for the reader to judge.

The study is based on a combination of two methods: analysis of documents, press reports and other written material and in-depth interviews with key informants. In all, eighty interviews have been conducted, with a minimum of seventeen interviews in and about each of the broadcasting corporations under study; many of these interviews were lengthy and most informative. Since in West Germany public broadcasting is decentralised into a relatively large number of broadcasting stations, interviews have been conducted with media experts on German public broadcasting in general and with key informants at West Germany's only domestic nation-wide broadcasting station, the second television channel – ZDF.

I would like to take this opportunity to thank the respondents for their co-operation, without which this study would have been impossible. The commitment to preserve anonymity makes it impossible to mention them all by name, and I must ask them to accept this general statement as an expression of personal indebtedness to each and every one of them. Also, because of the commitment to preserve anonymity, the authorship of respondents' statements – cited throughout the book – could be listed only where permission was expressly granted. And thus, unfortunately, the paternity – or maternity – of many colourful descriptions and many incisive insights must remain undisclosed.

Part of this study was conducted while I was visiting the Department of Sociology, Tel-Aviv University and the Department of Sociology, the Research School of Social Sciences, the Australian National University. I would like to thank these departments for their kind and friendly hospitality. I would also like to thank my own department, the Department of Sociology, the Faculties, the Australian National University for its continuous support and encouragement. Special thanks are due to the Australian National University Faculties' Research Fund for its generous financial support which has made interviewing, including interviewing overseas, possible.

Finally I would like to express my indebtedness to Dr Hanna Herzog of Tel-Aviv University, to Mr Yosef Lapid, formerly of the Israel Broadcasting Authority, to Mr Poppe Berg of ZDF and to Mr John Cain of the BBC for their invaluable comments, to Ms Manjula Waniganayake, for her most intelligent and skilful interviewing at the Australian Broadcasting Corporation, to Ms June Adams, Ms Allison Compston, Ms Michele Robertson and Mr Lee Byrgrave for their excellent research assistance and to Mesdames Julie Myers, Angela E. Grant and Beverley Bullpitt for their patience and skill in typing and retyping the manuscript.

Canberra   EVA ETZIONI-HALEVY

Abbreviations and Translations

ABC   Australian Broadcasting Corporation (before 1983: Commission)
Al Hamishimar – *On Guard* (an Israeli newspaper)
ARD   Arbeitsgemeinschaft der öffentlich-rechtlichen Rundfunkanstalten der Bundesrepublik Deutschland (the association of West German public broadcasting corporations)
ASIO   Australian Security Intelligence Organisation
BBC   British Broadcasting Corporation
BETA   Broadcasting Entertainments Trade Alliance (Britain)
BR   Bayrischer Rundfunk (Bavarian Broadcasting Corporation, Munich, West Germany)
Bundestag the West German Federal Parliament
CDU   Christlich Demokratische Union (Christian Democratic Union, West Germany)
CSU   Christlich Soziale Union (Christian Social Union, Bavaria, West Germany)
DLF   Deutschlandfunk (German Broadcasting – radio station for European listeners – West Germany)
DW   Deutsche Welle (German Wave – radio station broadcasting abroad, West Germany)
Frankfurter Allgemeine Zeitung – General Frankfurt Newspaper
FDP   Freie Demokratische Partei (Free Democratic Party – West Germany)
Freundeskreise – 'circles of friends'
Gremien   (supervisory) bodies
Ha'aretz – *The Land* (an Israeli newspaper)
HR   Hessischer Rundfunk (Hessen Broadcasting Corporation, Frankfurt-am-Main, West Germany)
IBA   Independent Broadcasting Authority (Britain)
IRA   Irish Republican Army
ITV   Independent television (Britain)
Länder   the West German states

xii　　　　　　　*Abbreviations and Translations*

Likud　　Union (a union of right-wing parties, Israel)
Ma'ariv – *Evening Prayer* (an Israeli newspaper)
Mabat – *Look* (a television news programme – Israel)
Mazpen – Compass (an extremist political group, supporting the Palestine Liberation Organisation – Israel)
MI5　　　Military Intelligence 5.
NATO　　North Atlantic Treaty Organisation
ND　　　No Date
NDR　　Norddeutscher Rundfunk (North German Broadcasting Corporation, Hamburg, West Germany)
NSW　　New South Wales (one of the six Australian states)
NUJ　　National Union of Journalists (Britain)
RB　　　Radio Bremen (West Germany)
Sat　　　Satellite
SDP　　Social Democratic Party (Britain)
SDR　　Süddeutscher Rundfunk (South German Broadcasting Corporation, Stuttgart, West Germany)
SFB　　Sender Freies Berlin (Broadcaster Free Berlin, West Berlin)
Shinui – Change (a small left of centre party, Israel)
SPD　　Sozialdemokratische Partei Deutschlands (Social Democratic Party of Germany, West Germany)
Spiegel, Der – *The Mirror* (a West German magazine)
SR　　　Saarländischer Rundfunk (Broadcasting Corporation of the Saar, Saarbrücken, West Germany)
SWF　　Südwestfunk (South-west Broadcasting Corporation, Baden-Baden, West Germany)
TDT　　*This Day Tonight* (a current affairs programme, Australia).
WDR　　Westdeutscher Rundfunk (West German Broadcasting Corporation, Cologne, West Germany)
ZDF　　Zweites Deutsches Fernsehen (Second German Television Station, Mainz, West Germany)

Part I
Introduction

This part of the book presents the analytical framework of the analysis, the historical background and the legal and normative frameworks of the broadcasting systems under study.

1 Framework of the Analysis

National broadcasting corporations are instruments of mass media and also bureaucratic-type organisations. In both capacities they are of major importance for the distribution of power in a democracy. My own interest in broadcasting stems from my interest in bureaucracy and its strategic but problematic role in a democratic regime. For this, the role of the national public broadcasting corporation furnishes an apt example.

THEORETICAL BACKGROUND: SOME FEATURES AND DILEMMAS OF DEMOCRACY

This role can best be analysed in the framework of a democratic–élitist (or demo-élitist) perspective. Concerned mainly with the manner in which élite power is exercised in a democracy, this is a well-established but recently neglected perspective in political science and political sociology. Since pluralist–democratic theories have fallen out of grace, two paradigms have recently been competing for centre-stage in these disciplines: Marxist class theory and élite theory. Both, however, have a common deficiency: they have failed to work out a coherent theory of political regimes in general and of Western democracy in particular. Indeed, both have had little of significance to say about democracy.

In general, both Marxists and élitists see democracy as preferable to other regimes. Yet both argue that democratic rules and democratic elections have mainly symbolic value, conferring no real power on the public. Both argue that democracy is merely a system where you vote for the people who rule you: the ruling class in Marxist parlance, the ruling élite in élitist terms. One may well ask: if democracy is so innocuous, if it affords no real power to the public, why is it preferable to other regimes?

The demo-élitist perspective as here presented, addresses itself precisely to this question. In doing so it attempts to

3

integrate elements of élite theory with elements of the pluralist theory of democracy. In this, it follows in the footsteps of Mosca (1939), Schumpeter (1976), Keller (1963) and Aron (1968, 1978). Its basic contention is that there is no inconsistency between democracy and élitism: élites are as necessary for democracy as they are for all political regimes. But the manner in which élites acquire power and exercise it are of the first order of importance. Following Schumpeter (1976) and Lipset (1965) democracy in its Western style is here defined as the institutional arrangement whereby two or more organised groups of people (or parties) participate in the contest for power and acquire such power through free elections by the whole of the adult population. Free elections, in turn, presuppose freedom of information, speech and organisation. Democracy, by this definition, is distinctive, because it is more effective than other known political regimes in curbing political élites' power, and therefore in the preservation of non-élites' rights.

Democracy restrains élites in the exercise of power, by certain 'rules of the game', whereby élites are confronted with an institutionalised, constantly recurring threat of replacement, with public scrutiny of their actions, and with constant exposure and demystification of their attempts to manipulate the public. Democratic rules also limit the political élites' power by confronting them in an institutionalised manner with the countervailing power of other élites, such as the opposition, the bureaucratic and judicial élites, or business élites and the leadership of trade unions.

At the same time, democracy is beset by dilemmas and internal contradictions which make it a rather precarious and fragile institutional structure. Also, and in connection with this, the rules of democracy are not always clearly defined; they are often ambiguous, inconsistent, controversial or all three.

The main dilemma that besets democracy stems from one of its major assets, from the fact that in it power countervails power: the power of incumbent political élites is counteracted by the power of other élites. This poses a problem for democracy, for while the incumbent political élite is democratically elected, the élites which countervail its power frequently are not, and their power is amassed in a non-democratic manner. As noted, however, this is also one of the major

Framework of the Analysis

devices through which democracy curbs the ruling élite's power. The absence or weakness of countervailing élites would thus obviate the very essence of democracy. The power of countervailing élites is thus one of the major weaknesses of democracy. But by the same token it is also one of the major assets of democracy: the power of countervailing élites poses a danger for democracy, but so does its absence.

This dilemma is well exemplified by the role of bureaucracy in a democratic regime. In previous analyses – *Bureaucracy and Democracy* (1985), *Political Manipulation and Administrative Power* (1979) – I have argued that bureaucracy has been widely (and justly) accused of jeopardising democracy because its non-elected élite frequently amassed great independent power as against that of elected politicians. Such accusations have been made by adherents to the 'technocratic' school of thought (see for instance Dogan, 1975; Ellul, 1965, Meynaud, 1964 and Peters, 1978) and by several Marxist scholars (see for instance Mandel, 1975; O'Connor, 1978 and Poulantzas, 1978). But although these scholars have not recognised this, a powerful, independent, bureaucracy is also necessary for the safeguarding of proper democratic procedures.

For the top of an independent, powerful bureaucracy is a major élite which countervails and thus curbs the power of the ruling political élite. Wherever the bureaucratic élite has lacked such independent power and has buckled down to the political élite – wherever bureaucracy has thus become party-politicised – it has become an instrument of political manipulation and corruption. In these cases it has been utilised for the handing-out of material benefits in return for political support, a type of manipulation which at times has greatly biased or obviated the democratic process. And only where bureaucracy has gained independent power as against that of politicians and has thus resisted the encroachment of party politics, has this electoral manipulation been eliminated and proper democratic procedures have come into force.

I have therefore presented the thesis that *bureaucracy poses a practically insoluble dilemma for democracy. A powerful, independent, bureaucracy poses a threat to democracy and yet is also a necessity for its proper functioning*. And because the role of bureaucracy in a democracy is so two-sided and problematic, the rules governing bureaucratic behaviour are unclear and even self-contradictory.

By democratic 'rules of the game' bureaucracy is supposed to be both politically neutral and under the control of elected politicians, both politically independent and politically responsive at one and the same time. And this ambiguity of rules, in turn, not only results in role-conflicts for both bureaucrats and politicians but is also instrumental in fostering actual struggles amongst and between them, as both politicians and bureaucrats interpret the rules to suit the promotion of their own interests.

To be sure, politics, by definition involves power struggles. Indeed, in a democracy these struggles are institutionalised and built into the very structure of the system. It has therefore been argued that the struggles between bureaucrats and politicians form a normal, 'healthy' part of the system. But as noted, in a democracy, power struggles are usually circumscribed by 'rules of the game' which mitigate them and many are arbitrated by the electoral process. By contrast the struggles surrounding bureaucracy occur at a point at which the rules and norms are ambiguous and controversial, and they cannot be resolved through elections. Hence, they have the potential of being particularly ruthless and disruptive.

DILEMMAS OF BROADCASTING IN A DEMOCRACY

In the present study I apply these arguments to national broadcasting. It is true that (unlike some other parts of the bureaucracy) broadcasting corporations are not in control of large-scale material resources and cannot allocate material benefits on any significant scale. Hence they cannot be utilised for electoral manipulation in the same manner as can be other parts of the bureaucracy, but since they are also instruments of mass media, they can be utilised for *symbolic* manipulation or propaganda both before and between elections.

Whether such manipulation may actually be effective is another matter. On the basis of research carried out in the 1950s and 1960s, social scientists had long argued that the effect of the media on public opinion is rather limited, and serves mainly to reinforce existing attitudes. More recently, however, the consensus amongst social scientists has been that the media, including the electronic media, do have a more substantial effect on public opinion than was previously believed, especially in making the public aware of, and focusing its interest on, certain issues which, for their part, may work in favour of or against certain parties, politicians or the government of the day. Moreover, whether broadcasting has an impact on public opinion or not, politicians generally tend to believe that it does – and act accordingly.

It follows that if a national broadcasting corporation is under the control of elected, incumbent politicians, it can be put under pressure by those politicians to adopt a political bent in its news and public affairs programmes designed to aid the ruling party or the government with the aim of keeping it in power indefinitely. Hence the crucial importance of the broadcasting corporation's independence from that government.

On the other hand, those staffing the broadcasting corporations (like bureaucrats) form a non-elected élite. Hence it would certainly be contrary to democratic principles if they obtained and retained significant power over, and exempt from, the control of elected politicians. This could occur, for instance, if the broadcasting corporation were allowed to espouse an overt or covert political line – authorised by no one but its own (senior or junior) staff.

Thus I argue that the same dilemmas which pervade the relationship between bureaucracy and democracy, reappear in the case of the relationship between broadcasting corporations and democracy.

SOME THESES AND HYPOTHESES

In this context I argue first, that for a national broadcasting corporation to be politically independent is both a necessity and a threat to democracy.

For the same reasons I argue that a national broadcasting corporation will be expected to be both politically independent and politically accountable; both controlled by the government and uncontrolled by the government at one and the same time.

This ambiguity of rules and norms makes it possible for politicians to promote their interest by exerting a variety of pressures on broadcasting people. The same ambiguity of rules and norms, however, also makes it possible for broadcasting people to promote their interests by resisting such pressures.

Hence, this self-contradiction of rules, is likely to bring forth or exacerbate a variety of tensions, conflicts and struggles between the political élites and the broadcasting élites, and also within the political and broadcasting élites themselves.

It has sometimes been argued that the pressures which politicians exert on broadcasting are legitimate in a democracy, as are the attempts of broadcasting people to resist such pressures. Thus the erstwhile BBC director-general, Hugh Greene, is often quoted as saying: 'There are no improper pressures; only improper responses.' And Kellner (1985, p. 10) wrote of 'the sacred right of ministers to tell the media "say this" or "ban that" and the equally sacred duty of the media to reply: "get lost" '. It follows that, as Kellner also wrote, it 'is not merely inevitable but *desirable* that those roles conflict'. In other words, the struggles between politicians and broadcasters are a normal, even desirable part of democracy.

My argument, however, is that because the rules and norms that surround broadcasting are ambiguous, it is never clear whether the political pressures exerted on broadcasters are indeed legitimate within the respective normative frameworks of their countries. Moreover, in many cases, while subtle and devious, such pressures can become quite pervasive. And since pressures from incumbent politicians are backed up by the power of office they can also become quite formidable – effectively putting national public broadcasting under siege.

To be sure, once pressures are applied, the attempts to resist them serve to countervail the power of ruling élites and the resulting struggles thus form a 'healthy' part of democracy and of broadcasting in a democracy. But because attempts to resist pressures (like the pressures themselves) are not governed by clear norms and rules, and because the resulting conflicts have no institutionalised resolution within a democratic framework, they can become quite relentless. They may exact a heavy price in terms of the sheer time and energy expended on altercation, in terms of undermining national broadcasting corporations' self-confidence and in threatening to diminish their public role and stature. To a large extent, this is precisely what has been happening in recent years.

Thus far the general framework of the study. In addition I have formed the following hypothesis: since a public national broadcasting corporation exists in the same normative framework and in the same political arena as the government bureaucracy, it is likely to have some features in common with it. Hence it is to be expected that countries that have party-politicised bureaucracies are also more likely to have party-politicised public broadcasting corporations as compared with other countries where the bureaucracies have become largely non-partisan. To put it differently: a country in which the bureaucracy is subject to party-political pressure and has not gained independence from politicians is also likely to have a public broadcasting service that is under greater political pressure and/or is more likely to buckle down to political pressure – as compared with a country where the bureaucracy has a position that is more independent from elected politicians.

To test this hypothesis, national public broadcasting corporations in two countries with largely non-partisan bureaucracies – Britain and Australia – and in two countries with party-politicised bureaucracies – West Germany and Israel – were included in this study. It is now generally agreed that no bureaucracy is totally non-political as the very formulation of policy – in which the bureaucracy is necessarily involved – has political and frequently party-political connotations. Nonetheless, when a comparative perspective is employed, some Western bureaucracies, particularly Britain and Australia, emerge as notably less party-politicised than other Western bureaucracies including West Germany and Israel.

The relatively non-partisan character of the British and Australian bureaucracies has been documented, for instance, in Etzioni-Halevy (1979 and 1985). With respect to the British bureaucracy, recently some commentators have seen in the top Thatcher appointments and promotions evidence of politicisation (Wass, 1985) and in Australia the present Labor government has introduced reforms that also seem to be leading to somewhat greater politicisation in the bureaucracy. These include granting power to the government to appoint and remove heads of departments (secretaries) at will, and the creation of a Senior Executive Service that is open to outside competition and whose members can be moved around more easily than senior public servants could be moved before. According to several observers, this has already led to a few scores of appointments which owe their genesis not to merit but to political affiliation (*The Australian*, 19 December 1984, p. 7;

Barnett, 1985). Still, the British and Australian bureaucracies remain less party-politicised than their counterparts in most Western countries.

The party-political character of the Israeli and West German bureaucracies has also been well documented. That of the Israeli bureaucracy has been documented, for example, in Etzioni-Halevy (1979, 1985) and that of the West German bureaucracy has been documented for instance by Seeman (1980, 1981); von Beyme (1983, p. 152) and Rowat (1985). On this basis, then, I have formed the hypothesis that West German and Israeli public broadcasting would be subject and amenable to political pressure to a greater extent than British and Australian public broadcasting.

PLAN OF THE BOOK

The book is structured around the outlined theses. The first part is introductory. Besides the analytical framework presented in this chapter it presents the historical and legal-normative setting of broadcasting, focusing on the ambiguity of laws, rules and norms surrounding broadcasting in each of the countries studied. The second and third parts of the book document the political pressures exerted on broadcasting: Part II documents the external pressures exerted *by politicians* on broadcasting corporations and their staff while Part III documents the internal pressures exerted *on behalf of politicians* mainly by the broadcasting corporations' upper echelons on their staff. Part IV reviews the resources and devices which broadcasters have at their disposal to resist such pressures, and the use they make of them; it also illustrates the resulting tensions and struggles. In the conclusion the book's theses and the hypothesis presented before are re-examined in light of the study.

2 Historical Setting

This book is concerned with the present – not with the past; it does not purport to offer a comprehensive historical analysis. This chapter's objective is more modest: to present the mere rudiments of the historical background of the broadcasting systems under study without which recent developments in them would be incomprehensible. For this purpose, a look at the historical setting of the British Broadcasting Corporation must be the first in line. For not only was it the first among the four broadcasting systems to be established, but it was also emulated by its three younger counterparts – though with varying degrees of determination and success.

BRITAIN

The British Broadcasting Corporation was established on 1 January 1927. It was the direct successor of the British Broadcasting Company which had been formed in 1922 as a consortium of manufacturers of domestic wireless receiving sets. The newly-established body was now set up as a public corporation under Royal Charter, deriving its authority from the King in Council. This constitutional device was adopted in order to distance the corporation from the government and from parliament, although ultimately it was to be responsible to them.

Designed to provide public service broadcasting of a high quality the BBC enjoyed a monopoly until 1955, when commercial broadcasting was introduced. Initially, the BBC was put under the control of the Postmaster General, but in 1974, broadcasting matters were transferred to the Home Office, and the Home Secretary became the minister responsible for broadcasting. As the minister in charge of the BBC at the time of its establishment, the Postmaster General assumed the task of framing its legal basis. And, despite the fact that the BBC was meant to be distanced from the government, he provided himself with overriding formal powers over transmissions and the content of programmes: among other things, he could require the BBC to broadcast or to refrain from broadcasting any matter as he saw fit.

The powers with which the Postmaster General endowed himself have only rarely been used in practice; they have never been used publicly or officially. This was hardly necessary, however, as a *modus vivendi* between the BBC and the government was eventually reached. According to Briggs (1961 and 1965), the director-general of the British Broadcasting Company, who then became the director-general of the British Broadcasting Corporation, John Reith, was particularly concerned that the BBC should not be subject to political interference. But according to Burns (1977, chap. 1) in 1926 Reith wrote a memorandum to the Prime Minister in which he made it quite clear that the BBC could be relied upon to support the government. And during the 1926 General Strike the BBC achieved a delicate balance: it insisted on defining its own position, while still giving support to the government against the unions (Briggs, 1961, pp. 360 ff).

Burns further reports than when the BBC was founded the Postmaster General instructed the corporation not to broadcast on matters of political, industrial or religious controversy, and not to broadcast an opinion of its own on matters of public policy. During the first years of its existence the government exercised fairly strict control over it in these matters (Howard, 1982), despite the fact that the Crawford Report (1926) and later on, the Ullswater Report (1936) recommended editorial autonomy.

Broadcasts by political parties effectively began in 1929. But it took seven years – including two years of a Labour government – for the situation to ease sufficiently for the opposition to be given a chance to respond to 'political' (as distinct from 'ministerial') broadcasts by government representatives. But in 1933 parliament established the principle that as far as elections and major political issues are concerned, broadcasting was to be shared equally between the major political parties; gradually this developed into a convention to which the BBC still adheres today.

This does not imply, however, that the BBC had now become independent from the government. According to Briggs (1979, chap. 4), in the 1930s there were cases of proposed broadcasts that were cancelled after government interference. Also, there were frequent objections in the House to what were labelled BBC errors in judgement and lapses in taste. This reinforced the propensity of senior BBC officials to exercise self censorship.

According to Briggs (1965, p. 422) in the 1930s Reith was extremely successful in his efforts to avoid detailed government and parliamentary control of the BBC and he had managed to ensure its virtual autonomy. But Burns (1977, p. 20) argues that at the time the BBC manifested its 'complete failure to wrestle free from its political swaddling clothes' and that this was because Reith did not make the attempt: he was ambitious for higher office and was loath to jeopardise his prospects. In the late 1930s the relations between the BBC and the government were exemplified by the fact that the newly established foreign news service was instructed to tell the truth, yet Foreign Office guidance was to be sought on all complex issues of policy. As will be seen later on, remnants of this system are still in existence.

Frederick Ogilvie succeeded Reith as director-general in 1938. According to Ezard (1985) in a revealing note in 1939, Ogilvie listed the frustrations with the government bequeathed to him by his predecessor, which still plagued the BBC:

> The transmission system (covered only by the blessed formula national security), the failure of MI5 to okay our artists at reasonable speed, racketeering by Cabinet Ministers over their talks, the important restrictions upon the Opposition.... etc.

In his reference to MI5 Ogilvie was alluding to security vetting of BBC candidates and personnel around which a scandal was to erupt in 1985 (see Chapters 4 and 13).

By the account of Ezard (1985, p. 17) at that time, plans were also set into motion for the BBC to be taken over during the war, and the corporation came 'within a sliver' of becoming a state propaganda outlet. In the event (although the BBC was put under the control of the Ministry of Information from 1939 to 1941) this did not happen, and a semi-independence was preserved. Briggs (1970, p. 11) described this semi-independence thus: 'The British government was in the background – with its own preoccupations and policies – yet the government did not broadcast itself. Each group within the BBC might be influenced ... by the policy of the British government ... yet each group had a measure of initiative and enterprise.'

In the post-war years, the BBC's tendency to distance itself from the government clearly increased, as became evident during the 1956 Suez crisis. At that time, Briggs (1979, chap. 4) recounts, when BBC radio refused to broadcast a talk by Australian Prime Minister Robert Menzies in support of government policy, the British Prime Minister Anthony Eden called up his friend the chairman of the BBC and matters were speedily rectified. Yet the BBC insisted on giving air-time to opposition as well as to government views despite a downpour from government politicians and threats of direct government takeover (Paulu, 1981, pp. 38–9). After 1959, with Greene as director-general, the BBC developed an even greater self-assertiveness. A new genre of talks and current affairs programmes was created, characterised by irreverence and criticism of the establishment. Not surprisingly, the BBC had to weather various traumatic storms, resulting not only from political pressures but also from public outrage over these programmes.

AUSTRALIA

In Australia both government-financed radio stations and private stations financed by commercial advertising had been in existence since 1923. In 1929–30 the former were taken over by the Australian Broadcasting Company. This company, in turn, was replaced by the Australian Broadcasting Commission, inaugurated on 1 July 1932.

According to the Dix Report (1981, vol. 2, p. 85) the ABC like most other Australian institutions which came into being before the Second World War, was modelled directly on its British counterpart. Like the BBC, the ABC was to provide high-quality public-service broadcasting, and to be distanced to some extent from government and from parliament, though ultimately accountable to parliament (Davis 1985, pp. 24–9).

One difference between the BBC and the ABC was that the former was distanced from parliament through its establishment under a Royal Charter. This was a constitutional device not available in Australia and hence the ABC was created by act of parliament, but distanced from it through its assuming the form of a statutory authority (Davis, 1985, p. 9). Another very real difference was that while the BBC initially enjoyed a monopoly over broadcasting, the ABC had to face competition from commercial broadcasters from the outset.

By law, the government could require the commission to broadcast, or to refrain from broadcasting, any matter. Apart from that, the commission would have the right to determine which political speeches were to be broadcast. Even so, up to the Second World War, there seemed to have been no clear conception within the ABC of either the right or the duty of preserving its independence. Thus, Inglis (1983, p. 31) recounts that in 1934 when a speaker submitted a draft commentary containing derogatory references to politicians as a class, the then general manager Walter Conder 'ruled that it was "scarcely the Commission's place to criticize the actions of the constituted government". Conder often invoked that principle . . . speakers got to know the rules.' And Thomas (1980, p. 91) wrote: 'it was a compliant institution during its formative years, and its compliance created a tradition . . . that has continued to affect ABC operations to this day'. In this context Inglis (1983) further recounts that in 1937, Judge A. W. Foster was invited to give a talk on the ABC on freedom of speech. In the script he criticised (among other things) provisions for wartime censorship. He was requested to remove the offending passages but refused writing: 'It is a little humorous perhaps . . . to contemplate a broadcast upon free speech under restrictions that are so obviously a denial of it' (Inglis, 1983, p. 62). And H. G. Wells, on a visit to Australia, made severe remarks on the censorship of broadcasting in this country, but concluded that the ABC was 'less degraded on the whole than the BBC' (Inglis, 1983, p. 63).

According to Inglis (chap. 2) the tradition nevertheless gradually developed whereby (more than the critics knew) the commission defended speakers, and the chairman stood up against political interference. By the late 1940s government guidance was still accepted for overseas broadcasts, but not for domestic programmes. In the early 1930s 'controversy was something to be either avoided or assembled with care' (Inglis, 1983, pp. 30–1) and the government occasionally intervened to stop controversial broadcasts. But by the late 1940s the convention had developed whereby the ABC took great pain to give representation to both government and opposition viewpoints and to avoid political bias, and in the post-war years arranged political debates on controversial topics – though in a moderate and balanced manner – were allowed on the air.

One of the differences between Britain and Australia was in the government departments that were responsible for broadcasting. Initially the ABC, like its British counterpart, had been under the auspices of the Postmaster General. After Labor's election in 1972 a new Department of the Media was created and made responsible for the ABC. The Liberal government, elected in 1975, scrapped that department and put the ABC back with the Department of Posts and Telephones, a decision once more reversed by Labor: when it came to office in 1983 it created a Department of Communications and put it in charge of the ABC. Thereby problems for broadcasting independence created in Britain by the BBC being in the charge of the Home Office (see Chapter 13) were avoided in Australia.

While the ABC had adopted an ethos of impartiality among political parties, there was nonetheless a view among respondents that until the 1960s the ABC had been a generally conservative institution. But as one respondent recalled, in the 1960s and 1970s, people were brought in with the express purpose of shaking the ABC out of its inertia. As a result, pockets of radicalism developed, especially in current affairs programmes. According to Inglis (1983, chaps 6, 7 and 8) this resulted in adverse reactions from rightist politicians and commentators but in supportive reactions from the left. It thus opened the ABC to pressures and counterpressures and brought about a new set of dilemmas for the commission and management, remnants of which were still evident in the 1980s.

ISRAEL

The Israeli Broadcasting Service had its beginnings in 1936, during the British mandate over Palestine. The Palestine Broadcasting Service (as it was then called) was 'very much a BBC creation' (Samuel, 1970, p. 198). But the British mandatory authorities made no attempt to accord it BBC-like independence. Initially, the service was part of the Department of Posts and Telegraphs. In 1945 a separate Department of Broadcasting was created, under the directorship of Edwin Samuel. According to Samuel's (1970, chap. 11) testimony he was concerned with maintaining control of the service while giving it enough leeway to develop its own high-quality programmes. Government control of the service is also attested by Gotliffe (1981, pp. 26–7), and by the testimony of an old-timer who was then a member of staff of the institution, there was strong censorship and total government determination of broadcasts. From the analysis of Mish'al (1978) we learn that this did not go over smoothly, as broadcasters had already developed strong aspirations for independence. Consequently, there was much tension between the government and the broadcasters, which occasionally peaked in a manifest rupture between them.

With the establishment of the state of Israel in 1948, radio – now called 'The Voice of Israel' – became a unit in the Prime Minister's department. The leader and Prime Minister at the time, David Ben Gurion, held a conception of statehood as a unifier of society, and of broadcasting as an instrument of such statehood. Hence he had no compunction in having the state – and in practice the government – press its stance on broadcasting and mete out continuous 'guidance' to news and current-affairs programmers. According to Mish'al (1978) the broadcasting staff, who had been rebellious under British rule, now accepted the government's authority voluntarily, not least because of their ideological affinity with that government. But by the recollection of the old-timer who had witnessed these events, broadcasting journalists did not always accept government control uncomplainingly and there were protests at times. Both agree that at that time there was far-reaching government control of both the organisation and the content of broadcasting.

In the 1960s this situation changed, as the ruling Labour Party suffered severe internal conflict and eventually split into two – with Ben Gurion now heading one of the rival camps. As long as the party's leadership had been strong and united it had had no great difficulty in eliciting obedience from the broadcasting service. But this was no longer the case when a rupture in the ruling élite emerged, and the broadcasting service became the focus of a struggle between the rival factions. As each faction – and especially Ben Gurion's supporters – had to face the possibility of broadcasting's subordination to its rival, greater broadcasting independence seemed the logical solution. As broadcasters sensed the new vulnerability of their political masters, and as they also perceived the need to guard their own interests by maintaining a balance between the rival camps they, too, pushed for greater autonomy. According to Mish'al (1978), this struggle was the beginning of the process which culminated in the creation of the Israel Broadcasting Authority as a public corporation.

By 1965, when the Broadcasting Authority Act was passed, Ben Gurion and his followers had seceded from the ruling Labour party forming their own splinter party. But the ruling party, now under the leadership of Levi Eshkol, was still faction-ridden. Eshkol's group wished to maintain a grip over broadcasting yet feared that its rivals would take over. For its part, the opposition both within and outside the party, pressed to remove broadcasting from the control of the establishment from which it was excluded. According to Mish'al the creation of the broadcasting authority was the result of a convergence of these opposing interests. The move for greater broadcasting independence thus resulted not so much from a clear ideological commitment but from a power struggle that created a balance among various feuding political forces. Nonetheless, Israel had adopted several aspects of the British legal tradition and, Mish'al further writes, the BBC's legal framework constituted the model on which the drafters of the Israel Broadcasting Authority Bill had drawn. The old-timer who had witnessed these events, testified that this had indeed been the case.

The new law, which provided that the Minister of Education and Culture be in charge of its execution, was rather vague. Hanoch Givton, director of 'The Voice of Israel', regarded it as 'topsy turvey' and as creating equivocal lines of authority (Gotliffe, 1981, p. 92) and many others seemed to agree with him. Following its enactment the struggle therefore focused on its interpretation. The result was a compromise – not provided for in the Act itself – whereby the authority's main controlling body, the board of directors, came to be composed of representatives of the major political parties in proportion to their strength in parliament. This composition has made it possible for broadcasters to manoeuvre between the opposing political forces on the board and thereby to gain a greater measure of independence from the governing body than would otherwise have been the case.

According to Salpeter and Elizur (1973, pp. 305–6) these struggles were reflected in the internal workings of the corporation as well. Instead of the institutional structure which was supposedly designed to ensure broadcasting independence but could not, the pressures and counter-pressures of different interest groups, both on the board and on the outside, came into play. Those, and the difficulty of controlling a rather unwieldy organisation, limited the government-appointed director-general's ability to introduce pronounced political bias into broadcasting.

By the testimony of Aharonson (1983) the same situation was reflected in the establishment of television as part of the broadcasting authority in the late 1960s. Neither the minister in charge of setting up the medium, nor those who actually undertook the task had a clear conception of what they aimed to achieve. Therefore the setting-up process was characterised by improvisation and the lack of clear guidelines for action. According to Gotliffe (1981, p. 462) newly-established television was an organisation where decision-making lacked consistency and assignment of responsibility was unclear. The result was disarray, lack of discipline and inordinate power wielded by employees and their associations. The further result was the clogging of channels for political pressures, and this constellation of factors has been exerting its influence on the medium – and on the authority – to this day.

WEST GERMANY

Regular radio transmissions in Germany began in 1923; within three years there were ten private broadcasting companies, each covering a part of the country. This regional character of broadcasting was terminated by the Nazis in 1933, when a central broadcasting organisation was established and put under the control of the Propaganda Ministry. But the West German broadcasting system as we know it today was established by the Western Allies in their respective zones of occupation. The Allies' main aim was to avoid a repetition of the Nazi experience and for this purpose they endeavoured to make broadcasting as independent from the state as possible. The British who were especially influential in shaping the system, endeavoured to follow the BBC model, although they recognised that this model could not be implemented in West Germany without far-reaching modifications.

The Allies framed a legal system which made broadcasting the concern of the Länder (states) rather than of the central government and which protected broadcasting from state control. They also provided broadcasting stations with constitutions (incorporated into state legislation) which were meant to ensure that broadcasting would be under public law, with control in the hands of representatives of the public, that is, of socially relevant groups (including political parties) rather than in the hands of the state (Williams, 1976, chap. 3; Wittich, 1983). The Allies supervised broadcasting directly until 1949, at which time they relinquished it into German hands. But the framework they bequeathed to West Germany – which Wittich (1983, p. 168) describes as a 'quasi-imposed democratic order' – in its basic elements, has been preserved to this day.

One of those elements was broadcasting's decentralised structure, as regional broadcasting stations were created. Most of these served only one state, or part thereof, the rest served two or more states (or parts thereof). The former were constituted by the enactment of one state alone; the latter were instituted by inter-state agreements. The size of the individual stations depended on the size of the audience in their respective regions. On this basis, the largest broadcasting concern now is Westdeutscher Rundfunk (WDR). Other large corporations are Norddeutscher Rundfunk (NDR) and Bayrischer Rundfunk (BR). Medium-sized networks include Hessischer Rundfunk (HR), Süddeutscher Rundfunk (SDR) and Südwestfunk (SWF). Small stations are Radio Bremen (RB), Saarländischer Rundfunk (SR) and Sender Freies Berlin (SFB). Besides the regional stations, two federal stations have been created: Deutschlandfunk (DLF) and Deutsche Welle (DW). Both broadcast only radio programmes, chiefly directed at other European countries.

Soon after their establishment it became evident that the stations would have to co-operate to surmount various common tasks. To this end, in 1950, the stations set up a working cooperative: Arbeitsgemeinschaft der öffentlich-rechtlichen Rundfunkanstalten der Bundesrepublik Deutschland (ARD). The co-ordination necessary for joint activities has been instituted through regular members' meetings and in special committees and commissions. Management of the ARD is carried out by its member-stations on a rotating basis, with the chairmanship changing biennially. ARD has been offering a joint television programme to which each member-station has been contributing in accordance with its size and financial resources.

According to Williams (1976, chap. 2) the 1950s were marked by a struggle over broadcasting between the broadcasting authorities and the states on the one hand and the federal government on the other hand. At that time the federal government under Chancellor Konrad Adenauer favoured federal legislation on broadcasting. Its argument was that standardisation was necessary to promote neutrality and fairness. But the move was opposed by the SPD, the Bavarian Party and the broadcasting stations' intendants. In the face of such formidable opposition the government did not press the point.

However, as Conrad (n.d.) reports, towards the end of the 1950s the Adenauer government was planning to establish a private television station financed by commercial advertising but under state control. In 1959 the government forged an alliance with a private company and commissioned it to start preparations for a second television channel. 'The alliance ... bore an uncanny resemblance to the Nazi link-up with big industry and the press' (Williams, 1976, p. 25). The regional stations objected and the states brought the matter before the Federal Constitutional Court. They protested against the contravention of the basic law edict whereby broadcasting was to be the concern of the states. In its verdict of February 1961 the court ruled that the federal government's attempt to establish television under private law violated the sovereignty of the states and the freedom of broadcasting anchored in the basic law (see Chapter 3). The court also confirmed the constitutional status of broadcasting as outside the control of the state. 'It is not difficult to detect in this an echo of the fear shared by the Allies that centralisation in broadcasting could be a first step on the road to another monopoly of German thought and life by a government or party' (Williams, 1976, p. 28).

Subsequently, the states decided to establish an alternative to ARD: a second joint nation-wide television broadcasting organisation which would be centralised, yet under state, not federal jurisdiction. This station was named Zweites Deutsches Fernsehen (ZDF) and was based in Mainz. It was set up on the basis of an inter-state treaty which came into effect on 6 June 1961; ZDF began broadcasting in April 1963, offering viewers a second television channel.

CONCLUSION

This brief and necessarily superficial retrospect has shown that, in one way or another, the BBC has served as a model for each of the other broadcasting corporations under study. In Australia the BBC model was followed as part of the British political tradition in general. In Israel, the antecedents of the present broadcasting system were established under British rule. Although the British authorities did not set out to transplant the BBC model of relative independence from government into that country, several aspects of the British legal system were adopted, and the BBC idea of broadcasting independence caught the imagination of broadcasters and legislators. And in West Germany the Allies (headed by the British) made an explicit effort to devise a broadcasting system which – like the BBC – would be public yet free from state control.

While all three broadcasting systems were influenced by the BBC, not all came to resemble it to the same extent. The ABC (despite some differences) developed most closely to the BBC model: in both Britain and Australia an institutional structure was set up designed to distance broadcasting from the state; in both countries (except in war-time) no attempt was made to bring broadcasting under direct government control. Yet in both countries the national broadcasting corporations were initially rather compliant institutions. Whatever traditions of independence eventually evolved, are thus of recent, generally post-war vintage.

The Israeli and West German broadcasting systems, though also modelled to some extent after the BBC, have had greater similarities to each other than they have had with their model: not only were both established under British rule, but in both countries the first leaders after independence – Ben Gurion in Israel and Adenauer in West Germany – endeavoured to keep or to bring broadcasting under direct government control. Eventually, both were unsuccessful, albeit for different reasons – in West Germany, because of the opposition of broadcasting personnel and state politicians and because of the steadfast position of the constitutional court; in Israel, because of power struggles in which the interests of major political factions and parties counterbalanced each other, yet converged in keeping broadcasting away from government control. In both Israel and West Germany direct government control was displaced by party-political representation on the broadcasting controlling bodies.

In all four countries, then, a certain distance of broadcasting from the state (or the government) has been achieved. In the following chapters it will be seen, however, that in none of the countries did a coherent legal and normative framework of broadcasting independence develop, and in none of the countries did broadcasting enjoy complete independence from government (and other political) interference in practice.

3 Ambiguities in Legal Status, Rules and Norms

It is a basic argument of this book that there are ambiguities in the legal frameworks and normative conceptions that govern broadcasting; that these ambiguities have made both political pressures on broadcasting and resistance to such pressures feasible; that they are thus a major factor in the creation of tensions and struggles that surround broadcasting. This chapter describes such ambiguities in the countries under study.

LEGAL AMBIGUITIES

Ambiguities are evident, in the first instance, in the corporations' legal status. Thus, the BBC has been constituted on a legal basis that would distance it to some extent from the government, but would yet grant the government some (circumspect) powers over the corporation. The form adopted for this purpose is that of the Royal Charter which sets up the broadcasting authority as a body corporate and requires it to acquire a licence from the Home Secretary.

The Royal Charter and the licence make no explicit provisions for BBC independence. Indeed, as Howard (1982, p. 6) clarifies, they contain provisions which contradict it and 'would make a nonsense of BBC independence if ever used in practice', but the BBC's own official handbook (BBC, 1985, p. 169) states: 'Subject to the law of the land and the obligations under the Charter and the Licence Agreement, the BBC is fully independent.'

The Licence reserves to the Secretary of State certain powers in relation to programmes. Under clause 13(4) of the Licence the Secretary of State may from time to time, by notice in writing, require the corporation to refrain from broadcasting any matters. But, the BBC handbook states: 'in practice, this has always been treated as a reserve power and ... the Corporation has enjoyed, and enjoys, complete freedom' (BBC, 1985, p. 170). A further requirement of the Licence (clause 13[3]) is that the BBC shall broadcast official announcements whenever requested to do so by a government minister. The BBC handbook, however, states that in practice the purposes of this clause are achieved without ministerial intervention.

Thus the Charter does not refer explicitly to BBC independence and the Licence provides for certain (albeit circumspect) powers of the government over the corporation and says nothing about BBC independence. By contrast, the BBC's own official publication emphasises the BBC's independence, while playing down the significance of the government powers over the corporation. These are differences in the definition of the situation, that may well open the door for clashes between the government and the corporation over the degree of its independence. According to Briggs (1979, p. 25) BBC independence is really based on convention rather than laws and regulations, and in the British tradition conventions are sometimes the more binding. But conventions must be anchored in norms, and as will be seen below, these too are ambiguous.

The ABC (like the BBC) is constituted on a legal basis that would distance it to some extent (though not completely) from the government and from political intervention. The form adopted in Australia for that purpose was that of the statutory authority, an instrument which 'allowed the organisation to be distanced from the government of the day while remaining subject to a measure of governmental – and parliamentary – control' (Dix, 1981, vol. 2, p. 85).

The legal status of the ABC is at present based on the Australian Broadcasting Corporation Act of 1983 which in turn is based on the Broadcasting and Television Act of 1942 and its successive amendments. Unlike the Royal Charter for the BBC, the Australian 1983 Broadcasting Act states explicitly that the duty of the ABC's board of directors is to maintain the corporation's independence. The board is obliged to ensure that any statement of policy furnished by the minister in charge shall be given consideration – but not that it shall be accepted or executed. However, under section 78 of the Act the minister may direct the corporation to broadcast any matter or to refrain from broadcasting any matter in line with national interest. Finally, the Act states that except as provided by this section or by another Act, the corporation is not subject to direction by the government, and it may determine by itself to what extent and in what manner political matter shall be broadcast.

According to some observers, neither the ABC's status as a statutory authority nor the pertinent legislative framework clearly define the degree of the corporation's independence. For although a statutory authority is expected to enjoy a degree of autonomy this is not always so in practice – as the Royal Commission of Inquiry into Australian Government Administration (the Coombs Commission) has acknowledged. While the legal definition of the board's duties requires it to safeguard the corporation's independence and permits it to make its own decisions as to political matter to be broadcast, it also enjoins it to consider ministerial policy statements and in some cases to accept ministerial directives.

The Report of the Committee of Inquiry into the ABC (the Dix Report) states that:

> A strong convention surrounding the ABC's editorial independence has provided additional support ... It is now accepted as a convention, irrespective of any legislative provisions ... that the Commission should not share responsibility with any other body for the content and composition of its programmes.

It adds, however, that '[t]his responsibility must be exercised within a framework of legal and other evolving standards' (Dix, 1981, vol. 2, p. 76). This addition, once more, seems to cloud rather than clarify the issue. What is more, some observers argue that in Australian politics conventions are not as firmly based as, for instance, in British politics.

The legal situation is even more ambiguous in Israel. The Broadcasting Authority Act enacted in 1965 (as amended in 1966, 1968 and 1973) provides that there shall be a minister, appointed by the government, in charge of executing this Act and that the government shall have the right to have its announcements and the announcements of the general staff of the military and of the civil defence authorities broadcast. The Act provides that in a state of national emergency the government shall be entitled to revoke the authority's powers as per this Act for no longer than 30 days (a time-span that the Foreign Affairs and Security Committee of Parliament may extend indefinitely).

Significantly, the Act lends the government no further prerogatives of interference. But by the same token (like the British Royal Charter but unlike the Australian Act) it makes no explicit provisions for the authority's independence from the government. Since the Act does not grant the authority any independence from government to begin with, it is not clear what there is to revoke in case of emergency.

The ambiguity of the Act is reflected in the variety of opinions expressed by various key informants on this Act. The opinion shared by several such informants was that the Israel Broadcasting Authority Act was modelled on the legal framework of the BBC, even though they all qualified this statement to some extent. Thus, a respondent who was himself a member of staff of the authority (and thus present) when the Act was passed testified: 'There was a clear conception at the time. The "Voice of Israel" would develop in continuity with the British pattern'; similarly Peleg (1981, p. 8) writes that from its inception '[t]he Israeli Broadcasting Authority sought, both in word and deed, to copy the British model of the BBC, with necessary modifications for conditions in Israel'.

Other experts, however, discern little resemblance between the legal framework of the Israel Broadcasting Authority and that of the BBC. Thus Hugh Greene (former director-general of the BBC) in his report on Israeli broadcasting (1973) wrote that the Israeli law lends much less independence to the Israel Broadcasting Authority than the British legal framework lends to the BBC. And a media expert Professor Shlomo Aharonson,[1] said: 'The Israel Broadcasting Authority Act is not modelled after the BBC. It is a hybrid creature, which came into being on the basis of a variety of political considerations', but former director-general, Yosef Lapid,[2] said: 'The independence of the broadcasting authority is expressed in that the law provides for a minister in charge of implementing the Broadcasting Act, but does not provide him with the authority to interfere in broadcasting'. Perhaps the experts' diverging opinions can best be explained by the illuminating comment of one respondent as follows: 'The Act is generally unclear. It is a masterpiece of hazy formulations.'

The basic legal framework for West German broadcasting

was created at the end of the 1940s under the influence of the Western Allies. Of these, the British had the clearest conception of the type of broadcasting they wished to construct. For that reason the legal basis of West German broadcasting is oriented chiefly towards the example of the BBC in its attempt to distance broadcasting from the state; it also drew on the beginning of radio during the Weimar Republic.

Though modelled on the BBC the West German legal framework for broadcasting differs from the British Royal Charter in that it clearly spells out broadcasting autonomy. Also, it makes broadcasting a matter for the Länder (the states) rather than for the central government, and thus sets the framework for a much more decentralised system of broadcasting. This is explicable by the fact that it was the Allies' overriding aim to preclude a repetition of the Nazi experience, and thus to make doubly sure that broadcasting enjoyed freedom from central state interference.

The constitutional basis for the freedom of West German broadcasting is article 5 of the Basic Law of the Federal Republic of Germany of 23 May 1949, which forbids the state (whether Federal or one of the Länder) to establish a broadcasting station or determine programmes; in other words it forbids state-controlled broadcasting. The article further states: 'Everyone has the right freely to express and to propagate his or her opinion in words, writing or images ... Freedom of the press and freedom of reporting by broadcasting and film are guaranteed. There shall be no censorship.' Further, the legal basis of broadcasting independence is to be found in the pronouncement of the Federal Constitutional Court of 1961 to the effect that: 'Broadcasting is the concern of the general public. It must be pursued in complete independence, in a non-partisan manner, and must be safeguarded against all forms of interference' (Federal Constitutional Court vol. 31, p. 327).

Within this legal framework the broadcasting corporations were thus constituted as self-administered corporations governed under public law (*öffentliches Recht*), in each state, or by inter-state agreements. For example, the ZDF's legal basis is the inter-state agreement of 1961. It provides that the ZDF be governed by public law and that it be legally independent.

It can thus be seen that of the four legal frameworks studied the West German one puts the most emphasis on broadcasting independence. Interestingly, however (as will be seen below) *it is precisely here, where the law is most adamant in safeguarding broadcasting independence, that broadcasting is beset by the most formidable political interference.* One explanation for this lies in the fact that the West German state laws and inter-state agreements governing broadcasting also provide for broadcasting to reflect the divergent political views existing in the community through the broadcasting corporations' supervisory organs (*Gremien*) in which those views (including the views of political parties) are to be represented (see Chapter 7). The German legislator has thus provided for an inherent contradiction: independence, coupled with political supervision.

AMBIGUITIES IN RULES AND REGULATIONS

Besides broadcasting laws, the broadcasting authorities investigated all have internal guidelines which go into more detail as to proper day-to-day broadcasting practice. Not surprisingly, ambiguities are evident here as well, although they have a different focus. They have to do mainly with the injunction upon broadcasters to maintain political objectivity, neutrality and balance, side by side with the injunction upon them to select, interpret and comment on political topics. It has to do with the injunction on staff to refrain from expressing their own opinions, side by side with the admission that complete desisting from value judgement is well-nigh impossible.

Thus, the BBC's *News and Current Affairs Index* (1980, p. 34) includes the injunction on the BBC 'to refrain from expressing its own opinion on current affairs or matters of public policy'. It further states that 'Specialist correspondents and reporters may, however, properly use their personal expertise to explain, interpret or summarise.' This raises the question how one may interpret without expressing or implying a personal opinion; whether the injunction to do the one without doing the other, is not a contradiction in terms.

In the Australian Broadcasting Corporation a new charter of editorial practice was adopted in July 1984. It includes the injunction on journalists to observe standards of balance, impartiality and fairness, and 'not to allow their professional judgement to be influenced by ... their own personal views'. Another guideline, however, states that '[i]mpartiality does not require editorial staff to be unquestioning ... News values and news judgements will prevail in reaching decisions, consistent with these standards' (*Journalist*, August, 1984, p. 7). This raises the question whether 'news judgements' can be made without being influenced by 'personal views'. As will be seen in Chapter 12 many staff members believe that this is impossible.

In Israel, a new edition of the Authority's *Guidelines for News and Current Affairs* came out in 1983. This document, too, is riddled with the same ambiguity. Among other things, it states: 'the broadcasting authority has no policy or viewpoint of its own. The authority will not broadcast "editorials"' (p. 3). It adds, however:

> In any case – it is mandatory to make a clear distinction ... between factual information ... on the one hand, and commentary ... on the other hand ... When professional reporting requires ... interpretation of facts, care ought to be taken not to come out with determinative statements (Israel Broadcasting Authority, 1983, p. 4).

Once again, these statements are inconsistent with one another. For in the first statement staff are enjoined to refrain from broadcasting 'editorials' and 'viewpoints', while in the second statement 'commentary' and 'interpretation' are allowed and even called for.

Perhaps the least ambiguous in this respect are the guidelines for programmes in the West German ZDF (of 11 July 1963) which state *inter alia*: 'The organisation is obliged to maintain non-partisanship ... when controversial views are expressed, expression must be given to the opposing views as well ... Value judgements must be identified as personal or editorial views.' But even here, the question of whose views must be expressed is left largely unanswered.

NORMATIVE AMBIGUITIES

Ambiguities are also evident in the norms held by the major participants: politicians and broadcasting people. In Britain, the norms affirming the independence of national broadcasting have been long-standing. But they have not necessarily been clear-cut. According to the BBC's own account (BBC, 1985, p. 170) the norms from which the independence of the BBC derives date back to the time before the Royal Charter was granted (in 1927) and have been reaffirmed by successive ministers on numerous occasions. But the lack of clarity with respect to BBC independence was also evident as early as the 1920s – for example, in the Crawford Committee's report which stated that the BBC should not be subject to 'continuing Ministerial guidance' but that the state, through parliament, must 'retain the right of ultimate control' (Crawford, 1926, Appendix II, para. 16). This, of course, raises the question where 'continuing guidance' ends and 'ultimate control' begins.

Respondents (including politicians) in this study generally expressed the view that the BBC should be independent. But a senior respondent qualified this view by saying that the BBC should be independent from government but accountable to parliament; independent in programming, but accountable financially. This gives rise to the question of whether these can, in fact, be kept separate. The same dilemma comes through in a leading article in the *Sunday Times* (25 August 1985, p. 14) on the Edinburgh Conference on broadcasting which took place at the time:

> The most fundamental question was never addressed: to whom are British broadcasters accountable? . . . although dependent on the favours of government, they do not think they should be accountable to it. Fine: few want state censorship . . . The alternative . . . is being accountable to the people . . .

This, in turn, raises the question, how can accountability to 'the people' be effected in practice? If 'the people' means parliament (where the government necessarily has a majority) the statement once again is open to the question: can accountability to government and to parliament in fact, be clearly separated in practice?

In Australia, according to Inglis (1983, p. 122) the first affirmation of broadcasting independence was made by the commission in the 1940s when it stated that it 'should not accept [the minister's] views as mandatory or accommodate itself to them against its independent judgement'. A similar affirmation came from Prime Minister John Curtin in 1945: 'the Government recognises that the intent of the Australian Broadcasting Act is to create a position of special independence of judgement and action for the national broadcasting instrumentality' (quoted in Dix, 1981, vol. 2, p. 72). Equivalent statements were made periodically in later years, for instance: 'The inquiry believes that the programming objectives set for the national service can only be achieved by maintaining the independent position of a Commission which is free from Government influence or intervention' (Green, 1976, par. 86). More recently, the leader of the (Labor) government in the Senate (Senator Button) said in the Senate: 'the Government is committed to the independence of the ABC' (*Canberra Times*, 5 May 1983, p. 1).

However, an alternative ideology has also been in evidence. For instance, in the Dix Committee of Inquiry into the ABC's Report (vol. 2, p. 71) we find the following: 'From the beginning of our review many people and organisations put the view to us that the publicly-owned ABC [should] not be a power unto itself. We share that opinion'.

There are thus differing views with respect to the ABC's independence. More importantly some pronouncements give direct evidence of the ambiguity surrounding the issue — for instance, the following statement in the Report of the Coombs Royal Commission of Inquiry on Australian Government Administration which pertains to statutory authorities (of which the ABC is one):

> The fact that a statutory body has been brought into being frequently signifies that a . . . decision has been taken to place the performance of a particular function outside the political sphere of influence or to relieve a minister and his department of immediate responsibility for it. But the fact that certain powers are reserved to the minister means that it is the Parliament's intention that the abdication of ministerial authority should not be complete . . . It has not been easy to devise statutory formulae which adequately express the desired balance . . . this difficulty has been compounded by the absence of any clear conception of what the minister's role should be (Coombs, 1977, p. 86).

Or the following statement from the previously-cited Dix

Ambiguities in Legal Status, Rules and Norms 33

Report (Dix, 1981, p. 71) as follows: 'while the public interest requires accountability of its instrumentalities, it also requires independence for a body such as the ABC'. The same divergence of opinion and ambiguity is evident in respondents' statements such as the following:

> I believe it should be independent. . . . to us it is the only really independent source [of information in Australia] and we have in the past and will in the future continue to defend it from attacks by politicians. I think, it should be right outside their fingers.
>
> It has to be accountable to the people . . . and I think the only practical way it can be is through the parliament. . . . I don't see any way around the proposition that . . . the ABC is publicly funded and therefore can't be a law unto itself.
> **Question:** So you are saying that it can't be completely independent?
> **Answer:** Yes I am.

Thus, some respondents were adamant that the ABC ought to be independent while another view was that it ought to be accountable. Still another view was that the ABC should be both independent and accountable. For example: 'Certainly I believe that the ABC should be independent but I also believe that it *has* to be accountable . . . for how it spends its funds . . . but [it should be able to] decide independently how [those funds are] utilised.' But is that, in fact, possible? In the opinion of some other respondents, it is not, and this creates a dilemma: 'I don't know what the answer to that is . . . I don't know whether there is any perfect solution.' Or in the words of a junior member of staff: 'The ABC should be independent. But it uses taxpayer's money . . . I really don't know.'

A similar divergence of opinions is evident in Israel. In a newspaper interview to mark his appointment, in 1968, the first director-general of the Israel Broadcasting Authority, Shmuel Almog, stated that the 'Voice of Israel' must be free of government or partisan interference, although it must preserve close co-ordination with the Foreign and Defence Offices on matters of foreign policy and security. Former director-general of the Israel Broadcasting Authority, Lapid, (whose term ran from 1979 to April 1984) made a similar, though more detailed statement in an interview: 'The essence of my role is to be independent from the government ... When you are appointed to a position like mine ... you know that for five years you must act so that later on you will not spit into your own face.' But a former right-wing member of the board of directors of the Israel Broadcasting Authority, Aharon Papo, (1980b) wrote:

> The astounding fact in the ministers' response is that they treat the broadcasting authority as if it were a natural disaster that must be put up with ... In their imagination – and only in their imagination – is the broadcasting authority conceived of as a fourth arm of government besides the legislature, the executive and the judiciary. The fact that the reporters and broadcasters have not been elected by the public and are only its servants has escaped their notice ... Broadcasting services are not the private mouthpieces of their staff – but belong to the public that funds them ... and since the public in a democracy elects a parliament which designates a government from its ranks – the government is the representative of the public through which it must exert its authority over the medium.

The same logic was evident, Lapid reported, in a query raised by a government minister (in a Cabinet meeting in which he participated) as follows: 'We give orders to the military, to the police. Why can't we give orders to the broadcasting authority?'

West Germany, it was noted before, combines a legal framework that adamantly protects broadcasting independence with provisions for, and massive political interference in practice. One convincing explanation for this inconsistency was furnished by a media expert in terms of the contrast between the normative conceptions on broadcasting held by the Western Allies (who set up the system) and those held by the Germans (who inherited it). The Americans and the British (though not the French) held the view that broadcasting ought to be free from state control. The Germans, on the other hand, had long held the opposite view. The origins of this conception are to be found in the Weimar Republic where broadcasting was state-controlled. Adenauer, who certainly was not a fascist, completely lacked understanding of what the Allies were trying to build up: he, too, thought broadcasting ought to be supervised by the state in the public interest.

The same point was also made by an eminent media

personality, Hans Bausch. He wrote (Bausch, 1983) that the Allies quickly realised the German inability truly to grasp democratic freedom, amongst other things, in broadcasting. This inability manifested itself, for instance, in the statements of a state premier, Dr Reinhold Maier who (although a sincere democrat) advocated state-control of broadcasting. On the occasion of the transfer of Radio Stuttgart into German hands in 1949 he stated that only with great difficulty could Germans accept the viewpoint that a radio station belonged to no one and that no one held responsibility for it. Bausch added that in the proceedings of state or federal parliaments one would look in vain for statements in support of broadcasting freedom.

Elsewhere in West Germany such voices can nevertheless be heard, although they are outnumbered by ambiguous voices or by voices favouring some sort of state or political supervision of broadcasting. Thus Willi Geiger, an erstwhile judge of the Constitutional Court wrote (Geiger, 1978, p. 38): 'The requirement for citizens' freedom of information basically dictates that the state refrain from exerting an influence on broadcasting.' But a CDU policy paper (CDU, 1976) includes only a vague statement to the effect that 'Freedom of information and plurality of opinions are preconditions for our free democratic order.' SPD policy papers are usually even more ambiguous. Although affirming media independence they add that in order to prevent misuse of such independence the state has the duty, through suitable bodies, to control the news coverage of the media (Kepplinger, 1983, p. 171). And according to Williams (1976, p. 126) several public figures have expressed themselves in favour of political influence on broadcasting, most notably the chairman of the CDU/CSU working party on broadcasting who described broadcasting as an inherently political activity in itself, which therefore could not be further politicised (or harmed) by outside interference.

A related explanation for the divergence between the West German legal framework and the situation in practice is to be found in what Wittich (1983) called the primary allegiance of the West German public to the political party. While allegiance to the state is an older, more established German tradition, the Nazi regime has led to a certain mistrust of the state coupled with pervasive party-loyalty. Yet state and party are not always clearly separable. According to Riese (1984, p. 11) Adenauer clearly identified the interests of his party with those of the state following the motto that 'what is good for the Union is good for the country', and he was not the only West German politician to see state and (ruling) party as intertwined. With respect to broadcasting in particular it is not clear whether the right to interference by incumbent politicians is to be seen as part of their role as representatives of the party or as part of their role as representatives of the state

All these ambiguities and ambivalences come through in respondents' statements. Some respondents expressed unswaying support for broadcasting independence, for instance thus:

> I think party influence [on broadcasting] is a disaster.
>
> ZDF must be politically independent ...

More common, however, were less adamant, or two-sided views:

> In a system of publicly-funded broadcasting, the interest of the public must be conveyed in some way. The next question is whether at present the public interest is conveyed in an acceptable manner. I think not. It is clear that there must be some supervision. The question is: how?
>
> For me this is an academic question. We cannot say: 'parties out', because we live in a party-state. Without parties, no party-democracy.
>
> I find that independence is the right thing ... but on the other hand I realise that with the existing institutions the clock cannot be turned backwards.

CONCLUSION

In all four countries studied there are marked inconsistencies in the legal frameworks, guidelines and norms that govern broadcasting. Some legal frameworks are designed so as to distance broadcasting from government – while 'ultimately' maintaining government control over it. This seems to resemble the design of a circle which 'ultimately' is really a square. And precisely where the legal framework makes the clearest provisions for broadcasting independence it also makes the clearest provisions for political intervention in broadcasting. Broadcasting corporations include in their guidelines not only the injunction to maintain neutrality, impartiality, objectivity, but also the injunction to provide commentary and interpretation – another circle that is really a square. There is – among broadcasters and politicians – a widespread normative conception that (as a German deputy intendant once wrote) the best government broadcasting policy is: none. There is also a widespread conception that (as one-time British minister Anthony Wedgewood Benn was quoted as saying) broadcasting is too important to be left to broadcasters. In other words, there is the conception that broadcasting ought to be independent. There is also the conception that broadcasting ought to be accountable. And frequently these two conceptions are held by the same people.

Since similar inconsistences recur in the legal frameworks, guidelines and norms surrounding broadcasting in all countries studied the conclusion must be reached that they are not the result of oversight on the part of the drafters of legal provisions and guidelines, nor the result of capriciousness on the part of politicians and broadcasters. Rather, they are the result of a deep-seated ambiguity ingrained in the role-definition of broadcasting in a democracy, the expression of a dilemma which broadcasting poses in this particular type of political structure. The manner in which this ambiguity is reflected in what actually happens on the ground is the topic of the following chapters.

Notes

1. Name cited by permission of the respondent.
2. Name cited by permission of the respondent.

Part II
External Political Pressures

This part of the book is concerned with pressures from outside the broadcasting corporations — mainly from governments and politicians — exerted on broadcasting corporations and their staff.

4 External Pressures through Direct Intervention

The most obvious political pressures exerted by politicians on broadcasting are attempts at direct intervention through complaints, suggestions and threats. These may be voiced privately or in public, that is, with the back-up of adverse publicity. Another variant of this method is the attempt to influence broadcasters through informal relations and contacts. In some of the countries studied politicians have disclaimed the use of such pressures. In *all* the countries studied they have actually used at least some of them − with relish.

BRITAIN

Despite declarations in favour of BBC independence, successive government (and other) politicians have exerted a variety of pressures on it. These include complaints to the board, to management, to key-position-holders, and to the broadcasters concerned, questions and adverse comments on the BBC in parliament, the press, party conferences and other public forums, and even threats and commandeering of BBC installations. The most celebrated cases of such pressures in previous decades were during the Suez crisis (1956); around the programmes *That Was The Week That Was* (1962−3); *Yesterday's Men* (1971) and *The Question of Ulster* (1972) (see Burns 1977; Briggs, 1979; Paulu, 1981 and others).

Such pressures were clearly escalating over the years. Prime Minister Harold Wilson was known to have been unhappy with the BBC; according to respondents he put it under pressure by withholding interviews from it and by appointing a chairman who he thought would 'dampen its exuberance'.

It seems nevertheless that the magnitude of the pressures

exerted on the BBC by Prime Minister Margaret Thatcher and her government was unprecedented.

In the view of some respondents these pressures have not taken the form of publicly voiced threats for those would be 'politically unacceptable.' But, as *The Sydney Morning Herald* (16 January 1982, p. 39) reported, after the BBC had shown a film on the revolt of a local authority and its 'brutal' putting down by the Prime Minister, 'though she remains discreet in public the *Blessed Margaret* is said to air some hair-raising views of what she would like to do to the BBC at Tory cocktail parties'. Here, then, privately expressed (but well-publicised) threats were added to adverse publicity in an attempt to intimidate the BBC.

According to a respondent, the BBC has had greater problems with political pressures under the Thatcher government than it has had under previous governments because 'the Thatcherites are a pretty crude lot of characters. They don't give a shit about the BBC'. A Labour MP said that not only Conservatives but some Labour politicians (including himself) were unhappy about the BBC. But another Labour parliamentarian explained:

> Mrs Thatcher is constantly bullying the BBC by attacking it in the House of Commons. To criticise the BBC in public is to put it on the defensive, isn't it? Labour MPs also criticise the BBC in parliament. But [when Labour was in office] I don't think it had situations where the Prime Minister actually attacked the BBC in the House.

Pressures on the BBC have also emanated from the SDP–Liberal Alliance. For instance, the minutes of BBC current affairs meetings (13 March and 14 May 1985) reported that members of the Alliance were constantly lodging complaints with the BBC about their own under-representation on programmes, and that when this had not borne fruit they were now pursuing their complaints through solicitors.[1]

What was the BBC's reaction to these pressures? According to a BBC spokesman the BBC had quite a few members of staff whose role it was to deal with complaints and smooth them over while at the same time insulating programme and decision-makers from such pressures. He added: 'The BBC likes to think that if these two roles are kept separate the BBC policy will not be influenced by politicians.' Other respondents, too, voiced the opinion that the BBC (in both its internal and external services) was not concerned about complaints and adverse publicity and that no traces of these pressures were evident in its output.

Briggs (1979) recounted that the BBC had been accused of reacting to external pressures by becoming excessively cautious, indeed, that the BBC was sometimes referred to an acronym for *Be Bloody Cautious*. Asked if, at present, the BBC was reacting to political pressures by caution, respondents generally agreed that this was not so:

> You obviously would not want to antagonise government and politicians all the time because at the end of the day they can damage broadcasting.
>
> Yes, this is the way it works. You ... are not unduly influenced [by politicians]. You're much more likely to be influenced because you're worried about the consequences of a row. It's a question of saying: 'Oh my God, do we really want to go through with the hassle? Do we really want the d.g. to phone up at midnight and say what the f--- are you doing?
>
> The BBC's outlook has become less bold in some ways. Its current-affairs reporting has lost a certain amount of its edge.
>
> In Greene's time there were quite a few programmes which mocked the government ... the BBC is not offending the government so much any more.
>
> It's become a very cautious institution ...

Government pressures on the BBC have usually been most adamant during and around national conflicts, because, as a respondent explained, during such conflicts the government could say to the BBC that it was not in the national interest to present views dissenting from those of the government. Thus, pressures on the BBC attained new heights during the Falklands War. Tory politicians attacked the BBC for not adequately reporting the government's peace initiatives, for questioning government statements, and for featuring opponents to the Falklands intervention on one of its programmes. An observer recounted:

that caused a big row in the sense of people getting up in parliament and attacking the BBC. And Milne, the director-general [elect], and Howard who was then the chairman . . . went along to a meeting of Tory backbenchers, and it was a pretty nasty occasion, with all the Tories getting very excited

and one of the staff said: 'We received threatening phone calls. The chairman and the director-general elect were almost beaten up in Parliament.'

During the Falklands War the government also commandeered one of the BBC foreign service transmitters. As one of the foreign service staff described:

We got a request from the Ministry of Defence to make special propaganda broadcasts to Argentina. We refused and they requisitioned one of our transmitters on Ascension Island. They started special broadcasts to Argentina to the derision of all concerned . . . The Foreign Office didn't mind. At that time they had so many flops – they didn't mind the Ministry of Defence having a flop of their own.

As to the BBC reaction to pressures during the Falklands crisis, the Glasgow University Media Group, on the basis of content analysis of BBC programmes, argued that they were not much better than rehashed government hand-outs with some background material from ministerial briefings (*Guardian*, 8 October 1985, p. 1). Some respondents thought otherwise, saying that in the case of the Falklands the BBC had told the government 'to stay away' or 'to get lost'.

The coverage of the conflict in Northern Ireland has been another focus of pressure on the BBC. Since coming to office in 1979 the government, and particularly Mrs Thatcher, have several times attacked the BBC for filming IRA gunmen. A key observer told of the occasion in which the BBC filmed some 'provisional people' and parliament was 'set alight'. Its proceedings were interrupted for Thatcher to make a statement about collusion between the BBC and the IRA 'which is all rubbish. But that's the sort of pressure that's on.'

Recently the most celebrated case of government interference on the issue was that of a 45-minute documentary scheduled to be shown on 17 August 1985 on the BBC series, *Real Lives*. The programme was to feature a lengthy interview with a senior

IRA man, reportedly the IRA Chief of Staff, and with a hardcore loyalist advocating armed conflict with the IRA. The BBC management decided to screen the programme despite an earlier remark by the Prime Minister that terrorrists ought to be starved of the 'oxygen of publicity'.

The Conservative Party chairman reacted by saying the BBC 'ought to be ashamed of itself' and a senior minister expressed amazement: 'The IRA Chief of Staff? On BBC TV? They must be lunatics' (*Sunday Times*, 28 July 1985, pp. 1–2). In a letter to the BBC chairman the then Home Secretary, Leon Brittan, condemned the programme as 'giving succour to terrorists' and requested that the BBC should not show it. In response, the BBC board of governors decided to postpone the screening of the film pending further deliberations in a calmer atmosphere.

This called forth a large-scale controversy. Thus, former BBC director-general Hugh Greene, condemned the decision; Mary Whitehouse, president of the National Viewers and Listeners' Association supported it. Readers' letters to the press were divided on the issue; but letters by the BBC people condemned the organisation for buckling down under pressure and, in protest, BBC staff went on a one-day strike. A group of BBC staff indicated that the incident had lowered their morale and increased their confusion as to the BBC's role, and a senior BBC executive said 'These are the most miserable circumstances most of us have ever had to work in. People feel terribly let down' (*The Times*, 2 August 1985, pp. 1 and 13).

Both *The Times* (2 August, p. 13) and the *Guardian* (19 August, p. 10) in leading articles condemned the Home Secretary, saying the incident had damaged the BBC's reputation though whether it had also damaged the IRA was left for the Home Secretary to calculate. Liberal leader David Steel expressed the view that the BBC ought not to be under the auspices of the Home Office for 'if the Bible came under the control of the Home Office it would get into trouble for publicising the devil' (*Guardian*, 19 August, p. 4), and Lord Annan accused the Home Secretary of behaving like a 'demented poodle' (*Sunday Times*, 29 December 1985, p. 7), but Kellner (1985, p. 10) argued that there was no point in attacking the Home Secretary, for he had only been doing his job; it was the BBC governors who had failed to do theirs.

Subsequently the BBC showed the film albeit (reportedly)

with some editorial changes. But the affair had a further consequence: in a Cabinet reshuffle, that took place about that time, Brittan was transferred to the Department of Trade and Industry – a transfer that was considered a demotion because of his involvement in the *Real Lives* fiasco. On this Zedaka (1985, p. 14) commented that what might well arouse the envy of Thatcher's peers was her ability to kick out any minister whose glory had dimmed 'especially for carrying out her own unpopular policy'. A few months later it was reported that the BBC had again been subject to direct government pressure, this time to scrap an interview with Brittan himself in relation to a political scandal that was threatening the Thatcher government. This time, however, the BBC resisted the pressure and staff felt that it had come out well from the encounter (*The Times*, 17 January 1986, p. 2).

The BBC, more than any of the other broadcasting corporations studied, maintains a network of informal relations with politicians at various levels. Thus the chief assistant to the director-general, and a whole array of other position-holders have the task of maintaining contact with politicians. More importantly, informal contacts occur on a variety of social occasions. People at the head of the BBC, top politicians and senior civil servants would all be of similar social background, and as respondents explained:

> At the head of British society, as at the head of any pyramid, the number of people diminishes. So the top BBC people and top politicians are likely to meet each other at parties, concerts, etc.
>
> It's just the way things work. People have lunches together. They have parties.

Could these relations be used to influence the BBC politically, to co-opt it, as it were, to the benefit of the political establishment? Several respondents assured me that they could not; that on the contrary, such contacts served to defend the BBC from political pressure and to aid it in influencing (rather than being influenced by) politicians. One respondent said: 'OK, people meet. What can we read from that? You need to present evidence that a set of consequences flow from that relationship.' However, when asked whether BBC people would be influenced by informal contact with policians, one respondent replied: 'Of course they would be.' Others amplified:

Yes. But it occurs in a million of tiny ways rather than in a small number of large ways.

A famous editor of *The Times* once said: 'I never have lunch with politicians. It is my job to evaluate what they do and I can do that better from a distance.' I have a high regard for this viewpoint. I always get rather suspicious when top BBC people and top politicians meet informally.

Recently there was an embarrassing disclosure in the press: by a heretofore secretive arrangement, confidential Foreign Office cables had been delivered daily to heads of departments at the BBC External Services. The director of External Services claimed that their output was not affected thereby. But several of the BBC staff expressed concern that the arrangement allowed Foreign Office views to outweigh other views of world events (*Observer*, 1 September 1985, p. 2). The *Guardian* (3 August 1985, p. 15) argued that straightforward Foreign Office interference would simply have met with a BBC invitation to 'get stuffed'. But the ingenuous and subtle device of letting senior BBC people in on confidential information, thereby making them part of the inner sanctum of the establishment was worse, for it could give an authoritative cue to Bush House output.

AUSTRALIA

In Australia, too, there has been a long-standing tradition of external pressures on broadcasting in the form of several variants of complaints and adverse publicity. Thus there were extensive pressures concerning the public affairs programme *This Day Tonight* (*TDT*), which made its debut in 1967. The programme was characterised by its irreverent treatment of the politicians it interviewed and it was frequently charged with leftist bias. Before the 1972 election, members of the (Liberal) government publicly accused *TDT* of a lack of balance, dubbing it Today's Distortion Tonight. Charges of left-wing partisanship on *TDT* continued into the late 1970s, and in 1978 it was terminated. But this may have been done because morale in the making of the programme had already been low (Harding, 1979, chap. 5; Inglis, 1983, chap. 6).

Complaints by politicians about political bias on the ABC continued into the 1980s. For this we have the testimony of Clement Semmler, the erstwhile deputy general manager of the ABC, in an article entitled 'As difficult as ABC' (Semmler, 1983, p. 2): 'Most of the senior officers of the ABC will be leaned on from time to time as they have been in the past . . . by politicians in power. I know I was – as head of programmes, as deputy general manager, as acting general manager.'

The respondents concurred that attempts at 'leaning' on ABC staff were still common as illustrated by the following statement:

> Politicians on both sides make a wide range of contacts with the ABC most of which are to try to influence the programmes

Who usually complained? One respondent said: 'Any minister, if he feels he has been unfairly treated complains.' Respondents believed Communications Minister, Michael Duffy, to be scrupulously fair. But not all members of government received a clean bill of health. Several respondents stated that complaints had come 'from the very top':

> The PM might say 'what are you doing to me. You're ruining me.'

> There's been suggestions that right from the top there's been dissatisfaction expressed and that can be a signal – if there are any faint hearts . . . to tailor themseles accordingly . . . there was some hullabaloo [about that]

While there was unanimity amongst respondents about the origin of the complaints, there was less agreement as to the recipients. Some respondents thought complaints went mostly to the chairman or the board; others thought that politicians normally approached the managing director, while still others thought that complaints more frequently went to regional managers, editors, heads of programmes or the staff concerned.

Occasionally (though not too often) ABC staff have also been subject to threats: 'if you're just having drinks down in the bar and a politician is there and he'll say "it's not going to end here" and "we're looking into it", etc., etc.' More frequently the

ABC has been subject to adverse publicity. For instance, *The Australian* (4 April 1984, p. 1) reported that both the Prime Minister and the Minister for Foreign Affairs, Bill Hayden, had launched 'scathing attacks' on the ABC at an Australian Labor Party Caucus meeting, probably knowing that their attacks would be reported in the press. Mr Hawke had said: 'Freedom of the press is freedom to lie, I suppose', adding that the ABC was taking a consistent line against the government, and that the ABC should start to look seriously at itself. Foreign Minister Hayden had begun by saying that the ABC should be independent, but concluded by saying that it was 'out of control, second rate and fragmented'. However, the Minister for Communications, Duffy, told caucus they could not have it both ways. The ABC could not remain independent, while at the same time having people attacking and threatening it. According to *The Australian* the argument developed (or deteriorated) into a 'bitter clash' interspersed by shouting and four-letter words.

In November 1984 the Prime Minister again publicly criticised the ABC. He said he did not want to conduct himself in a way which appeared to involve some attempt at intimidation or direction. But he got around this hurdle by ostensibly speaking as a private citizen. He then felt free to say: 'I think the operations of the ABC leave a considerable amount to be desired' (Grattan, 1984, p. 6).

Asked how the previous Liberal government and the Labor government at the time of this study compared with respect to the pressure they put on the ABC, respondents expressed contradictory views, as illustrated by the following statements:

> The attitude of the present government against the ABC doesn't seem to be anywhere as harsh as it was under the previous Liberal government.

> There are occasions when politicians complain. In fact, the Labor government more so than the Liberal government.

> I can't distinguish major differences . . .

What was the ABC's response to such pressures? According to one respodent, politicians 'must apparently be getting a responsive approach to their complaints or why would they be doing it'. However, a board member expressed a different opinion: 'On a senior executive level – I feel I am a senior executive – that sort of pressure is not responded to!' The same board member thought that the lower level of the ABC might be more responsive to political pressures: 'For instance there's a current affairs producer and he's canvassing a particular issue and Joe Bloggs says "well, why aren't I on it?" And the producer owes Joe Bloggs a favour . . . that sort of thing probably does happen.' Other respondents believed that all levels of the ABC would now be resistant to political pressures:

> because the ABC hears complaints from politicians and considers them, that doesn't mean that it . . . buckles down under such pressure . . . Despite the PM's calls to several different sections of the ABC, his request was simply not granted. So I'd be very careful in assuming that every *attempted* influence correlates with actual influence. It doesn't.
>
> I think the ABC tends to stand up for itself.

One respondent thought reactions to complaints depended on the person who received them. Some would check the complaints and 'stroke people' without compromising their ethics – others were 'cringing'. While rebutting the complaints they would still give the complainants the impression that the ABC had slipped. Many respondents believed that pressures resulted in clashes and blow-ups:

> If the board have to pick a fight with the government that's probably what they'll do.
>
> Hawke (and other ministers) . . . were stood up over the last election and it was just thrown back in their faces . . .

But while *fending off* political pressure led to conflict, so did *giving in* to political pressure: 'and the odd occasion when someone has been unwise enough to respond directly to the pressure then what tends to happen is that you get a blow-up within the organisation'.

Informal relations between ABC people and politicians were not entirely absent. According to observers, some ABC journalists had 'superb contacts' and 'open access' to politicians. But close relations with politicians were far less extensive at the

ABC than they were at the BBC. Two respondents who had connections with both the BBC and the ABC were in full agreement on this point. One said: 'The ABC has nothing comparable.' The other amplified: 'In Australia people would be a lot more suspicious of such meetings because people are generally more suspicious of the chaps at the top.'

ISRAEL

In Israel, no less than in Australia, pressures on broadcasting through direct interference via complaints have been very common, and according to the respondents they were applied to practically all levels of staff: management, heads of department and reporters. These pressures, prevalent under Labour governments as well, seemed to have been exacerbated under the Likud government (1977–84). As respondents in 1983 explained:

> During the Likud term interference has become more straightforward.
>
> During Labour there was much interference but we did not feel the boot as we do today . . . pressures are brutalised.

One explanation for this may lie in the fact – noted by several respondents – that the majority of broadcasting staff were left-wingers and thus Labour supporters in any case, while the Likud government had to confront mainly hostile staff. Another explanation was offered by a media expert: 'Labour did not set out to defend the freedom of the press. Far from it. But Labour was pragmatist while the Likud has a strong ideological thrust to its interference.'

Especially common has been interference through publicity, parliamentary debates and well-publicised investigations. Thus Hugh Greene who came to observe broadcasting in Israel, reported (1973) that at that time the Education and Culture Committee of the Israeli parliament was conducting an extensive investigation into broadcasting – prompted by no more than a minor error in one news broadcast. A decade later, politicians had not eased off and there were frequent discussions and adverse comments on broadcasting in parliament, in parliamentary committees and in government meetings. As a respondent corroborated: 'government and other politicians constantly busy themselves with the broadcasting authority'.

A similar point was made in 1983 by the then director-general Lapid: 'In cabinet meetings, especially when the budget is about to be renewed, ministers bring up a tirade of complaints.' He added that at one such meeting, at which he was present, the then Prime Minister, Menachem Begin said (and saw to it that this was later publicised): 'Your appointment has been a poor bargain.' According to another respondent, at a Cabinet meeting, a minister remarked: 'That's not a broadcasting authority but a broadcasting devil.'

Under the Likud government pressures on broadcasting were thus quite formidable. But after the 1984 election, with the advent of a broad coalition government in which both major parties, Labour and the Likud ruled jointly, the name of the game changed considerably. Political pressures from Labour and the Likud were now counteracting each other and, to a certain extent, were cancelling each other out. These developments are discussed at greater length in Chapter 12.

Under all recent governments, the pressures brought to bear on television have been more forbidable than those applied to radio. This has to do with the difference of broadcasting-time which each of the media has at its disposal. At the time of writing, television broadcast on one channel, for a few hours a day only, while radio broadcast on several channels and (as a respondent explained) 'for so many hours that it can give coverage to all political views'. Also, television was more at the focus of national attention: its relatively few news and current affairs broadcasts were both widely viewed and widely discussed. Most importantly, radio had a strong, and professionally highly-qualified director who (as a respondent explained) 'refuses to let politicians push their noses in'.

The manner in which the Israel broadcasting authority dealt with political pressures through complaints was described by a respondent as follows: 'We check, and if, indeed, the complaint is justified we broadcast a correct version or a response . . . If the complaint is not justified we say to the person: "you are wrong." ' According to other respondents, political pressures merely led to a more careful political balance; and the more brutal the pressure the less the tendency of staff to succumb to it. However, according to one respondent, things were not always so simple and, as a result of political pressures, things got on the air that should not: 'Sometimes pressures come from party headquarters to give coverage to certain party events. For instance, following such a phone call, I got instructions to cover a party convention that was of little interest to the public. It was a boring programme.'

As in Britain, in Israel too, there are extensive, informal relations between broadcasting people and politicians. The Israeli establishment is generally small, and in it not only politicians, but media people are included as well. The members of this élite live in the same areas, meet socially, and – not infrequently – intermarry. There is also a movement of media people into politics and vice versa. There is, therefore, as a respondent put it, an 'incestuous inbreeding' within this élite in which senior broadcasting people also take part. In addition, political correspondents work closely with politicians and, as the years go by, informal social ties develop. Respondents adamantly denied that such ties could influence their work. But, through such informal channels, a variety of (partly classified) information reaches certain key-position-holders within the broadcasting authority, although it is difficult to assess the impact that has on actual broadcasts.

WEST GERMANY

In West Germany, no less than in the other countries studied, external political interference is a well-established custom and one, moreover, which has been strengthened in recent years. According to several media-experts, the explanation for this trend is to be found in the growing conviction of politicians that broadcasting has an impact on their political fortunes.

The milestone in this development was the Federal election of 1976 which the CDU lost by a small margin of a few hundred-thousand votes only. Professor Elizabeth Noelle-Neumann conducted a study on the basis of which she subsequently claimed (1980) that the Union had lost the election because of broadcasting, specifically television. According to Noelle-Neuman this was so because television had given the public the impression that the CDU was not capable of winning the election. Swinging voters were thus convinced to go on the winners' bandwagon. A standing commission on broadcasting, the ARD–ZDF Media Commission, took up the mater on 21 April 1977. According to an expert:

> There was a meeting in which I ... participated. There was a spectacular appearance of Profesor Noelle-Neumann in which she reported the results of her study ... And in the protocol of that meeting there is a brutal passage in which ... the then business manager of the CDU said: 'We will not allow a partisan television to narrow our electoral chances as was the case in 1976.' And since then the CDU has made an effort to gain more influence inside the broadcasting houses (see also Bausch, 1980, p. 768).

As other respondents concurred, the CDU has recently shown the most pronounced tendencies to interfere in broadcasting, and this is so for three reasons. First, the CDU has been more disgruntled than other parties with the manner in which its case has been presented in broadcasting; second, it imputes more political importance to broadcasting than other parties; third, it is the most professional in its public relations work. Several broadcasting journalists, however, felt that not only the CDU but politicians in general were now more nervous and touchy than before because they had accepted the view that if public opinion turned against them, the culprit was to be sought in broadcasting.

According to practically all respondents direct intervention took the form of complaints from the Federal Chancellor, ministers, the states' premiers and governments, party officials, members of parliament, and public servants. Politicians directed their complaints first and foremost at their members and sympathisers on the boards and – as a respondent put it – at 'their darlings' in key positions within the broadcasting organisations themselves. But intendants, directors and editors-in-chief in general, were also frequent recipients of political complaints. In addition, politicians also voiced complaints publicly, in the Bundestag, in state parliaments and in the press.

Sometimes politicians named specific members of staff in their complaints and sometimes they even demanded that these people be disciplined or punished. In response, respondents agreed, politicians' complaints were examined and if anything had really gone wrong, an appropriate correction and reply would be made. But beyond that, several respondents insisted, politicians' complaints had no direct effect on programmes for as one respondent said: 'We don't wish to make programmes that are popular with politicians. That would be a mistake.' Another participant in this study, however, expressed a more qualified view: 'One would have to examine each case separately. On the one hand it will be felt that it is to the benefit of the house to fall into line. But it will also be felt that in some single cases it it necessary to stand up on one's hind legs and say: not this way please.'

Another respondent said that because of constant complaints and also because politicians could grant or withhold interviews and information, broadcasting stations have let themselves be intimidated to a certain extent. An article in *Der Spiegel* (13 February 1984, p. 13) noted that because of political pressures the independence of broadcasting has been 'trampled' and destroyed.

On one point there was unanimity amongst respondents: demands by politicians to discipline or punish someone were usually rebutted and did not bear the desired fruit. Respondents cited several examples of journalists who were attacked by politicians without this doing any damage to their careers. A recent example was cited by several respondents. This was the case of the state secretary in the Department of Interior, C-D. Spranger (CSU) who voiced an attack on public broadcasting. In an article and an interview in the press, as well as in a debate in the Bundestag, he complained that both ARD and ZDF tended to the left, that they put the main emphasis on the negative aspects of reality, and that they spread anxiety, hopelessness and a disaster mentality.

Voicing his complaints, Spranger had also named several names and demanded that the people involved be punished. Asked whether this would damage those people's careers, a respondent reassured me that not only would this not be the case, but that on the contrary, it would lend them publicity and would further, [rather than hinder] their careers. I happened to be present when one of the staff was notified of the fact that he had been named and attacked by Spranger. He seemed entirely unconcerned. One respondent later commented:

You could see how Mr ? reacted [to Spranger's attack] – namely, not at all. It just bounced off . . . even if the intendant wished to discipline him, he would not be able to because it was a political and not a professional matter.

In West Germany, as in other countries, informal relations form another connection point between broadcasting and politics. On the basis of a research on the German élite by the Mannheim Elite Study Group, Kutteroff (1984) concluded that a dense network of informal contacts between broadcasting journalists and politicians existed and that it created a role conflict between broadcasting people's professional commitments and their socio-political loyalties. In the same vein a respondent mentioned the fact that the chairman of the ZDF administrative board was also a senior politician, adding: 'There is a friendly togetherness there.' Another respondent said it was 'only natural' that party members in broadcasting and other party members met informally, and a third respondent stated:

> There are relations between the intendant and politicians. And since these people are frequently on the boards which supervise the intendant this is bad. But nobody will be able to provide proof for this. Journalists [too] would not admit that there are such tight relations between themselves and politicians, that they play cards together . . . or that a journalist works for several decades in Bonn, for instance, and knows everybody well, and is no longer in the position to see things objectively . . . where [the journalist] says: this fellow has given me information in all these cases. Now I'm not going to make him trip when I've found out something unfavourable about him. This is undeniabe. But it is imposible to prove.

CONCLUSION

At the outset of this study my expectation was that political pressures would be more formidable and pervasive in the countries with party-politicised bureaucracies – Israel and West Germany – than they would be in the countries with non- or less party-politicised bureaucracies – Britain and Australia. With respect to pressures through direct interference, this expectation has not been borne out: such pressures were extensive in all countries involved. Moreover, the direct but largely imperceptible pressure brought to bear on broadcasters through the collusion of informal relations and the passing of inside information was at least as prominent in Britain as it was in the countries with partisan bureaucracies, and while views on the effect of this device on broadcasting were divided I would side with Kellner (1985, p. 101) who offered the following comment: 'Few things corrode democracy faster than private deals among the great and the good, quietly eroding away our right to judge for ourselves what is happening.'

Note

1. The Alliance in fact brought court action for unfair treatment by the BBC – which was later withdrawn.

5 External Pressures through Funding

Another classical instrument of political pressure on the public broadcasting corporations is the control of funding. Governments have utilised it, evidently working on the well-known presupposition that, if you hold them by the purse-strings, their hearts and minds will follow.

BRITAIN

It is a distinctive feature of the BBC that so far as it has been financed largely by licence fee (although its external services are financed by grants-in-aid from the Treasury). According to the BBC's handbook, this system of funding guarantees the independence of domestic broadcasting. In fact, however, the situation is not as simple as that, for the government determines the size of the licence fee. Once the licence fee has been set, it will not be reduced, and this has given the BBC a long run of financial independence. However, because of inflation, which has taken off especially in the past thirteen or fourteen years, the real value of the licence fee has been eroding and the BBC has been dependent on the government periodically increasing it.

Moreover, recently, the BBC's financial situation has worsened in other respects as well. For as *The Economist* (14–20 September 1985, p. 40) informs us, between 1975 and 1983 the cost of television-time went up by 68 per cent in real terms; in addition, the BBC has been constantly expanding its operations and for this, too, it has been requiring larger funds. Yet, between 1968 and 1985, the colour-television licence fee was not increased in real terms. What has kept the BBC going has been the growing number of colour-television licences (which are dearer than those for black-and-white televisions. This bonus is now largely exhausted and the BBC's dependence on the goodwill of the government is therefore increasing.

When the licence fee comes up for review, the government usually does not grant the BBC the full increase it has requested. Thus, in 1984, the BBC requested that the fee be raised to £65, but in 1985 when the decision was made, the fee was raised to £58 only. The difference amounted to £350 million over the coming three years (*Scan*, 6–19 May 1985, p. 7). But the BBC has usually pitched its demand as high as possible knowing that it would be bid down. Hence it is difficult to tell whether it had sustained a real cut-back and if so, whether this was based merely on an administrative judgement of the Home Office, whether it was based on government assessment that the licence fee was unpopular with voters, or whether there were any sanctions implied, or political warnings involved.

The BBC has occasionally been threatened over the licence fee. This was the case under a Conservative government during the Suez crisis. Also, under a Labour government in the 1960s, Prime Minister Wilson took offence at some BBC offerings, and Hill (1974, p. 84) reported that he subsequently heard through the Post Office that the prospects in relation to the licence fee had never been worse. By the account of a key informant, during the licence negotiation, Wilson himself had indicated that if the BBC did not mend its ways the fee would be affected. Similarly, under a Labour government in the 1970s, when the licence fee once more came up for review, and the BBC had displeased the government over its coverage of Northern Ireland, there was a threat from the Secretary for Northern Ireland that government displeasure would be reflected in the licence-fee settlement.

In more recent years the government would have been wary of holding the stick or the carrot of the licence fee directly over the BBC's head. But subtler ways of utilising the device have not been ruled out. Thus the Annan Committee reviewed with BBC officials the question of whether the government utilised the licence fee as a lever of control over programmes and got a negative reply. But one official pointed out that producers and directors were aware of the tensions involved in the fee negotiations with the government and might well modify programmes of their own accord (Paulu, 1981, p. 26).

Also, once the licence fee has been set, the government requests the House of Commons to provide the agreed amount[1] for the BBC. This has always been done as requested, although the occasion has been used to debate and criticise BBC policies. Thus it was reported in the press that Conservative MPs 'whooped and jeered' when the Home Secretary announced the last rise in the licence fee. BBC staff are thus made aware of the trend of opinion in parliament in conjunction with the issue of funding and this, too, might well lead them to curb their own tendencies to annoy the powers-that-be. So the implied financial pressures of recent years may have been as effective as the financial threats of previous years.

On this, there were two schools of thought amongst respondents. Respondents of the one school expressed the conviction that it was difficult to pinpoint direct financial pressures on the BBC recently, that things simply were not so transparent, that the acid test of financial pressures would have been 'volatile fluctuations' in funding in conjunction with political criticism, that such fluctuations had been absent, and that the BBC was simply too well-established and influential to 'soft pedal' before each decision on the licence fee.

Respondents of the other school of thought maintained that the funds which the government has been granting the BBC have been too little and too late, and that this has kept the BBC in a constant state of money shortage. It has not been necessary for the government to apply threats of the kind voiced earlier, simply because the BBC's constant money-squeeze and consequent growing dependence on the government have made it more mindful of government wishes, have caused it to lose much of its earlier self-confidence and have reinforced its general trend towards greater caution and avoidance of trouble. Respondents who were of this view also maintained that the present government was especially sensitive to criticism. Current affairs programmes were the most likely to irk the government, and since they also were not large audience-getters, financial pressures of several kinds have converged leading to the BBC to cut them down. Thus, as one respondent summarised the situation, there was now a combination of an especially-touchy government with an especially-dependent BBC – two factors which had combined to increase BBC nervousness and caution.

AUSTRALIA

In Australia, initially, the broadcasting corporation had been funded by licence fees supplemented by *ad hoc* grants from the government. Since 1949–50 the ABC has been dependent entirely on parliamentary appropriations for its funding (and in 1974–5 the licence fee was abolished altogether). In January each year the ABC submits forward estimates of expected expenditures for the next three years. These are then subject to negotiation with the department of finance. If an agreement is reached it is likely to be incorporated into the budget. Otherwise, the final arbiter of the appropriation is the Expenditure Review Committee, composed of senior cabinet ministers, including the Prime Minister. The allocation for the ABC decided upon by this committee is then submitted to, and passed by parliament as part of the budget appropriation bills. Hence, although the level of funding depends in part on bureaucratic advice, the final decision is a political one, and made by the government.

When submitting forward estimates the ABC also submits estimates for supplementary funds for the previous year. Prior to the bills for these appropriations going through parliament, senior ABC managers appear as witnesses before a Senate Estimates Committee where they have to render an account on how the government's money has been spent. These funding procedures open the door for political pressure as well as for a large measure of uncertainty. The previous chairman, Dame Leonie Kramer, noted: 'the greatest difficulty for the ABC is caused by the uncertainty of funding. And by that . . . I mean the annual hand-out system. Every year senior management people have to go to Canberra with the begging-bowl and then argue down to the last dollar and cent' (Simper, 1983, p. 12). Periodically, proposals for triennial funding – which would exempt the ABC from pressure at least for some of the time – have come up, but have been rejected.

The most well-known utilisation of funding as a political weapon occurred under the Liberal–Country Party (Fraser) Government. For instance, in early 1976, the ABC was suddenly informed by that government that the expected supplementary funds for 1975–6 would not be forthcoming. The

ABC thus was A$8.4 million short of what it had expected. Severe cuts and retrenchments became necessary. The government gave no explanation for its decision but it is likely that this was not unrelated to the fact that some of the ABC's public affairs programmes had assumed a left-of centre, antigovernment political line, for while, at the same time, the government (through funding limitations) imposed a 5 per cent reduction on the overall public-service ceilings, it imposed a 15 per cent reduction on the ABC staff's size. Another 10 per cent cut in funding came into effect in the 1977–8 budget, and another 3 per cent in the 1978–9 budget (Dix, 1981, vol. 2; Inglis, 1983, chap. 8).

A Liberal Minister for Communications, Tony Staley, in 1979, practically admitted that funding squeezes had been used to pressure the ABC, saying in an interview on an ABC programme 'The ABC admittedly has had a difficult time in the last few years.' The interviewer then asked: 'Is it an admission from the government that it has been too hard on the ABC?' The minister replied: 'In effect it is' (Williams, 1982, pp. 6–7).

Labor governments have also exerted their influence on the ABC through funding. In 1974/75 the Labor government expanded the ABC budget to enable it to finance two new stations: 2JJ in Sydney and 3ZZ in Melbourne. The first broadcast explicit sexual material and rock music for young people. The second was devoted to broadcasts by minority groups. Thus 'by efficiently launching 2JJ and 3ZZ' the ABC demonstrated its ability 'to faithfully mirror the intentions of the media policy formulated by the government' (Davis, 1984, p. 41). In summary: 'When Liberal-Country Party governments chose not to respect the independence of the ABC they stopped it doing things. Labor governments tended rather to *make* it do things' (Inglis, 1983, p. 379).

This, however, is no longer true, for the present Labor government has not desisted from using the weapon of funding cuts at least in an implied threat. At the beginning of April 1984, Prime Minister Hawke, after criticising the ABC, made the following statement: 'People in the community are asking why we are funding an organisation like this, and if this feeling builds up, then it should be reflected in a number of ways' (*The Australian*, 4 April 1984, p. 1). Subsequently the Prime

Minister denied that he had threatened the ABC (*Australian*, 13 April 1984, p. 1). But if the previous report in the *Australian* is correct, a threat was clearly implied. As Crisp (1985, p. 24) saw it: 'the irony is that the ABC's life support system is being squeezed by the very Labor government many thought would be its salvation'.

In actual fact, the Labor government did not cut down the total ABC allocation in the next financial year, that is, in 1985–6. In the budget brought down by the same government for 1986–7, it was announced that the ABC would be amalgamated with a public, ethnic broadcasting station (the Special Broadcasting Service) and that savings of 4 per cent in nominal terms (and 12.4 per cent in real terms) over the ABC's previous allocation would be achieved. But this was, in any case, a tough austerity budget and it was difficult to tell whether the ABC was singled out for especially adverse measures.

Moreover, even with respect to previous cut-backs, it is not clear that they were always made for political reasons; sometimes they were a response to inefficiencies within the corporation. For instance, one respondent thought that Fraser bore down on ABC funding among other things because he thought management had inadequate control over the organisation in financial terms, adding: 'And I think he had some reason for that.' Another member of staff concurred that during Kramer's chairmanship the ABC was conspicuously lacking in efficiency in using the resources it did have. Also, various press reports in 1984 concurred that an ABC funding crisis – necessitating major cuts in the ABC's operational expenditures – arose mainly because ABC staff levels had grown uncontrolled over the previous months, that the ABC did not know how many staff it had, nor how much it paid out for them.

Nonetheless, broadcasting staff believed financial cut-backs were used by the government as an instrument of political pressure and took a dim view of the process. As Williams in an article entitled 'Starving Auntie' (Williams, 1982, p. 6) put it – top government personalities 'are mean, unsubtle bullyboys who see us not just as some political threat . . . whatever that could possibly be . . . but as somehow alien'. Respondents held similar views, as illustrated by the following statements:

> If the ABC upsets the ... government, next time they have to go there for a year's appropriation the government can say: you haven't behaved yourself, so you get only a little bit ... so they can influence the ABC because they are holding the purse-strings.

> I think funding is the biggest sword, the sharpest sword that's hanging over [the] organisation's head

> I don't think [the ABC] can ever really be independent ... while it has to go cap-in-hand to the government ... for its money. I mean ... if it's seen to be a bad boy it gets whacked in the pocket and usually the hip pocket.

Comparing the ABC's lot under previous (Liberal) and present (Labor) government, respondents made the following statements:

> Under Fraser ... [the] ABC was very nearly crippled by having staff and funding cut ... [it] meant that lots of the good people who saw the writing on the wall, left ... their equivalents could not be recruited from outside.

> As I understand they've been having great problems getting money out of the Labor government.

Several respondents mentioned the adverse effect funding-cuts had on the ABC's technical equipment, which by now was twenty years behind that of commercial stations. A number of reports in the press also concurred that because of government-funding cut-backs, the ABC had been sliding down a slope of technical incompetence, with its equipment becoming more and more outmoded, ineffective and prone to unexpected breakdowns. Thus, Humphrey (1984, p. 15) reported:

> Recently it was the rule rather than the exception for 90 per cent of the video machines needed for the nightly news ... to be out of order ... The technical foul-ups that resulted gave the ABC's enemies hours of endless fun counting the ways newsreaders and presenters could blush, stammer, swallow their curses and apologise yet again to their steadily diminishing audience. Sadly, they got very good at it although it is fair to say that none has yet equalled the [current affairs] anchorman who, left definitively stranded by snowballing technical disaster and no help in sight for the last four minutes of the programme, got up and danced a Maori *haka* complete with eye-rolling and tongue-poking.

ISRAEL

Here the broadcasting authority has been financed from the licence, from advertising, and from a grant by the Treasury. The government has been gradually decreasing its participation in the authority's budget, and by now its contribution has ceased altogether. But the authority's budget has to be ratified by the government and the Finance Committee of Parliament, while the licence fee has to be ratified by the same committee. In practice this means that the authority is dependent on the government and on the major parties' politicians for its funding.

Indeed, in this respect the situation in Israel has been worse than in the other countries, for the political establishment has been using the weapon of funding more blatantly, and at the shortest possible possible intervals, to exert political pressure. Thus, previous director-general Lapid recounted in 1983, when he was still in office:

> While the budget for all government departments is ratified once a year, the broadcasting authority's budget is ratified for six months, sometimes for three months, and sometimes for one month only — to keep us on a short leash so that I will have to come and ask for the money, so that they can tell us what they think of us.

Director-general Porat gave a similar account:

> We are the only ones whose budget is ratified four times a year. Every three months we come crawling to the Finance Committee and we are thrown a bit of money — until the next crawling. And this is called an independent broadcasting authority (Baum, 1985, p. 5).

Here, too, the broadcasting authority owed at least some of its difficulties to financial mismanagement; but this was hardly the whole story. The authority had suffered a budget cut-back of 20 per cent in real terms from 1982 to 1984. At the beginning of 1985, it had a budgetary deficit of several million dollars which the government was refusing to cover. At that time it was announced that under the 1985 budget the authority would have to sustain a further budget cut-back of 20–30 per cent in real terms, employees would have to be retrenched and programmes would have to be drastically curtailed. The authority's financial situation was thus pretty grim and it was widely believed to be on the verge of collapse. By the account of key observers, this was to be attributed in part to the fact that the authority's management had let expenses escape its control. To this, however, must be added the generally precarious economic situation in Israel at the time, which made proper fiscal administration of any public institution well nigh impossible. Perhaps for that reason, the Treasury eventually relented and awarded the authority an emergency grant to cover its deficit.

In autumn 1985 the authority's budget once more came up for review before the Parliament's Finance Committee. The committee met several times but refused to ratify the budget. Partly, no doubt, this was in response to an unfavourable report by the committee's economist on the authority's finances. But political factors were obviously at play as well. For the committee was neatly divided between Labour representatives who pressed for the ratification of the budget, and Likud and Religious Party representatives who opposed the ratification and – being in the majority – prevented it. They also used the committee meetings to denigrate television and accuse it of bias against their own parties. They clinched the argument by making it very plain that they would not be sorry to see television shut down. Not surprisingly, staff expressed the view that under the cloak of substantive deliberations, the committee was really acting on the basis of political considerations.

The previous broadcasting budget had been for the period ending on 30 September. From then onward the Finance Committee had left the authority to function (or malfunction) without a budget. Subsequently the state Attorney General advised that in so doing the committee had acted in contravention of the Broadcasting Authority Law. At the time of this study it was therefore expected by respondents that willy-nilly the committee would eventually have to ratify the authority's budget.

WEST GERMANY

Here, too, the public broadcasting corporation (with the exception of DW and DLF which are state-funded) are sustained by licence fee in combination with advertising revenue. The fee is determined jointly by all eleven state parliaments and consolidated in an inter-state agreement. Advertising revenue at present averages some 30–40 per cent of the total broadcasting budget.

This arrangement ensured financial stability and independence for German broadcasting for quite a number of years. Until the late 1960s the stable licence fee was sufficient to cover the post-war reconstruction of broadcasting because the number of viewers grew steadily. Only after 1967, when that number steadied, did it become clear that an increase in the licence fee would be necessary to finance broadcasting. It is from then onward (writes Bausch, 1983, p. 25) that financing became the Achilles heel of broadcasting independence.

The independence afforded to broadcasting corporations by the licence fee is still greater in West Germany than it is in other countries because rather low inflation maintains the value of the fee (in real terms) for longer time-spans. The issue of increasing the licence fee nonetheless comes up periodically. This is so because even here creeping inflation eventually nibbles away at the value of the licence fee. Also, as a respondent explained, broadcasting stations are not content merely 'to vegetate' and are intent on expanding their operations and keeping up with technological developments.

The last licence-fee increase for public broadcasting was granted in 1983 and the agreement runs until 1987, at which time, the issue is expected to come up again. The previous increase in the licence fee involved a protracted struggle and it is expected that this will be the case next time around as well, for all eleven states will have to reach agreement on the level of the fee – a difficult feat in the best of circumstances. Also, as in other countries, raising the licence fee is not exceedingly popular with the voters and poiticians would be wary of imposing this increased financial burden on them.

While much of the politicians' motivation to curb licence-fee increases has little to do with the degree to which public broadcasters satisfy their and their parties' expectations, this factor is not entirely absent from their deliberations. This was once more illuminated by Bausch when he wrote (1980, p. 87) that public broadcasting can hardly be independent when the people who are to be criticised on its programmes are the very same ones who also decide on its finances.

That party-political considerations are in fact involved is evident from the fact that (with some exceptions) CDU representatives and CDU governed states generally opposed licence-fee increases more adamantly than SPD representatives and states. It will be recalled that the CDU is also more disgruntled with public broadcasting than the SPD and it may be presumed that these two facts are not entirely unrelated. Since at the time of writing most states and the federation were CDU-governed it is not surprising that broadcasting personnel were less than confident concerning the outcome of the forthcoming licence-fee struggle.

The next question is whether politicians could use financing to influence broadcasters and whether broadcasters could do anything to appease politicians and thereby tip the scales of the forthcoming finance decisions in their favour. On the face of it, there was little that either could do. For anything that CDU politicians might demand, and anything that broadcasters might do, to curry favour with the CDU, might well antagonise the SPD. Yet the hegemony of the CDU was by no means assured; there are state elections practically every year: the balance might be tipped in favour of the SPD at any time and public broadcasters might thus find themselves out in the cold.

There was nonetheless something that broadcasting stations may be pressed to do, and could do, to find favour with politicians: to be generally cautious and 'well behaved'; to criticise as little as possible and thus to refrain from antagonising anyone on either side of the political fence. This was in fact the manner in which Bausch (himself an experienced intendant) perceived the situation when he wrote (1980, p. 744) that broadcasting institutions 'must constantly plead for the means of their financial subsistence through good behaviour'. With regard to the ZDF one respondent lent support to this view in the following words: 'With the licence fee there is, in fact, a political price that we must pay, namely [to display] a certain general, favourable attitude. With every critical decision we must ask ourselves: what impact will this have when the decision for raising the licence fee comes up again.'

Another respondent at first expressed a different view. Asked if it was to the financial interest of the ZDF to be generally less critical he replied: 'No, I would not say so.' The respondent then qualified his statement: 'Well, its logical. We don't have the intention of quarrelling with all politicians from morning till night. That would be stupid. It is impossible to swim totally against the current ... [but] our experience shows that politicians can never be satisfied.' Paradoxically the clearest answer to the question of whether the ZDF would do anything to curry favour with politicians in order to ensure a licence-fee increase in 1987 was given by another respondent – who said: 'Yes and no.'

CONCLUSION

In Britain public broadcasting has been financed largely by licence fee, in Australia by parliamentary appropriation and in Israel and West Germany by licence fee in conjunction with advertising revenue. In practice the method of finance makes little difference: in all four countries broadcasting corporations have been dependent on parliaments and in practice on governments for their funding. The time intervals at which the financial decisions concerning broadcasting are made have been a better indicator of the severity of financial pressures: in Britain and West Germany these decisions come up only periodically; in Australia they come up annually and in Israel – quarterly, or even monthly. Indeed, in Israel political pressures through funding (or lack thereof) have been the most blatant and aggressive, and have verged on the attempt to force the national broadcasting corporation into closure. In Isarel the purse strings have thus been used in an (albeit unsuccessful) bid to choke the broadcasting corporation.

It can be taken for granted that financial cut-backs for broadcasting corporations have their source not only in veiled political pressures. Financial mismanagement, particularly in Australia and Israel, has played a role as well; some cut-backs have thus been borderline cases between administrative necessities and political prerogatives. But even in these cases it is beyond reasonable doubt that political motives for financial pressures have not been absent. Hence the conclusion that funding has indeed been widely used as a formidable political instrument, not only to cut down broadcasting budgets, but to cut broadcasting corporations themselves down to size.

Note

1. This may be the whole of the licence net revenue or a percentage thereof, as determined by the treasury.

6 External Pressures through Privatisation

Privatisation in broadcasting refers to the introduction of commerical financing (through advertising or private subscriptions) on public broadcasting on the one hand, and the establishment or expansion of private broadcasting (usually in conjunction with technological developments such as satellite and cable broadcasting) side by side with public broadcasting – on the other hand. At the time of writing all the countries studied already had one or the other of these – but none of them had both. The political pressures and struggles involved in attempts to impose the second of the two features – generally against the wishes of the public broadcasting corporations – are the topic of this chapter.

BRITAIN

In Britain private competition to the BBC from what came to be the Independent Broadcasting Authority (IBA)[1] has been in existence since 1955. But the system of public–private duopoly has been working satisfactorily and the BBC has been able to maintain a high reputation. Some recent inroads into this system, however, may well lead to a new – and much diminished – role for the BBC.

One such development is the introduction of direct satellite broadcasting which by some accounts the government has been attempting to rush through. Trying to keep pace with developments, the BBC expressed an interest in this project by forming a joint venture consortium with some private companies. But by summer 1985, the consortium had collapsed, and the private companies were planning to join a French satellite due to be launched in July 1986, and to start broadcasting on four channels three months later (*Scan*, 23 September 1985, p. 11). Because of rapid technological developments it was expected that, within a few years, many more satellites would fill the skies and dozens of channels would become available. Satellite television was thus emerging as a major private competitor for the BBC.

Another such competitor was proliferating cable television. Since 1972 there have been several experiments in this area; in 1980, twelve new pilot projects were introduced (Kepplinger, 1982, p. 86). For some time such projects have been suffering from financial and other difficulties. By 1985 the government was pushing cable television which was expected to reach 30–40 per cent of the homes in the areas covered within the first four years of operation (Brooks, 1985). By 1986 cable developments slowed down again but certainly did not stop.

The most important development, however, was the establishment of a review committee, chaired by Professor Alan Peacock, to assess the effects of introducing advertising, sponsorship or alternative ways of financing the BBC. Established in the spring of 1985, the committee was required to make its report in the summer of 1986.

The establishment of the committee raised a furore in Britain for it was widely believed that the results of the committee's efforts were a foregone conclusion. Professor Peacock declared that the committee consisted of independent-minded individuals, and that its conslusions had not been pre-ordained (*Guardian*, 19 August 1985, p. 4). But the reactions to this statement were generally sceptical. The independence and integrity of the committee were not in question. Nonetheless it was widely believed that its conclusions could lead in only one direction – the greater exposure of the BBC to market forces – for several reasons.

First it was well known that Peacock himself was a free market economist and so, too, were some other members of the committee. Also, one member of the committee had previously been head of BBC Scotland, who had subsequently fallen out with the BBC. So, as one respondent put it, 'there you have a committee largely made up of people either hostile to the BBC or ideologically committed to advertising.' Second, although the majority of submissions the committee had received from organisations and indidivuals were opposed to the idea, successive opinion polls – including one conducted for the committee itself – showed that the public was overwhelmingly in favour of advertising on the BBC (*The Times*, September–

November 1985). By the end of 1985, it was rumoured that Peacock had been forced to accept the impossibility of forcing advertising on the BBC. But he was still 'casting about frantically' for a system that would expose the BBC to 'some cold blast of market forces' (Watt, 1985, p. 16).

Moreover some people argued that Mrs Thatcher had already made up her mind in favour of advertising or an equivalent, and hence the committee's conclusions would not really matter. As a respondent claimed: 'The Peacock Committee is required to present a series of economic models, and there's a cynical belief about that the Prime Minister has already made up her mind to put some advertising on the BBC, and that she will pick the model which is most convenient.'

The establishment of the committee also raised a political furore because the attitudes towards it were divided along partisan lines. Conservative politicians were by and large supporting the establishment of the committee and the introduction of advertising into the BBC while Labour and Liberal–SDP/Alliance politicians were opposing both. One respondent, for instance, himself a member of the IBA, quoted Conservative members of parliament as saying to him: 'Rotten old BBC. They say that advertising will spoil their service. It doesn't spoil yours, does it? So let them have some. Jolly well serves them right. They will [finally] have to compete for something.' The respondent insisted that some Conservatives have eventually been convinced to reject advertising. But, by and large, the above citation well reflects the Tory viewpoint at that time. *Per contra*, Labour and Liberal politicians have adamantly rejected the idea of advertising on the national public broadcasting system. Thus, the Labour Shadow Home Secreary said that if the BBC was made to take advertising then when Labour came to power it would reverse that. And Liberal Party leader David Steel, declared that the committee was clearly 'intended [by the government] as a wedge to break up the BBC' and 'to muffle the independent voice by which they feel so threatened' (*Guardian*, 19 August 1985, p. 4).

Another reason for the furore around the Peacock Committee was the fact that the BBC, the IBA and its affiliates all opposed advertising on the BBC. Thus the then chairman of the BBC, Stuart Young, warned that commercials would demean BBC programmes. And representatives of the IBA cautioned that the heightened competition for advertising money would lead to programmes gravitating towards the lowest common denominator in both systems.

Finally, and most importantly, the establishment of the Peacock Committee was traumatic because it was believed by a variety of people (though not by all concerned) to have been set up in order to exert political pressure on the BBC, and to diminish the stature of the BBC by effectively destroying its traditional role and self-image. Some respondents pointed out that the setting up of the committee constituted political pressure in its own right, no matter what its conclusions might eventually turn out to be. In the words of one respondent, a union representative, 'the Peacock Committee – that's a pressure to conform'. Or in the words of another respondent, a Labour member of parliament: 'The Peacock Committee, that's a further form of pressure . . . the lesson is: behave yourself or you'll get advertising. So now for a year or so we shall have a Peacock Committee of enquiry and the BBC will again be on best behaviour.'

Some respondents added that this pressure was intended to make the BBC excessively cautious and had already had this effect, for instance by cutting down current-affairs programmes as much as possible or 'putting them back' to late hours. In connection with this the *Journalist* (London) (June 1984, p. 1) reported that the BBC was about to scrap a daily current affairs programme *Sixty Minutes* and replace it with 'soft' news (an independent check with BBC archives showed that this had in fact been done). This seemed to the writer of the article to be in line with a general trend of cuts in current affairs air-time on the BBC. Ten years previously the BBC had had about 35 minuted devoted to current affairs in the early evening (in addition to news coverage) plus a late-night current-affairs programme of about 45 minutes. At present there were about 5–10 minutes of early-evening current affairs, and the BBC was not planning to put on another current-affairs programme after *Sixty Minutes* was dropped.

The fact that some current-affairs broadcasts were to be replaced by news could not be seen as a consolation, for (as has been pointed out to me by respondents in more than one country) in the news the government normally emerges more favourably than the opposition because they are the ones who make the news and announce them. In current affairs, on the other hand, the opposition frequently comes out more favourably than the government because the task of such programmes is to be questioning and critical. So it is political criticism which is most likely to suffer under the pressure of privatisation.

It was also pointed out that the government attitude toward the BBC – of which the Peacock Committee was but an indicator – was pressing the BBC towards commercialisation, 'Americanisation', and emphasis on light entertainment. One respondent summarised: 'The present government wants a more popular, more commercial minded [system] ... approaching a mass audience ... [but the BBC] doesn't want to be transformed into a second and perhaps inferior IBA.' Respondents voiced the opinion that the setting up of the committee was generally intended to cut down the BBC, and that it had already succeeded in impairing its self-confidence:

> The BBC is in a mood of intense defensiveness because of the Peacock Committee ... In a subtle way there have [already] been changes since Mrs Thatcher came to power. ... I think it's now becoming a much more cautious institution, much less eager to assert itself; much less willing to offend anybody, less vigorous and lively than it was. I think the BBC is very nervous now.

> the [whole idea] of a public institution is being challenged by the government ... the BBC faces the problems of how it [now] defines its role ... its purpose ... The BBC was always brilliant in rethinking its role ... it's going through a very bad time now.

Did the pressures thus being applied to the BBC reflect the prime minister's displeasure with the BBC? Most respondents thought the pressures were more closely related to the prime minister's free-market ideology, her dislike of the unpopular licence fee, and her belief that the BBC should 'stand on its own feet'. But one respondent added: 'Maybe there is something at the back of Thatcher's mind saying: "Yes, I'll screw the BBC because they've made my life difficult over the Falklands." I don't know. But how do you find out?'

In the event, the Peacock Committee, whose report was released at the beginning of July 1986, demonstrated its independence by rejectig advertising on the BBC and proposing yearly indexation of the BBC licence fee. But it also proposed the eventual replacement of this licence fee through funding by direct subscriptions, privatisation of Radios One and Two, the auction of direct broadcasting by satellite franchises, and complete deregulation of cable television. As expected, it thus opened the way for a free market in broadcasting, and for a system in which (as a leading article in *The Times*, 4 July 1986, p. 13) put it, public broadcasting would play 'an important but definitely secondary role'.

Although some commentators considered the proposals too radical even for the Tories, and although the government announced that the pay-as-you-view system would not be implemented before the next election, other commentators believed that several ministers favoured the proposals and *The Times*, in the same article, commented that the Peacock Report 'can hardly fail in the longer run to exercise strong influence on thinkng and policy about broadcasting'.

AUSTRALIA

At the time of writing privatisation was not a central item on the Australian agenda, although the tolling of the bells could be heard in the distance. The ABC had long been faced with competition (mostly private) which had been increasing over the years. In Sydney and Melbourne (Australia's major metropolitan centres) the ABC was currently competing against four television stations. As private competition had been increasing, the number of prople watching ABC programs had been decreasing: the ABC lost between one third and a half of its audience within the last decade.[2] According to a senior executive this had happened not only because of the growing number of private stations, but also because the private stations were more in tune with the mainstream of the audience, while the ABC had been 'marginalised' in Australian society.

The Labor government which came into office in 1983 made it clear that it expected the ABC to shape up and increase its attractiveness to the audience. And the organisation has in fact been making strenuous efforts of respond to this demand. But it has not really been forced into a new mould. For the time being the parliamentary appropriation would continue to ensure its subsistence. The ABC could thus permit itself to broadcast at least some quality programmes (including political programmes) even if they were not large audience catchers.

At that time also there were no prospects of commercial advertising being imposed on the ABC. The Dix Committee of Enquiry on the ABC (1981) had recommended commercial sponsorship of some ABC programmes. More recently, the idea had been floated again – and rejected by the ABC board and by the government.

Satellite broadcasting was also being introduced in Australia but at the time of writing was not looming as a threat to the ABC. Satellite broadcasts, begun at the end of 1985, gave 300 000 Australians in remote areas access to television. The private broadcasting stations were users of satellite broadcasting. But the ABC had a substantial share in satellite broadcasts as well: when the first Aussat satellite became operational, ABC satellite broadcasts became operational with it. Hence, as a respondent informed us, there was no 'undue fear' in the ABC because of satellite broadcasting.

The situation may be quite different, however, in the near future. Firstly, private competition was about to expand even further: in May 1986, the Minister for Communications announced the government policy of speeding up the licensing of three commercial television signals for most rural areas (where previously the ABC had had only one private competitor). Also, the ABC is generally modelled after the BBC. Hence it is quite possible that if a pay-as-you-go-system is eventually inflicted on the BBC, it will be imposed on the ABC as well. It is at this point that problems similar to those in Britain would be likely to occur: the parliamentary appropriation for the ABC might well be decreased and it would be incumbent on the ABC to increase its audience in order to gain a substantial share of the subscription market. The ABC would thus be forced to adapt to market demands and quality programmes (including current affairs) might well fall by the wayside, be shortened, or have to change their character to suit the taste of the audience. The ABC might even have to model some of its current affairs offerings after one of its private competitor's (semi-) current affairs programmes 'Sixty Minutes'. In it, human interest stories, frequently with sexual connotations, have largely supplanted political analysis.

From this viewpoint satellite broadcasting might also pose a greater problem in the near future. By mid-1985 the ABC staff union was already complaining that the corporation was undertaking to develop such broadcasting without obtaining additional funds for this purpose. This meant a A$20 million cut in the ABC budget in real terms, and that expenses on existing programmes would have to be trimmed: 140 hours of Australian television production would be lost and staff ceilings would be affected (*Scan*, 15 July 1985, pp. 7–8). With the further development of satellite broadcasting, this trend would most likely be exacerbated. Unless the ABC was able to increase its budget through advertising or subscriptions it would have to divert more of the existing funds to satellite broadcasting development, productions would have to be trimmed, and small audience catchers such as the more serious but less entertaining political programmes would probably be amongst the sufferers.

ISRAEL

Unlike the situation in Britain – commercial advertising on public broadcasting had never been a major issue here. Israel Radio had long featured advertising on some of its channels, and recently television quietly adopted commercial sponsorship of programmes to help to overcome its escalating financial difficulties. In contrast, the prospective introduction of a competing television channel, most likely a privately-financed one, has recently become the focus of intense political struggles. Perhaps this is so because Israel Television has so far enjoyed a monopoly. Israel Radio has had to face competition from a high-quality military station. Since 1973 it has also had to face competition from 'The Voice of Peace', a pirate station run by the famous peacemonger, Abie Nathan, and transmitting from a ship off Israel's shores, but at the time of writing Israel's public television still enjoyed its unrivalled position as national broadcaster.

A second television channel had been on the agenda for many years; as far back as 1969 some people believed its introduction to be imminent. But until 1985 this channel was much like the weather. Everyone discussed it but no one was able to do much about it: the political struggles surrounding the issue had led to a stalemate (Paz-Melamed, 1985b).

The matter had been high on the government's agenda since 1977, but because of intra-coalition wranglings it was stalled until 1984. At that time the Likud government was replaced by a national unity government and the Ministry for Communications fell to the small Shinui Party and its representative, Amnon Rubinstein. The coalition agreement stipulated that the second channel be established under the auspices of his department. Rubinstein speedily drafted a proposal for the introduction of such a channel, but the government failed to act on it for several months.

In the autumn of 1985, the proposal to set up a second channel was still stalemated because many divergent political interests impinged on the issue and counteracted each other. It was in the Likud's interest to stall for another year when (according to the coalition agreement) the premiership would fall into their hands. At that time – they hoped – they would be able to put their own people in control of the channel. It was in Labour's and Shinui's interest that the second channel go ahead immediately, albeit in different forms. The Labour Minister of Education and Culture was intent on establishing the channel as an extension of existing educational television which was under the sponsorship of his department, and run by his own people. The Shinui Minister of Communications, on the other hand, was intent on establishing a private commercial station, financed by advertising. Ostensibly this would remove the new channel from political interference. But, according to press reports, the new authority would be supervised by a board composed of representatives of the public, of government departments and of political parties, and this board would be directly in charge of the new channel's news programmes. And Rubinstein had already founded an 'Authority for the Establishment of a Second Channel' headed by a member of his own party.

Also a party to the struggle were the Israel Broadcasting Authority and its board of management. These feared that the new channel would impoverish the existing one by attracting huge advertising monies and the most talented of the authority's employees. According to the chairman and some members of the board, establishing the second channel under the present Broadcasting Authority Act would be an elegant solution to the problem. Other members of the board went further and demanded that the second channel be established within the framework of the Israel Broadcasting Authority.

On the other side of the fence were the private producers who did all they could to promote the proposal. They pointed out that many dissatisfied Israeli viewers had been tuning in to the television stations of the neighbouring Arab countries, chiefly Jordan. One producer complained: 'Hussein has no board of management, and no responsible minister, and his parliament does not have to reach a decision. And he has two channels already over which he broadcasts to the multitudes of the house of Israel. But I, an Israeli producer, am to be forbidden from doing so?' (Ron'el and Cohen, 1985, p. 6).

In October 1985 the government finally decided to give Rubinstein's proposal for a second, commercial, channel the go-ahead. According to Paz-Melamed (1985b) there had been so many calls of 'wolf' in the past that many people simply would not believe the 'wolf' was really on the threshold. Nonetheless many observers offered the opinion that this time the matter was really heading for a breakthrough. For Rubinstein was so determined to push through his proposal that he threatened to resign unless action was taken. Also, politicians were fully aware that an Arab satellite, recently put in place over Jordan, was being used by the neighbouring countries to occupy the television frequencies in the Middle East. Unless the government acted quickly there would be no frequencies left for the new channel.

At that time the introduction of private cable television in Israel was also on its way. In 1985 some pirate cable stations were already in existence. The government favoured cable television not only in its own right but also because it would offer the public a higher standard alternative to the low quality programmes (including pornography) presented by the pirate stations. Accordingly, in June 1986, the Parliamentary Finance Committee passed a bill for the introduction of cable television in Israel.

Clearly, in one way or another, private, commercial television was about to be introduced in Israel. It was not clear as yet what shape it would take, what political programmes it would feature, and how Israel television's own political fare would be affected. But one thing was beyond doubt: with the introduction of the second channel and of cable television the importance and stature of the existing television channel would diminish proportionately.

WEST GERMANY

While in Israel the main political struggles concerned the introduction of a second television channel, in West Germany there were two national broadcasting systems (running three television programmes) already in existence. And unlike the situation in Britain the introduction of commercial advertising was not an issue here, as public broadcasting was partly financed by limited advertising. Nonetheless, public broadcasting in West Germany had long enjoyed a complete monopoly (or more precisely a duopoly) on broadcasting. In 1985 the writing on the wall was for breaking that duopoly through the introduction of privately run 'new media' in the form of cable and satellite programmes.

For a long time the duopoly of public broadcasting in West Germany had been maintained because of the scarcity of available wavelengths. Because of this, the German Federal Constitutional Court had ruled in 1961 that pluralism was to be maintained within the public broadcasting system itself, and that the establishment of a joint private–government broadcasting corporation was unconstitutional.

In recent years the Federal Constitutional Court has still been insisting on broadcasting pluralism. But technical developments in the areas of cable and satellite broadcasting have made a much larger number of frequencies available – and it thus became possible to meet the requirements for pluralism through the participation of an increasing number of broadcasters including private ones (ARD, 1984, p. 136). Consequently, the new verdicts of the constitutional court have been becoming less restrictive, and in its verdict of 1981 it recognised the possibility of private broadcasting (Wilfert, 1984, p. 1).

But it was left for the Länder (states) to pass the necessary legislation to introduce satellite and cable television, mostly through private broadcasters, in their domains. By 1986 most states had already done so, and the development of the new media was going ahead. Cable television had been under discussion since 1974 and in 1978 the state premiers agreed on the introduction of four pilot projects in local areas. Concomitantly, satellite television was also developing. In 1984 ZDF, in co-operation with the broadcasting corporations of Austria and Switzerland, started a satellite channel – 3 SAT – intended for German-speaking countries. In January 1985 another satellite channel – the first privately run television programme – SAT 1 – was established. Research had shown that in the areas in which it could be received it could successfully compete with the ratings of national public broadcasting (Kaltefleiter, 1985). And in the Spring of 1986 ARD began transmission of a satellite programme of its own: *One Plus*.

Even so, the laying of cables (into which satellite television was to be fed) was expensive, and hence proceeded rather slowly: by the beginning of 1986 SAT 1 and 3 SAT sould be received by only about one million households. Private broadcasting therefore was not yet a serious threat to ARD and ZDF which shared twenty-two times as many households with television sets capable of receiving their programmes between them. It was expected, at the time, that it would take ten years or more for private cable and satellite television to reach comparable numbers of viewers. But a new satellite which could be received without cable networks – TV SAT – was expected to become operational in 1987. And it was clear, that somewhere around the turn of the century there would be several widely received private television programmes in West Germany (Haagen, 1985). At that point, private broadcasting would have become a formidable competitor against the public broadcasting system.

As soon as the development of private broadcasts through the new media became technically and legally feasible political struggles developed. The CDU – which was dissatisfied with existing public broadcasting and expected that its case would be more favourably presented on private stations – promptly came out in favour of the new media. The SPD – whose politicians believed that their own cause was best served by public broadcasting, while private broadcasting would give over-representation to the capitalist circles – opposed the new developments. However, the SPD was gradually changing its attitudes and by mid 1986 the state of Hessen ruled by the

SPD-Greens was the only one in which the introduction of private broadcasting was still prevented.

Since most SPD politicians were resigning themselves to the inevitable, the introduction of private broadcasting as such was no longer a major issue. But there was still a jockeying for position, with public broadcasters backed by SPD states attempting to put as many new programmes into place and to gain as much advertising time as they possibly could, and CDU/CSU states doing their best to promote private broadcasting. A few cases of litigation on such issues were before the Federal Constitutional Court during the first half of 1986 (*Frankfurter Allgemeine Zeitung*, January–July 1986).

Importantly, some question marks remained as to the effects which the introduction of private broadcasting would have on public broadcasting. Asked what these effects would be, some respondents said they did not fear competition, as the 'private ones' would be showing mostly bought foreign programmes whereas the German public preferred to see its own programmes, politicians and artists. But most respondents admitted that with the added offerings the market would be divided and the number of viewers for public broadcasting would shrink. The bright side of this development would be that politicians would be less motivated to exert pressure on public broadcasting. So far, as a respondent explained, all politicians have had to do was to try to influence ARD and ZDF and they would have got hold of the entire German public. With the proliferation of private broadcasting there would simply be too many points on which to exert pressure on – to make it all worthwhile. This silver lining, however, also has a cloud: with public broadcasting losing some of its audience to private broadcasting, it would also lose in importance. So the price to be paid for diminished pressure would most likely be diminished stature.

While some respondents said they did not shirk the competition of private broadcasting in general terms, all agreed that it posed a financial problem. For some advertising funds would certainly be lured away from public to private broadcasting while concomitantly the licence fee might not be raised. Several respondents converged on this point, but one most fully clarified the situation:

> Private broadcasting is financed by advertising and therefore needs

a programme for the masses. The masses want light entertainment. Public broadcasting on the other hand is obliged by law and by the inter-state agreements to provide programmes for minorities as well. So once the private ones manage to push themselves through, we fear we will feel it on the advertising market . . . We also fear that once the private ones have come through [we will have problems with the licence fee]. Viewers will say: 'I can see SAT 1, etc. and it costs nothing, and they bring two entertainment films every evening and that's cool. And here come ARD and ZDF; they bring [fewer] entertainment films, and they bring minority and political programmes which I don't want to see. And now the licence fee for ARD and ZDF is to be raised – I won't buy that!' And politicians will be under pressure not to raise the fee

Could the introduction of private broadcasting be used as a spectre hanging over the public broadcasters which ought to convince them to fall into line politically? At the time of this study it was clear that the process could not be reversed. Hence, it could no longer be used as a stick with which public broadcasting could be intimidated into compliance. But the financial issues surrounding this process certainly *could* be used as such a stick. Several respondents concurred on this, although they also concurred that politicians would never admit it openly. One respondent had this to say:

Yes there is a material threat there . . . If [they] now say: under no circumstances may you bring more advertising than before; the most attractive times go to the private [broadcasters] . . . this is of course material pressure that may become massive. If the word goes out that public broadcasting does not get a Mark more than previously, but the cost of living rises, this is of course a circumcision. There is a threat there from one political side: we want to support the private [broadcasters] because they are closer to us.

So in 1985 the introduction of private broadcasting as such was no longer a source of political pressure. But it was making public broadcasting corporations more vulnerable to financial pressures, a situation which politicians may well be using to their advantage for years to come.

Public broadcasting corporations now had to work out an appropriate response to the new developments. Initially their representatives reacted by opposing them altogether. Thus

SDR intendant Bausch (1980, p. 969) wrote that politicians had appeased public broadcasters by saying that:

> the intention was merely to place at the side of the public broadcasting cow a little private calf. [But] this biological metaphor is instructive . . . [for] the cow grows old and ends up in the slaughterhouse while the calf develops and owes its deliverers a debt of gratitude.

Thus intendant Bausch opposed private broadcasting on the ground that it would lead to the demise of public broadcasting coupled with the politicisation of the new system. And even as late as 1984 ZDF intendant Stolte – in the ZDF yearbook – came out strongly against private broadcasting. But by then it had become eminently clear that merely opposing private broadcasting would be but a futile exercise and that additional ways of coping with the problem had to be devised. One such way was to participate in the new media – by having a major share in SAT 3 and by taking part in cable pilot-projects in order, as a respondent put it: 'to be with it from the beginning, for in 5–10 years the train may have left the station and we may not be able to jump on board'. In the words of another respondent: 'Better to mount the horse than be trampled by it.'

This raises the question of how one mounts the horse. According to the overwhelming majority of respondents public broadcasters would have to do so – and indeed were already doing so – by adapting themselves to the taste of the mass audience. As one respondent explained: 'For political reasons it is becoming more and more important to show that we are just as attractive [to the audience] as the private ones.' What was attractive to the audience was first and foremost entertainment; and to some extent the public broadcasters were already gearing themselves to this priority: the ZDF was transmitting more entertainment films than previously, including those which – for reasons of quality – it would not have touched five years earlier.

Apart from affecting the public broadcasters' standards, the advent of private broadcasting was also expected to affect their political programmes. Most respondents thought that these programmes would now be apt to lose large numbers of viewers who – when given a choice – would opt for entertainment.

So, to maintain a share of the audience, public broadcasters would have to shorten such programmes. Some respondents also thought that private competition would lead to the 'Americanisation', or the popularisation of current-affairs offerings. A senior member of staff at ZDF said: 'There is some anticipatory identification with the aggressor. Why shouldn't we make political programmes entertaining? It would be possible to introduce association games, cartoons, surprise guests, things like that.' Political programmes would thus feature entertainment which could include anything short of politicians performing a striptease for the edification of the audience. Thereby they would undoubtedly become more popular but lose much of their political sting.

According to some respondents only the news was not likely to suffer 'circumcision' because it had high ratings. But the news could be expected to suffer from the new trends in a different way. A study by Krüger (1985) found that in comparison with news on public broadcasting stations, news on West Germany's private channel had a much smaller proportion of political items, much more sport and human interest stories. The private station was evidently shaping the news to the taste of the audience. Once public broadcasters have to compete with private ones, they may well have to shape their news along similar lines.

All in all, then, political contents are likely to be reduced and 'softened' and the remaining political contents are likely to be watched by fewer people than was previously the case. Is this what politicians had in mind when they pushed for the introduction of private broadcasting? According to some respondents this is dubious to say the least:

> They are cutting into their own flesh – for the simple reason that the ... losers will be the political programmes. Whether the politicians are interested in having potential voters who are even less politically educated than they are anyway is still an open question.

> They remove their own possibility of reaching voters. And this certainly has not been anticipated and desired by politicians – it is a side irony.

CONCLUSION

In the mid-1980s in all the countries studied, privatisation was on the march. And despite individual differences there were some features of this process which the four countries had in common:

- The public broadcasting corporations were faced with the prospects of having competition from private broadcasters, or commercial financing imposed on them.
- These prospects were regarded by public broadcasters as a threat because they jeopardised their existing financial basis.
- These prospects were also regarded as a threat because they were likely to lead to a commercialisation and a popularisation of programmes.
- In particular, they were expected to lead to a diminution, a popularisation and a 'softening' of political programmes.
- The combination of these trends was perceived as likely to lead to a shrinking of the public broadcasters' influence, importance and stature in society and to a weakening of their self-confidence.

It may be argued that all these fears were groundless. For were not the British and the Australian broadcasting systems coping with private competition already? And did not the Israeli and the West German broadcasting systems have commercial advertising without their stature having been diminished? But so far none of these broadcasting systems has had to face private competition *and* commercial advertising or some other form of private financing. It was quite possible that the threat of a weakening financial basis, and the consequent popularisation and shrinking of political programmes would become greatly exacerbated when the features of private competition and commercial financing were combined. For then public broadcasters would have to compete with private broadcasters over *both* the audience *and* the advertising market, or, if financed by subscription, the competition for the audience would become much fiercer than it is at present.

It has been argued that there is nothing wrong with popularisation, that opposing it is merely a remnant of the elites and snobbishness of bygone days, that competition enlivens the business and pluralism invigorates democracy. The fact remains, however, that the representatives of public broadcasting perceived these developments as a threat. They could therefore be used by governments – and in some countries have already been used explicitly or implicitly – as a source of political pressure, to put public broadcasters 'on best behaviour', a pressure to which public broadcasting with its financial dependence on government has proved to be especially vulnerable.

This problem was most acute for the BBC which was already facing an identity crisis, and was becoming increasingly nervous, defensive and cautious. But whether this was intended or not, it might be expected that the same pressures would lead to political timidity in the other countries as well. And in all countries concerned – this may well work in favour of politicians and parties of whichever government may be in power – that is, in favour of the political establishment and the status quo.

Notes

1. The Independent Television Authority until 1971.
2. In 1984–5 one of the ABC's news and current affairs programmees, *The National*, was a spectacular failure and caused an especially pronounced 'dip' in ratings. With the elimination of this programme the 'dip' was overcome. But the general decline in the ABC's share of the audience has not been convincingly reversed as yet.

7 External Pressures through Appointments

The use of appointments is a time-honoured device to achieve political compliance. In several Western democracies it has been – and in some is still – used, in the government bureaucracy. It is no less popular in broadcasting corporations, where it has been applied with respect to the boards, their chairmen and the directors-general.

THE BOARDS

In all countries studied the broadcasting corporations are governed by boards whose formal role is to represent the public in broadcasting. The BBC is governed by a board of governors consisting of twelve members. These are appointed by the Queen-in-Council – that is, in practice, by the government. But the convention is that once appointed, the governors lose their political identity and become non-partisan in the performance of their duties. Another unwritten convention is that the board includes at least one financial expert, a diplomat, an educationist and a trade unionist.

While governors can escape political partisanship they cannot as Briggs (1979, p. 20) put it 'escape the influences of their own backgrounds'. Hence it is significant that most of the the governors have tended to be public school, 'Oxbridge' graduates, with a median starting age of 58–9 (Paulu, 1981, p. 133) – in other words, established and establishment-type persons. In 1977, the Annan Report expressed wonder at the fact that so few members of the board had their roots in the working class. Respondents in this study confirmed that the present governors continud to be part of the establishment, and that they were generally conservative in their outlooks.

Some respondents claimed that the governors, who had been appointed by the Thatcher government were now more overt political appointees than they used to be, 'with a majority who are pro-government', 'the PM's friends'. Also, A. Singer, a former managing director of BBC television, attacked Mrs Thatcher's unprecedented packing of the governors with 'placemen of her own disposition' (*Guardian*, 25 August 1985, p. 6).[1] A respondent testified:

> The government has tended to put people [on the board] who are sympathetic to its views in greater numbers than has been the practice in the past. There is a question that the PM is said to ask about every appointee to a public body: is he one of ours? . . . And you have in the space of one government, as it were, destroyed a tradition which has been very valuable. The appointments are not party-political but possibly it's even worse. Because if it were political each party would claim its right to representation. [As it is] they are . . . establishment people and therefore they may be much more prone to be the servants of whatever regime is in office.

So far (as Paulu, 1981, p. 24) explained, the convention was that once appointed, the governors 'then somehow miraculously became independent guardians against political pressures' and indeed 'the miracle really does happen in at least some cases'. Also, Annan (1977, p. 15) wrote that in the 1960s when the board repeatedly asserted its independence, politicians were wondering whether they had not appointed an admiral who habitually turned a blind eye when the Admiralty made a signal.

Have times changed since then? According to some respondents the governors still took their responsibility of preserving the independence of the BBC very seriously indeed, and as one respondent added, while as individuals the governors might be favourably oriented to the government, when they met as a board, something happened to them and they became better than they were as individuals. Other respondents thought that the governors no longer stood up for the BBC. One respondent expressed the view that what a truly independent board should have done would have been to resign over the issue of the government intending to impose advertising on the BBC.

According to many observers the board's ability to stand up for BBC independence had been put to the test over the screening of the *Real Lives* programme and they had not passed the test with flying colours. True, the board did not ban the film but merely postponed its screening. True, also, the proper procedures of referring the matter upwards to the board apparently had not been followed. But these mitigating circumstances did not prevent the former director-general, Greene, expressing the view that the board had bowed to government pressure, a thing which former boards would not have considered doing (*Guardian*, 31 July 1985, pp. 1 and 30). *The Times* (2 August 1985, p. 13) similarly expressed the view that the governors 'were acting under heavy political pressure, which no amount of protestation to the contrary will make invisible'. *The Daily Telegraph* (24 August, p. 2 reported that even right-wingers and conservatives were criticising the governors for folding up under the government's onslaught. And, most importantly, BBC management fell out with the board and criticised its retreat under government fire. Eventually the decision was taken to show the film at a later date. But whether this decision had restored the governors' reputation as guardians of BBC independence is still an open question.

In Australia, under the 1983 Broadcasting Act, the erstwhile Australian Broadcasting Commission was transformed into the Australian Broadcasting Corporation governed by a board of seven to nine directors. Like its predecessor – the commission – the board of directors is appointed by the government for a fixed (but renewable) term. Its members are customarily drawn from different groups and organisations such as universities, trade unions and organised religion.

The importance of the board (commission) lies in its power to map out broadcasting policy and to appoint the managing director. Consequently all governments so far have made attempts to staff it predominantly with their own sympathers. This was attested, for instance, by former deputy general manager, Semmler, who wrote of the 'blatant stacking of the national broadcasting instrumentality under both Labor and Liberal governments' (Semmler, 1981, p. 30). And the Dix Report (1981, vol. 2, p. 87) bears witness that 'since the early 1970s governments of both political complexions appear to have more overtly appointed to the Commission people who, in their view, are politically "acceptable" '.

When Labor came to power in 1972 it found the commission staffed with Liberal Party sympathisers. But as vacancies appeared, it introduced its own people. When the Liberal government came back to office in 1975 it looked for a way to reverse the trend. To this end it introduced into parliament a bill which would have removed all commissioners from office. Widespread adverse reactions forced the government to back down. But while the existing commissioners were to stay on, this was to be counterbalanced by an increase in the commissioners' numbers so that Liberal appointees could be introduced as well. In addition, the government renewed none of the Labor appointments so that eventually, the commission was once more staffed by people sympathetic to its views – indeed, according to one respondent, mostly by 'ultra-conservatives'.

When the Labor government returned to power in 1983, it replaced the existing commission by a corporation. It took this opportunity to dismiss the Liberal-appointed commission and replace it by a board of directors of its own choice. Interestingly, while the Liberal government's attempt to dismiss the commissioners before their term had expired gave rise to widespread indignation, the Labor government's feat to achieve a similar aim – did not. A respondent expressed his concern about this saying 'This is a precedent. Previously it couldn't be done. Now it can be done.'

Respondents were canvassed about the political composition of the Labor-appointed board. A few thought the board did not show a clear trend. The majority, however, thought that although most directors were not official members of the Australian Labor Party they were broadly sympathetic to its policies, somewhat left of centre, small-'L' liberals. As to the board's stand *vis-à-vis* political pressures, some thought the board was open to pressures because it was politically appointed. More often, however, the view was expressed that the government was having some 'blues' with the board.

> I don't know whether the board is resisting [pressures]. I think they probably would. They are fairly independent-minded.
>
> I think that the government is disappointed with the way they chose the board.
>
> The present board is probably as little loved by the government as any ... that has gone before was by any previous government.[2]

In Israel the law provides for a broadcasting authority

composed of a thirty-one-member plenum and a seven-member board of directors, appointed by the government for a three-year term. The plenum is to reflect the variety of views within the mainstream of Israeli society and convey them to the broadcasting corporation. In practice it has no real power and acts as a rather toothless parliament. The board of directors is the public body which actually governs the broadcasting corporation; although it does not appoint the director-general it supervises him and is entitled to issue instructions to him. It is appointed from within the plenum and composed of party representatives selected by a 'party-political key' that reflects the parties' weight in parliament. This means that the government and its coalition partners have a majority on the board. Members of the board have always represented first and foremost their own political parties and according to various reports and observations this has become more flagrant recently.

In West Germany the broadcasting laws of the various states and the various inter-state agreements provide for broadcasting corporations' supervisory organs (*Gremien*) which are to reflect the divergent political views existing in the community, and represent them in broadcasting. Accordingly, the broadcasting corporations are to be governed by the following organs:

1. The *Broadcasting Board* (*Television Board* in the ZDF) consisting of eleven to sixty-six members – which has the task of supervising the basic programme policies. These boards are divided into two basic models: the first is the pluralist model in which board-members are nominated primarily by various 'socially relevant' groups such as employers' associations, trade unions, parties, churches and the like (BR, HR, RB, SDR). The second is the political–parliamentary model, in which board-members are elected by the state parliaments and governments (WDR, DW, DLF). There is also a mixed model which combines elements of both types (SFB, NDR, SR, ZDF) (Kepplinger 1982, p. 82).
2. The *Administrative Board* – usually composed of between seven and nine members, all or some of whom are appointed by the broadcasting board. Its task is to oversee the management of the corporation; it is usually involved in

senior appointments. Of the two boards, the broadcasting boards are usually the less powerful as they are relatively large and cumbersome, and meet only intermittently. However, unlike the plenum of the broadcasting authority in Israel, they are by no means powerless.

As in Britain, board-members tend to be of privileged social background, but here this is less salient, for it is the overt and growing politicisation of staffing that is the focus of attention. The broadcasting corporations that came into being under Allied rule were constituted according to the pluralist model; those that were established after the Allies withdrew followed the political–parliamentary or the mixed model. The earlier stations seem to have obtained and maintained more political independence than those established later on. According to most observers, however, even the early corporations have not remained as they were originally meant to be, and party-politicisation has become pervasive in practically all boards: the representatives of the 'socially relevant groups' who were meant to be politically independent have frequently joined one political camp or another thus creating clearly delineated political blocs.

For this the ZDF furnishes an apt example. Its television board was constituted according to a mixed model with around two-thirds of its members selected from amongst non-party groups. But the representatives of these groups in fact show affinity to one or the other of the major parties. In this manner party-political blocs are created which render the ZDF board practically indistinguishable from the political–parliamentary model.

Generally speaking, the party that holds a majority in the relevant state parliament or parliaments will also hold a majority on the relevant board. Since at the time of writing there were more CDU (CSU) states than SPD states, most boards were CDU-dominated. The CDU has also had an advantage in manoeuvring its members and sympathisers into key positions on the boards because of its greater efforts and talents in this area. As Williams (1976, p. 135) put it 'the SPD is not so much innocent of manipulation as inept at it' or as a respondent supplemented 'the SPD simply sleeps through the whole process'.

This general situation was reflected in the ZDF. Since the CDU dominated both boards, it could push through its own decisions on all matters. However, as several respondents informed me, it was not the custom on the boards to overrule minorities unilaterally. The tendency was usually to seek a compromise so as to reach consensus.

In some broadcasting corporations poilitical pressure groups calling themselves 'circles of friends' (*Freundeskreise*) have established themselves. These circles are composed of each party's members and sympathisers on both boards and amongst the key-position-holders within the broadcasting stations. According To Williams (1976, p. 124), '[t]he black humour of the name may be totally unintentional. They are certainly nobody's friends.' In ZDF, for instance, the members of those circles usually meet before every board meeting to discuss the issues which then come up at the formal meeting. According to Williams, board-members attend the party circles to receive their orders; in this manner, they pre-empt the important decision of the board meetings.

CHAIRMEN OF THE BOARDS

In Britain, the chairman (like the board) is appointed by the Queen-in-Council – that is, by the government. By convention this is a non-political appointment. This convention seemed to have worked until the appointment of Lord Hill, who had been a Conservative politician. Because of that – respondents thought – no Conservative Prime Minister would have dared to appoint him, and only a Labour Prime Minister could do so. His appointment was nevertheless seen as a 'definite intrusion of politics', because it was aimed at 'taming the BBC' (Schlesinger, 1978, p. 138), and rendering it more responsive to the government's wishes. In the event Hill shaped up as a disappointment to his appointer, Prime Minister Wilson for, in the words of a respondent, he 'was an extremely vain man and the desire to have his own ideas accepted was greater than his desire to impose Wilson's ideas'.

Since then, no chairman has had an active political background (Paulu, 1981, p. 130). But the chairman at the time of this study, Young, though not active in politics, was known as a Conservative. As a Labour MP told me, he was appointed because he was part of the Conservative clique. If Labour came to power he would soon find himself out of a job. Respondents further stressed the fact that the chairman had a background in finances and accounting, and that the government felt that the BBC ought to be led by someone who could take a 'hard look' at its finances and trim it down.

Besides being a Conservative, the chairman was also the brother of a Cabinet Minister (although he was appointed before his brother). Some respondents assured me that this was 'pure coincidence', that things just didn't 'work in this crude way here'. Another respondent said with a smile: 'Yes, very small society, isn't it? This is not by chance.' Another respondent offered: 'It's not considered the done thing, but it is in fact done. *She* does it.' One respondent applied a comparative perspective: 'It's the sort of thing that we in Britain used to laugh at countries such as Spain for having twenty years ago. We thought it quaint that a country should have the audacity to put members of the same family in positions where there ought to be . . . a proper, healthy hostility. Now it happens in this country.'

These matters, of course, are not unrelated to the chairman's ability (or otherwise) to stand up for BBC independence. Some respondents thought the strength of the British tradition was that even if the chairman had a political background he would detach himself and be there to defend the BBC, and that this was evident with Young who had plainly defended the BBC over the licence fee and the Falklands controversy. Moreover, if the chairman were not to stand up for the BBC this would cause 'a rumpus . . . an enormous row'. This, however, is precisely what has in fact happened later on in the case of the *Real Lives* programme.

In October 1986 a new chairman was appointed to succeed the recently deceased Young. He was Marmaduke Hussey, a previous chief executive of *The Times* newspapers. He, too, was a conservative, establishment figure, and the relative of a government minister. It was widely believed that he was brought in in the hope that he would exert firmer control over the BBC.

In Australia, chairmen of the commission (board) have been appointed with a view to ensure broad sympathy for the government's aims. Thus Professor Richard Downing,

External Pressures through Appointments

appointed by the Labor government in 1973 had supported Labor at the previous election. Sir Henry Bland, appointed by the Liberal government in 1976, had previously been an informal adviser to Liberal PM Fraser. J. D. Norgard, also appointed by the Liberal government in 1976, was a former executive of a major corporation and thus could have been expected to be sympathetic to Liberal views; and Professor Dame Leonie Kramer appointed by the Liberal government in 1982 was known as a right-winger.

Kenneth Myer, appointed by the Labor government in 1983 was a prominent businessman who had supported Labor in the 1972 election. But according to practically all respondents his Labor Party allegiance has not been assured later on. Nonetheless, as one respondent saw it, there was no doubt that he had various links, through influential figures, in the Labor Party.

Though politically appointed, Australian chairmen have sometimes surprised and disappointed their appointers. Of this, according to Inglis (1983, chap. 8) chairman Bland became a prominent example even though this was not apparent initially. He furiously rebutted an attack by Prime Minister Fraser on the ABC, and when the Cabinet subsequently increased the number of commissioners so as to be able to introduce its own supporters, Bland resigned.

In various letters to the press in 1984, Tony Bond, the vice-president of the ABC staff association, expressed the view that the chairman, Professor Kramer, did not do her share in rebutting attacks on the ABC. However, several respondents testified that as chairman, particularly under the Labor government, she was pretty adamant in resisting pressures:

> Kramer was a strong-minded chairman in this respect.
>
> When Hawke and Button called Leonie Kramer she didn't pass it on.
>
> Kramer's responses were always proper ... it was her professionalism and her integrity she put to the foremost rather than her political leanings.

Chairman Myer has once been widely criticised for not being a staunch defender of ABC independence. In 1984, following a complaint by the government of Papua New Guinea on an interview with an Irian Jaya rebel which was to be screened on the *Four Corners* programme, Myer supported a management decision to ban the interview saying the 'ultimate consideration' had to be Australia's relationship with the country involved. He was subsequently overruled by the board. But other than that, the prevalent view was that (like his board) the chairman had been standing up for ABC independence. At the end of April 1986, chairman Myer resigned – because of internal divisions in the board.[3] The new chairman – appointed in July 1986 – was David Hill, chairman of the New South Wales Rail Authority. Hill was known to have close connections to the right wing of the Labor Party with which prime minister Hawke was also connected. But he was also known as a capable and tough administrator. A few months later he was appointed as managing director of the ABC and was to resign his post as chairman.

In Israel, the chairman of the authority is appointed by the government and is usually a representative of a government party. The previous chairman, Professor R. Yaron was a Likud activist, though also known as a prominent legal expert. He was instrumental in conveying political pressures downwards, but he would reject any suggestion that he considered unlawful. The present chairman, Micha Yinon, is also a legal expert. He is a faithful of the National Religious (coalition) Party. According to an informant, his main concern is that there be as many religious and as few anti-religious programmes as possible.

In West Germany, chairmen of boards are sometimes not merely political appointees but senior politicians in their own right. This holds especially for the ZDF where the chairman of the television board is the mayor of Mainz, Yokel Fuchs (SPD) and the chairman of the administrative board is the premier of the state Rheinland-Pfalz, Bernhard Vogel (CDU). As one respondent quipped: 'The Chairman of the administrative board is – what a coincidence – the premier of the state.' By now this 'coincidence' is more in the nature of an established tradition.

When chairmen (or even members) of the board are themselves active politicians, this raises the question of where their primary loyalties lie: with their parties or with the broadcasting stations. In the opinion of one respondent: 'One must justly say that the chairmen feel an obligation to the welfare of the institution . . . of course it is not always easy [to reconcile the different interests of the party and the ZDF] but so far they have always been successful.' Most respondents, however, offered a different opinion as illustrated by the following statement: 'my impression is that they are primarily politicians. It is clear that they speak for their parties.'

THE DIRECTORS-GENERAL

One difference between the various countries is in the appointment of the broadcasting corporations' one-person executive, their director-general (managing director in Australia, intendant in West Germany). In Britain the director-general is appointed by the board of governors and his appointment is not a political but a career-professional one. Considerations with subtle political connotations are nonetheless not completely absent.

Thus one of the past directors-general, Sir Hugh Greene (1960–9) was known as energetic and daring. During his term programmes became aggressive and *avant garde*, and political satire (*That Was The Week That Was*) flourished. He, certainly, was not a comfortable director-general for the government to have around. Hence, as Tracey (1983) shows, subtle ways and means were found to squeeze him out. The key move in the manoeuvre was the appointment of Lord Hill as chairman. The Prime Minister, Wilson, adamantly denied that he wanted to get rid of Greene. He must have realised, however, that Greene would never be able to get on with Hill. And constitutionally the chairman is superior to the director-general. So Greene eventually retired.

According to respondents this signalled the end of an entire epoch at the BBC and the beginning of a much more conservative, cautious one. In the words of a participant 'daring individuals just don't get appointed anymore' and directors-general tend to be more conservative. Certainly Ian Trethowan, who preceded the present director-general was conservative in his outlook and the present director-general Alisdair Milne, while not affiliated to any political party, was also reported to be 'bearing towards conservatism.'

Greene was known not only as a generally daring director-general but also as one who stood up for the BBC. Milne has not been able to build up a similarly outstanding reputation; it was reported (Summers, 1985) that in the recent BBC crises he had not been as steadfast in defending the BBC as staff had expected. It was even claimed by some critics that one reason for the crisis surrounding the *Real Lives* programme was that Milne had been perceived as a weak director-general. Otherwise the governors would not have dared to schedule the critical meeting in which the programme was banned during his absence. And in his presence the meeting's outcome might well have been different.

Upon his return he made no secret of where his sympathies lay – with his staff who wanted the programme screened, to wipe out any doubts about the BBC's independence. But for some time little was heard of his action to bring this about. Also, when the storm surrounding MI5 vetting of BBC staff broke loose, Milne attempted to play down the issue (see Chapter 13). Eventually he announced that vetting in the BBC domestic services would cease and that the *Real Lives* programme would be screened, albeit with some editorial changes. However, had he done so *before* pressures from the public, from his own staff and from unions had been building up, his action would have been more effective in restoring confidence in BBC independence.

In Australia, the managing director is appointed by the board for a limited (renewable) term. But while the appointment of the board itself has usually been a covertly politicised process, the appointment of the managing director has either not been political or only marginally so. This is attested by the fact that the supremos of the ABC have usually served for long time-spans under different governments. Sir Charles Moses and after him Sir Talbot Duckmanton have served under a succession of governments until their retirement. The general manager appointed after that (Jennings) was only temporary, and the appointment of the managing director at the time of this study, Geoffrey Whitehead, was once more non-political.

A decisive testimony to the latter is the fact that he was not even an Australian when appointed. According to one respondent the reason for his appointment was that 'the ABC needed an axe so an outsider was brought in to do it for them'. There is no evidence, however, that this was to be a political axe. The respondents in this study, too, believed that Whitehead was not a political appointment. Indeed, most respondents stated that they knew nothing about his political leanings:

> He's a bit of an enigma.
> We work very closely together but we've never discussed it . . .
> Whose side he's on would only be known to the ballot box.

Respondents have also testified to the fact that the process of appointing the managing director by the board was non-political – for instance:

> I know [his political views were not taken into account] because I was on the committee that appointed him . . . political considerations were taken into account but not his. [Other candidates had] clear political leanings towards the Labor Party and [their appointment] would've gained the board some kudos in Canberra . . . So I think the board did bear in mind political considerations and decided really that it couldn't be seen to [make] a political appointment . . . But the preparation had been done by the management consultants. We would've been expected to have been alerted to any problems there. I mean, it would've been irresponsible to have appointed someone and discover later that he was a member of a Communist party or a Nazi party or something like that.

In October 1986 Whitehead was succeeded by Hill. Since Hill had close Labor connections the Opposition claimed (with some justification) that this time the appointment of the managing director had been a political one.

In Israel the law provides for a director-general appointed by the government for a five-year (renewable) term. Since the government makes the appointment it is, not surprisingly, politicised. Thus, the first two directors-general after the broadcasting authority was established, Shmuel Almog and Yitzhak Livni, were choices of Labour governments and accordingly had Labour or general left wing affinities. The next director-general, Yosef Lapid, appointed by a right-wing Likud government in 1979, was known as a right-winger but not as a party member. Since then there has been an increasing politicisation of the appointment: the director-general at the time of writing, Uri Porat, also appointed by the Likud government, was well known as a party faithful who had previously been media adviser to the Prime Minister, Menachem Begin, and indeed was appointed (in the term used by a respondent) as a '*politruck*'.

However, the political appointment of the director-general does not necessarily ensure political compliance. For example, the first director-general of the broadcasting authority, Almog (appointed in 1968) at times transmitted external political pressures downward by intervening to prevent certain broadcasts from going to air. Even so, the pressures he received far exceeded the pressures he conveyed. Thus he served as a brake on, more than as a conveyor of, political pressures (Salpeter and Elizur, 1973, p. 305). As another example, former director-general Lapid clearly disappointed his appointers as is evident from the accusations levelled at him by government personalities (see Chapter 4). Several respondents voiced the opinion that when his term was about to run out he did a variety of things designed to appease the government so as to increase the chances of his re-appointment. But, in the event, whatever Lapid may have done did not meet the government's expectations, as is proved by the fact that he was not actually re-appointed.

The present director-general, Porat, was also a major disappointment to the Likud government, which appointed him. Porat was appointed to replace Lapid, because he was expected to be more faithful to the government's political stance. And, indeed, according to a key observer of the broadcasting scene, Porat initially intended to live up to these expectations, but he soon discovered that this led him to a constant confrontation with his employees. He therefore decided to side with the employees. But whatever the reason, from the Likud's viewpoint the result was still unpalatable.

In West Germany broadcasting legislation provides that each corporation have an intendant appointed by the broadcasting board, the administrative board or both for a (renewable) term of between three and ten years. The ZDF's intendant, for instance, is elected by secret ballot by the television board for a five-year renewable term, on the basis of a 3:5 majority. The administrative board may dismiss the intendant before the expiration of his term with the approval of the television board but so far this has never happened. The intendant is responsible for the entire programme of the corporation and makes senior appointments (with the approval of the administrative board).

The intendant is thus quite a powerful figure (according to a respondent, a 'monarch' in his institution). Not surprisingly, political parties make great efforts to secure an influence over his appointment, which consequently involves a great deal of inter-party bargaining and manoeuvring, though with a tendency to seek some compromise between the major parties. This is evident for instance in the ZDF which so far has had three intendants. The first, Professor K. Holzammer, was a CDU supporter, but as counterbalance an SPD person was selected as deputy intendant and programme director. Holzammer held office until 1977, when Karl Günther von Hase was elected. By all accounts his was a political appointment effected as a compromise when two other candidates were unable to gain the required majority in the television board.

Von Hase served for one term only, after which, in 1982, the present intendant, Professor Dieter Stolte, took office. Known as a CDU-sympathiser, Stolte was nonetheless selected unanimously by the representatives of all parties and continues to enjoy their support. This is so not only because of his well-known professional qualifications, but also because of his adeptness in manoeuvring between the parties – in the words of one respondent 'in bringing all interests under one hat'.

How firm are West German intendants in standing up for their institutions' independence? While the intendant is quite powerful within his institution, he is also dependent on the supervisory organs. He must maintain a majority there for his own eventual reappointment and as a respondent remarked, 'where one ogles reappointment it is very difficult [to preserve independence]'. He must also achieve support for the senior appointments he wishes to push through. In addition, he must take account of the political constellations and pressures from within the organisation (Bausch, 1980, p. 790). The intendant is thus caught between the twin pressures of party-political incursion from above and political pressures and counter-pressures from below (Wittich, 1983). Perhaps it would be exaggerated to say with Mai (1978, p. 591) that 'the intendant has become the punchbag of the nation'. It is nonetheless true that the situation of multiple pressures and role conflicts in which the intendant finds himself makes it difficult for him to be truly independent. So the intendant who fends off political pressures from all sides and simply makes them 'bounce back' is a rather rare phenomenon.

Nonetheless, such figures do appear occasionally. For instance, according to one respondent there used to be such a grand old man by the name of C. Wallenreiter in BR (1960–72). Another intendant who was widely reputed to be especially independent, was Hans Bausch, for a long time intendant of SDR. According to a respondent 'SDR is an island of the happy ones.' Another respondent noted in greater detail: 'Bausch is the strongest man in defence of broadcasting. He comes from the CDU but he makes it very clear: "I have a mass media instrument here; I am not a party representative; I must do things on my own responsibility." He is a shining exception.'

On the subject of ZDF-intendant Stolte, an article in *Der Spiegel* (13 February 1984, p. 13) claimed that while some intendants, when faced with political pressures, formed 'umbrellas' for their staff, in ZDF 'it rains through'. Asked about this, one respondent mused: 'it is hard to tell. Things may be better than they look.' Another respondent testified that the intendant might reproach a member of staff after a complaint – but he would always defend his staff against the outside. Yet another respondent summarised the views of many others by saying that Stolte was pragmatic. His approach was that the ZDF's independence could best be served when conflicts with politicians were minimised.

Summing up the situation with respect to West German intendants in general, a respondent aptly said: 'They are no slaves. And neither are they party functionaries. But there is a relationship of dependence there.'

CONCLUSION

One difference amongst the countries studied is in the appointment of the broadcasting corporations' director-general: in Israel he is appointed directly by the government, in the other countries by the board. The boards themselves, of course, are appointed by the government or are in other ways politically appointed. But since the appointments they make are a step removed from governments or political parties, one would have expected them to be at least somewhat less politicised than those made by governments or parties themselves. In fact this is not the case: in West Germany where the intendant is appointed by the board, the position is no less politicised than in Israel where the director-general is appointed by the government.

There are also differences in the manner in which the boards themselves and their chairmen are appointed. In Britain, Australia and Israel, they are appointed by the government, in West Germany by parliaments, governments and 'socially relevant' but highly-politicised groups. In all four countries the boards reflect the main, established, political forces in their respective societies. In Israel and West Germany the links between the board and politics are direct, overt and institutionalised; in Australia they are by now well-known and semi-institutionalised; in Britain they are the most covert and subtle.

Political appointments at senior and publicly visible levels cannot always be counted on to ensure compliance. And in all countries studied there are cases in which chairmen, boards and directors-general have stood up against their appointers and defended their corporations' independence. In general, however, the political establishments have been able to use staffing in order to structure the governing bodies of the broadcasting corporations to their advantage. Even in Britain where these bodies have traditionally had the greatest degree of independence, this independence has recently not been as clearly visible as before.

Moreover, where politicisation of the board is open and above-board, it is subject to scrutiny and representation by all major political parties. But where politicisation is subtle and elusive there is less opportunity for scrutiny and for the counteracting power of the opposition to make itself felt. This is unfortunate, for it may well invite the suspicion that nibbling away at broadcasting independence has been greater than has actually been the case.

Notes

1. However, by August 1986 Lord Barnett, a former Labour MP, had been appointed as vice-chairman of the BBC.
2. In July 1986 some directors' terms had run out and three new directors were appointed. At the time of this study it was not known as yet how they would shape up politically.
3. These were not directly related to politics, hence are not relevant for this study.

Part III
Internal Political Pressures

Besides external pressures (exerted by governments and politicians)
there are also internal political pressures
(exerted on behalf of governments and politicians)
by the different echelons of the broadcasting corporations themselves,
and bearing down on broadcasting staff.
This part of the book reviews various forms of such pressures.

8 Internal Pressures from the Board, from Management and from Peers

This chapter is concerned with internal pressures through intervention by the board, by management and by peers. It shows that – like the ambiguity of norms with respect to external intervention (see Chapter 3) – there is also ambiguity and controversy with respect to internal intervention. In addition, the chapter is designed to answer the question whether broadcasting staff enjoy autonomy or whether, in actual fact, they can do what they like – as long as they do what they are told.

BRITAIN

Here normative ambiguity and controversy as to internal political autonomy is well-documented by Swann (1978b) who quotes two views: the Conservative view that the (leftist)junior staff are *inadequately* controlled by the hierarchy, and the Labourite view that junior staff are *intolerably* constrained by the (rightist) hierarchy.

In fact the political influence of the board on the BBC has only occasionally been blatant. According to Burns (1977, chap. 1), the BBC's first director-general established the tradition that the board had little power in practice. O'Brien (1985, p. 23) wrote that the board resembled the God of the eighteenth-century deists: it presided but was incapable of intervention. 'Its authority in the word of a former director-general, Sir Charles Curran – is "immanent". "Immanent" is a euphemism for "impotent".' And Briggs (1979, Introduction) wrote that the board's important decisions have usually concerned matters of development rather than routine matters of programmes.

This account is supported by Semmler (1983, p. 32) who wrote that the BBC board had previewed the current affairs programme, *Yesterday's Men*. But 'the ensuing brouhaha between Wilson and the BBC governors' had convinced the board to leave programme decision-making alone and exercise their authority retrospectively.

Schlesinger (1978, chap. 6) wrote that the Reithian tradition (weak chairman, strong director-general) persisted into the 1960s, when it was broken by Lord Hill, who set out to assume direct control of the organisation. Respondents in this study thought that as a rule, even later, the board did not directly interfere in programmes. It was nonetheless politically influential by 'setting the tone', by creating the general atmosphere which permeated the entire organisation. One respondent explained: 'They create an atmosphere of caution. Daring producers know they'll be criticised by their own governors.' Interestingly this respondent, a Labour MP, added that the rot had really begun under Lord Hill, under a Labour government, because he had turned the board into an institution which – instead of standing as a defence between the BBC and the government – had tried to run the organisation.

This view was subsequently borne out by the instance of the *Real Lives* programme in which the board's interference had once again been blatant: it had previewed a programme and reached the politically-relevant editorial decision to postpone its screening, to the chagrin of the director-general and BBC staff. If, as Briggs (1979, Introduction) put it the traditional role of the board was 'to appoint and never disappoint' a director-general, in 1985, the board had clearly not fulfilled this role.

Pressures from management have usually been more concrete than those from the board and according to Burns (1977) have taken the forms of:

1. Official policy statements;
2. Referrals upwards;
3. meetings and discussions.

This was similarly confirmed by Francis (1977), Swann (1978a) and Hetherington (1985).

Likewise Schlesinger (1978) wrote that although BBC staff espoused a myth of internal independence, there was actually unobtrusive but very pervasive internal guidance. It consisted of an acknowledged system of referrals upwards, but also of an unacknowledged system of referrals downwards which (though largely invisible to staff) was omnipresent. The system focused on weekly meetings of senior editorial staff in which reactions to programmes were given and policy guidelines were laid down. The deliberations of these meetings were diffused through minutes which were formally restricted but whose wide dissemination was ensured through deliberate leaks.

Additional evidence came from respondents who emphasised that all complex matters that were in doubt were routinely referred upwards. With respect to referrals downwards, respondents said that although people further up the hierarchy would not issue instructions on programmes, they would give general guidance and review what had been done. Two respondents said there was an extensive system of internal guidance at the BBC but that it was not respressive, that there was nonetheless much internal freedom because of the tradition of open discussion in British society which had shaped the tradition of the BBC. A third respondent was convinced that there used to be much more liberty in the BBC but that recently control had tightened and professional staff had become like clerks, doing what they were told.

Even more direct evidence for the system of guidance through editorial meetings came from perusal of their minutes. In these meetings the importance of referral upwards was strongly emphasised. Thus, in the minutes of one such meeting, the chief assistant to the director-general said that she preferred over-referral to under-referral. For 'referral was crucial in ensuring that senior staff knew of potential problems [so] that breaks could be put and warnings given, which would avoid damage to the BBC' (Minutes, News and Current Affairs Meeting, 23 April 1985, p. 7).

Schlesinger (1978) wrote that the monitoring system was designed to make people conform to the BBC ethos of balance and strict impartiality. This impartiality, however, was premised on a commitment to the existing order of parliamentary democracy; it was a balance between established parties, while non-parliamentary forms of political opposition were viewed with suspicion. This was well-epitomised by director-general Curran who cited with approval the words of an editor, 'Yes, we are biased; biased in favour of parliamentary democracy (Schlesinger, 1978, p. 167).

Asked whether Schlesinger's analysis would apply today, respondents generally said that it would. A union representative added that the BBC was indeed a supporter of the state mechanism. One respondent expressed surprise at the question. 'Of course it's slanted within certain parameters of parliamentary democracy. It would be amazing if it wasn't. It's not Maoist. It would be very strange if it was.'

Schlesinger also wrote that the system of monitoring from above was made even more effective by a prior process of socialisation whereby staff internalised the mores of the BBC and could be relied upon to make the 'right' decisions without being told. In line with this, the *Guardian* (31 August 1985, p. 15) cited foreign service producers as saying:

> It's hard to put your finger on cases of censorship. It's more a case of self-censorship. You instinctively know what will be acceptable.

> It's the electric fence school of journalism. Once stung, you don't put certain ideas up again.

Respondents in this study held similar views:

> People are familar with the parameters within which the BBC works and will self-censure their output accordingly.

> I don't think they issue instructions to be nice to the government or anything as crude as that. It's just a general climate of caution, and this is more oppressive that anything else.

> That general pressure to comply is the way the BBC functions.

AUSTRALIA

The ABC charter of editorial practice adopted in 1984, provides that 'authority for editorial decisions will be vested in editorial staff'. Ostensibly, this clear guideline should have solved any possible ambiguity in this area. However, according to the *Australian Financial Review* (7 August 1984, p. 2) this is not the case:

Taken literally, that injunction would prevent ABC management, or the ABC Board from exercising authority over sensitive programme matters ... Of course, that will not excuse the ABC Board when a wrong decision is made by the editorial staff ... the board will have to bear ultimate responsibility for what the ABC broadcasts.

There were also differing interpretations of the board's role in practice as evident, for instance, from an altercation in the press, between Peter Bowers and Tony Bond, then vice-president of the ABC staff association. Bowers characterised the previous board (commission) and its chairman, Kramer, as non-interventionist. (*Sydney Morning Herald*, 31 May 1984, p. 14). To this Bond responded: 'This nugget of nostalgia for the good old Kramer days does not assay true ...contrary to what your columnist says, she was extremely interventionist' (*Sydney Morning Herald*, 7 June 1984, p. 8).

In his letter, Bowers also attacked the then existing board for being interventionist, adding 'the consequence of an interventionist board, inevitably, is managerial paralysis'. But Davis (1985, pp. 200-10) in his study of the ABC reached the conclusion that while that same board had been active in its attempt to restructure the ABC (see below) boards generally have not been too interventionist. Indeed, board-members were often characterised by staff as having 'hearts of gold and boots of custard' (Davis, 1985, p. 206).

Respondents in this study were unanimous that the board did not interfere in programming decisions unless they had major political implications – and then conflict was the result:

> The board doesn't interfere ... in the production process. It would only be when there was a question of ... the highest political nature

> There was one case where Leonie Kramer interfered quite badly ... A Western Australian commission for something had requested an apology for an item which was broadcast. The programme controllers believed that the apology was unnecessary ... Kramer stepped in and said that an apology should be made ... the staff went up in arms ... it was resolved by a backdown by Kramer ... but this would happen very, very seldom

Another, more recent, case concerned intervention from

above after a complaint by the Papua New Guinea Government about an ABC programme (discussed in the previous chapter). Respondents commented:

> Now that I think was wrong and it breached a basic journalistic principle.
>
> The board should have stayed out of it. This can happen. That's when you get a clash.

Ambivalence and dissent also existed with respect to the propriety of managerial intervention and in regard to the situation in practice. Left-wingers were apt to accuse ABC management of an attempt to impose their views on staff. For instance, Ashbolt (1980, p. 159) characterised the ABC as

> an institution where the weight of intellectual repression bears . . . down from its own self-constituted upper echelons, on the creative programme makers, diffusing an ethos of political orthodoxy, cultural gentility, social conformity and hierarchical obedience.

Many left-wingers within the ABC staff shared this view and blamed management for the alleged timidity of the ABC.

Ashbolt himself, however, also expressed a different view when he wrote (Ashbolt, 1980, p. 153) 'there are times when the ABC leviathan begets a radical under-belly and seems to change course, almost in defiance of its predominant and prescribed purpose'. This view was shared by right-wingers, who believed that the ABC management ought to be criticised for not bearing down on staff − or for doing so ineffectively. Thus Lipski (1981) wrote of a belief amongst Liberal backbenchers that an ABC's bias to the left could be put down to a lack of effective management. Or as McAdam in an article entitled 'A Red Scare on Radio' (McAdam, 1983a, p. 27) wrote: 'What ails the ABC, above all is [that] . . . staff are no longer effectively accountable to management, nor is management to the Commission.'

Respondents in this study, too, were divided over the issue of management intervention. Some took a positive view, saying for instance: 'The managing director obviously has an absolute right, and indeed a duty, to be personally satisfied about the

adequacy of what we are broadcasting.' Other expressed more qualified views such as the following: 'He's got the power and the managerial prerogative to do it . . . but he should be delegating and only in extreme circumstances should programmes need to be referred to him for a decision.'
Still others took an explicitly negative view of managerial intervention. One respondent said management used control over resources as a source of political pressure, adding:

> it could be that to a programme director, the issue doesn't seem important enough to risk getting offside the person who controls the budget. And so you will not make a fight of it. People tend to make fights on the principle only when the issue is very important. But a slower erosion can be even more dangerous.

Another respondent offered the opinion that with regard to news the relationship between Sydney and the regions was 'a bit like the Warsaw Pact – you do what you are told'. She added that some regional bureaucrats, too, were 'meddling' in editorial decisions, although they tended to be ignored by editorial staff. Therefore, there was no real political guidance.

But another person interviewed thought guidance from above *did* have political implications:

> There's not a memo or a letter that comes down from on high . . . I mean it can be a conversation [with politicians]. Then, maybe, the general manager talks to the editor: 'what's happening?' . . . Maybe it comes that way . . . or 'Look I don't want you to write it that way, you've got to write it that way' . . . Yes there is such pressure . . . I don't think the ABC is free of it.

It can be seen, then, that respondents' views over what management ought to do, shaded over into views on what was actually happening, and on both counts there was no unanimity of opinion. In this context, it is worth citing the testimony of two respondents who were familiar with both the BBC and the ABC. As they saw it, meting out guidance to staff took place in the ABC as well, but there was far less of it than there was in the BBC.

In Australia (as in Britain) some internal pressures are never voiced, but are implied, so that staff know (or think they know) what is expected. This type of implied pressure is sometimes described as pressure by 'osmosis' (Deamer, 1981, p. 46) and frequently leads to a 'pre-emptive buckle' (Davis, 1985, p. 232). It has been described by one respondent (a staff member in the News Department) as follows:

> There is no overt pressure. It's subtle. Stories on women, welfare and the like are stacked at the end. You soon get to know what the priorities are and you pander to them. Any inclination I might have had to dig into problems I gave up – because conservative values are subtly pushed into you.

ISRAEL

Here the board of directors, whose members are party representatives, has been making considerable efforts to influence the minutiae of broadcasting. This has raised problems because in the words of a respondent:

> The board of directors ... is supposed to be in charge of policy, not in charge of performance. But the distinction ... is very unclear, especially the closer we approach the area of politics ... everyone sees it as it is most convenient for him.

The interventionist tendencies of the board were evident as early as the beginning of the 1970s. Thus Greene (1973) wrote that the board was interfering with minor details of operation such as participants in certain broadcasts, which rightfully ought to be a matter for the producer (and not even for the director-general) to decide. The situation has not changed much since then, and one respondent testified in 1983 that the board of directors went as far as to interfere in the staffing of specific programmes. Former director-general Lapid, in 1983, also testified that the board put him under great pressure, although he resisted the tendency of politicians to meddle in managerial affairs.

With the appointment of a new board in 1984, some interesting developments occurred. Whereas the previous board consisted of political representatives who were not professionals, the new board included several political representatives, who were also professional journalists. Hence, as one respondent commented 'each board member thinks he can run the authority better than the d.g.' In addition, the new director-general, Porat, was not adamant in resisting board interference. When he had problems with staff, he sought the board's support. Thereby he himself opened the door to the board, introducing it into domestic wrangles. As one respondent explained: 'They said: "You wanted us inside, so here we are." It will now take years to get them out again.'

Radio was subject to less interference than television. Thus, Sarah Frenkel,[1] the head of the radio news department, testified in December 1984 that the board of directors did not interfere in the details of programmes, although there might be a complaint occasionally. But at that time, people in the television News Department were complaining that the discussions at the board's meetings increasingly resembled those of the news department itself, as the board got into the habit of analysing in detail items that had been broadcast a day or two before.

In general, then, the board was now interfering selectively – but in more minute detail – in the authority's day-to-day work. This made life rather difficult for the director-general who reportedly commented in an interview to the press that there were now eight directors-general to the broadcasting authority: himself and the seven members of the board.

Another change, however, was that because of the advent of a broadly-based coalition government in July 1984 the political representation on the new board was more balanced. On the previous board, under the Likud government there had been a clear (5:2) majority of Likud supporters. Under the broad coalition government, the division was 4:3, with four Likud and three Labour sympathisers. Since Likud and Labour sympathisers on the board almost balanced each other out, they tended to neutralise each other and greater political autonomy for the broadcasting authority ensued. Thus, paradoxically, there was now a state of more minute interference, coupled with a state of greater political freedom, than there had ever been before.

Just as there was ambiguity in Israel with respect to the board's right to interfere in the work of management, so there was also ambiguity with respect to management's right to interfere in the work of professional staff. Former director-general Lapid indicated that he saw it as his duty to give guidance to staff who could not expect to form 'a state within a state'. A senior member of staff expressed a similar opinion: 'Of course there are pressures from management on staff but I think this is entirely legitimate. . . . The director-general is also our editor-in-chief.'

A key observer, Professor Aharonson, commented in 1984 that this claim was not based on the Broadcasting Authority Act but on Lapid's interpretation of it:

> When there is a strong diretor-general, a 'fighter' of Lapid's type, he can interpret his role as one of editor-in-chief. But when . . . a man of a different callibre appeared, the staff . . . were no longer willing to accept this.

Even before this, not all the staff accepted management's intervention as legitimate. Thus, a staff association representative said in 1983:

> Some members of management attempt to further their own political interests . . . by using incorrect administrative channels – directly from the head of the pyramid to its bottom. This takes the form of an informal approach: 'Perhaps you could interview this or that person; perhaps you could give a reaction on this or that topic.'

In 1984, management's prerogatives of interfering were further questioned by a member of staff: 'Political pressures by management are not legitimate. Management itself does not see them as legitimate . . . whenever such pressures are publicised management feels pushed into a corner.' Another respondent added that intervention from management was illegitimate as 'political pressures . . . [were] usually disguised in professional terms'.

With respect to what was actually happening on the ground, the consensus amongst radio staff was that interference from management had recently become more oppressive. According to one respondent, until a few years ago, heads of department would have considerable autonomy 'Then a director of radio came in who saw himself as editor-in-chief, and political interference began in every single programme. Today radio people are not allowed to act according to their professional judgement.' This respondent added that interference was even worse in the news department, where management was listening in constantly and 'breathing down their necks'.

A respondent further clarified that the director's policy was to eliminate controversial issues: 'for instance, the issue of relations between Jews and Arabs. The director said: "leave that one alone. It's problematic." ' Another member of the radio staff concurred, saying that until a few years ago, staff had much more freedom in the creation of programmes:

> Then a new procedure came into effect, according to which every proposal for a programme must come before the director of radio. Each proposal must include details on content, who is to be interviewed, etc. Part of the proposals he rejects without giving reasons. Programmes on relations between Jews and Arabs, between the religious and the non-religious, and other controversial topics are rejected. Only *parve* (bland) topics remain. There is much discontent amongst staff about this.

In 1985 I was also informed that the director of radio was constantly listening in and if there was a mishap, he would call in immediately, keeping staff in a state of anxiety. This, of course, would also make staff exceedingly cautious politically.

Surprisingly, the same member of staff said that people interviewed on his programmes had severely denigrated the government, yet no directorial reprimands had followed. Other respondents, too, reported that the government was frequently criticised by those interviewed on radio programmes, by panellists and freelances, that there were programmes in which a great variety of political views were freely expressed. As one respondent explained, the director's manner of responding to political pressures was to give both sides on all issues or as a senior American broadcasting personality had described the procedure: 'one – yes, one – no, one – funny'. Thus, the director of radio was holding staff on a short rein but granting much freedom of expression to outsiders – the result being by all accounts a high-quality medium.

The situation on television was entirely different. By the end of 1985 the medium had been without a director for an entire year and therefore the filling of other managerial positions had been deferred, and a power-vacuum had been created.

In this vacuum political pressures, particularly from the

board, had been exacerbated. Thus the board had effectively succeeded in pressing television to terminate its major current affairs programme, *The Week – a Diary of Events*, because of its allegedly negativistic stance. Eventually respondents reported that the programme would be reinstated but in a different format; it would be briefer, mainly a summary of the week's events – no longer would it be a 'fighting' programme; no longer would it pose a 'threat' to politicians; 'its wings [had] been clipped off'. For their part, employees' councils were also attempting (mainly successfully) to fill the power-vacuum – by augmenting their own power to unprecedented dimensions. Thus, respondents reported, the councils had succeeded in 'forcing their will' on television and in 'dictating' what was to be done. For example, on 6 September 1985 the technicians' council made the unprecedented decision to delete a report from the evening news because it had been recorded on video rather than on film, and there was no agreement between management and themselves on video transmissions.

Not surprisingly, politicians and many staff were displeased and some said television was now run by employees' 'Soviets', and that it was in a state of pandemonium and anarchy. A senior member of staff, when asked to whom he would turn if he encountered a problem, retorted that not only did he not know the answer to that question, but that he did not even know who *would* know the answer (Paz-Melamed, 1985a).

Surprisingly, television still managed to present professional, informative news programmes, as well as a high-quality programme of political interviews, *Focus* (although this was almost the only political focus left). Asked how this was possible, respondents said that routine had kept things going even though major decisions had to be swept under the carpet.

In Israel, as elsewhere, there were also invisible pressures by 'osmosis'. Thus, a member of staff, Yitzhak Roeh, in a newspaper interview expressed the opinion that broadcasts were characterised by 'stick-to-ism'. He added: 'It's a matter of offering or withholding encouragement and support, depending on whether you work within the conventional mould or not. It's not just a matter of politics but of keeping things quiet, of not rocking the boat' (Segal, 1983, p. 5).

Pressures by osmosis do not necessarily work in a conservative direction, however. On this, one member of staff commented:

'There is a certain [leftist] journalist consensus. Conservative journalism is the minority of the minority. And hence there are doubtless [internal] pressures ... if you have conservative views you've got a problem ... you are labelled as a flatterer, as sucking up to the establishment.' It is not considered *bon ton* to agree with the establishment.

WEST GERMANY

The ambiguity and controversy surrounding the issue of internal control *v.* autonomy for broadcasters has come to the surface particularly in the 1970s. Thus on 2 July 1971 the assembly of NDR programme staff approved the following principle: 'The internal freedom of broadcasting ... does endow the individual programme worker ... with the legal power not to have to do or be responsible for anything that is contrary to his conviction' (Williams, 1976, p. 145). To statements such as these SDR intendant Bausch gave the following reaction:

> I have to protest ... the ... intendant can surely not be the only employee of a broadcasting station who for the sake of pluralistic diversity of opinion is daily more or less forced to ... be responsible for contributions which contradict his own opinion (cited in Williams, 1976, p. 153).

Following a similar line of thought one respondent, a (rightwing) media expert said:

> The balance of the programme is controlled by the intendant. [Accordingly] the intendant may instruct a journalist to express his (the journalist's) opinion. But he may also say 'that's enough. Now I'm going to instruct someone else to express his opinion ... '
> Hence in broadcasting, journalists are not entitled to unlimited freedom of expression ... but they don't like to hear that.

Another respondent, however, expressed a less clear cut view: 'According to the programme regulations anybody is entitled to express his opinion. ... [but] freedom in an enterprise like this cannot consist of everybody doing whatever he wants. That would make it impossible to put a programme together ... '

In practice, by the account of several ZDF respondents, the television board's powers to supervise programmes were frequently utilised as a basis for political interference. In general supervision was retrospective: mainly programmes that had been on air were taken to task – 'They might say: can you justify that?' But for new programmes the consent of the board was also required. A respondent reported: 'The board intervenes not only in the content and shape of programmes but even in their placement and frequency. In my opinion they have now overstepped the limits.'

According to some respondents the board's influence was limited by its lack of professionalism. One respondent gave his assessment as follows:

> I am unhappy about the lack of professionalism of the people who sit on the board. Sometimes they have no idea of what they are talking about . . . [But] this, again, is also our chance. I would not want these people to be professional supervisors of programmes. The less the boards understand of broadcasting – the smaller their influence.

Another respondent, however, admitted that constant board interference could grind away broadcasting independence: 'If [board] members constantly reiterate their complaints about a certain programmer, in the end the editor-in-chief will call him and say: 'Mr X: does it always have to be like this? Isn't it possible to do it any other way?'

Political guidance from management, senior staff and peers took the form of planning and review of programmes, of discussions and referrals upwards, of reprimands to staff who had overstepped the limits, and of cutting, postponing or deleting offending programmes. Thus Greulich (1976) wrote of the cases in which the SDR intendant terminated an inconvenient programme, in which the ZDF intendant publicly reprimanded an editor; in which the SR intendant changed a politically non-conformist programme and added: 'All this is bearable [because] . . . it is publicly observable and controllable. Devious, however, are the innumerable cases that happen almost daily, but remain secret, which only a small circle of colleagues knows about and is afraid to publicise . . . ' and Donner (as cited in Williams, 1976, p. 140) expressed the view that 'programmes are stopped, reworked, ... cut, postponed, placed in the archives; producers ... are "convinced" in discussions.'

Some respondents believed incidents such as these still happened, and one gave the example of a journalist whose (politically uncomfortable) programmes had been constantly cut and censored; another respondent added that journalists had to adapt to the organisation if they wished to prosper. Another respondent, however, took a more lenient view: 'Of course ... the journalist must adapt to the organisation. ... There are of course limits. But anyone who argues that the limits go as far as to take on the form of censorship is either a liar or an idiot.'

With respect to the ZDF, respondents pointed out that programme planning was done at the top of the hierarchy and that any material to be broadcast which ran for over 30 minutes had to be referred upwards all the way to the intendant. One respondent commented that the material thus referred would be examined from all points of view:

Question: From political viewpoints as well?
Answer: Good heavens, actually, yes ...

The planning and review of programmes also took place in weekly conferences of editorial boards in which programmes of the past week and for the coming week were discussed. One respondent explained that *what* was presented in programmes was determined from above. But *how* things would be presented in programmes was determined by the editorial boards. Another respondent described the meetings as follows: 'Materials are presented at a pretty early stage, and this is where the process of opinion formation begins. Some people may say: "What is this nonsense?" Or: "Excellent", and the chief editor is also consulted and possibly the editor-in-chief.' Asked whether political influence was exerted, a respondent replied:

It is impossible to make the distinction. For example, recently there was a strong critique of the Federal Chancellor, and several colleagues proposed: let's have a programme: 'Is the chancellor about to be toppled? Other colleagues opposed the idea on the ground that the crisis was not big enough to warrant such a programme. It was a 20 per cent political but 80 per cent professional argument ... But I must admit, when things are sharpened, such a discussion can certainly become political.

Several respondents emphasised that although programmes would have to have the blessing of the hierarchy or 'however high it may have to go', this did not hold for things that were expressedly characterised as commentaries. Here, personal opinions could be expressed and it was up to the ZDF to present different commentaries so that the overall programme remained balanced. However, there were very few such commentaries and only a minute minority from amongst ZDF's 3800 employees would ever have a chance to express their opinions.

Respondents with right-wing leanings argued that despite general guidelines from above, the most important decisions were taken at the bottom of the organisation. Left-wingers, however, argued that people at the bottom had their political autonomy eroded not only by censorship from above, but also by what had eventually become self-censorship or anticipatory censorship. This idea was most prominently expressed in a book edited by Broder (1976a) entitled *Die Schere im Kopf*, that is, *Scissors in the head*. In it Greulich wrote (p. 20) that censorship had eventually led to 'preventive good behaviour of people simply refraining from touching 'hot irons' for fear of getting scorched. And Broder himself (1976b) wrote: 'My basic equipment as freelance writer includes not only a typewriter, sound equipment, [etc.], ... but also "scissors in the head" that function so splendidly that by now I hardly notice them.'

While leftists were concerned about self-censorship created by pressure from above, rightists emphasised the imperceptible pressures for conformity from peers. In the words of a right-wing media expert: 'Anyone who presents himself as a conservative will be isolated ... while leftists are highly regarded.' Another right-wing media expert amplified: 'It is made clear to right-wingers that they are not appreciated. "Go elsewhere – we don't need you here." As simple as that.' People from different sides of the political spectrum nonetheless stressed that journalists on the ground could still have a large measure of freedom provided they created it themselves:

A good journalist created his own freedom.

There remains a lot of free space, and the fact that this is not evident is in the first place the fault of the journalists who do not utilise it as much as they could.

There are people who, through their stature, have forced their colleagues to tolerance.

This was well illustrated by the following occurrence related by a respondent. A few years ago, when the issue of abortion was at the focus of public opinion, the ZDF produced a programme which gave information on the topic to youngsters and showed an abortion in detail. Before going on the air it was previewed by the head of the department who demanded some cuts. But the producer insisted: 'This is my programme. Either we broadcast it as it is, or not at all.' The matter was then referred to the programmes director and the intendant who decreed: 'We'll put it on.' This created a storm with the church and the family organisations up in arms. The television board sent for the intendant and the programmes director and demanded that the producer be punished. But the then intendant, von Hase, was adamant, and the programmes director (now the intendant Stolte) backed him up. The intendant said: 'This was a very important programme. There is no cause to punish anyone. Thank you gentlemen.' And – according to the respondent – that was that.

CONCLUSION

This chapter has dealt with political pressures through intervention and 'guidance' emanating from inside the hierarchy of broadcasting organisations themselves. It showed that there was much normative ambiguity and controversy as to the extent of control the hierarchy was entitled to have $v.$ the extent of autonomy which members of staff were entitled to enjoy. The discussion then addressed itself to the situation in practice. It raised the question whether staff doing politically relevant programmes had a degree of autonomy or whether they could do what they liked only as long as they did what they were told.

In Britain, the conclusion was, that staff could do what they liked as long as they did what the political ethos of the BBC dictated. And although it was an ethos of strict impartiality between existing parties, it slanted BBC work towards caution and the existing political establishment.

In Australia the board did not go overboard in exerting its authority: generally it did not intervene in programmes and the rare cases in which such intervention did occur usually resulted in clashes. Managerial political intervention, though not absent, was also less noticeable than in Britain.

In Israel a distinction had to be made between radio and television. Radio was run by a strong director who had created an unusual combination of dictatorial intervention with freedom of expression – resulting in a high-quality medium. Television, at the time of writing, had been functioning without a director for a year the result being pressures and counter-pressures pitted against each other – a situation in which television still managed to survive. In the words of a respondent 'Radio is a one-man show; television – a no-man show.' At the time of writing there were no clear indications yet as to how the situation would change with the appointment of the new director.

In West Germany right-wingers and left-wingers differed in their views on internal political pressures. But all agreed that such pressures were pronounced, although broadcasters with integrity and stature could still snatch some autonomy from the jaws of the ferociously politicised system.

In all countries the system included imperceptible pressures from management and peers that were eventually translated into self-pressures. Referred to as 'socialisation' in Britain, as 'pre-emptive buckles' or pressures by 'osmosis' in Australia, and as 'scissors in the head' in Germany, such pressures would work in both a right-wing and a left-wing direction and it was agreed that they were generally the most effective, hence, also, the most oppressive of all pressures. This implied that in many cases broadcasters could do what they liked as long as they did what they were told – by themselves, as co-representatives of the system.

Note

1. Cited by permission of the respondent.

9 Internal Pressures through Appointments and Promotions

In all the countries studied there were implied pressures from the government on the broadcasting authorities through the staffing of the top supervisory positions and these have been dealt with above. This chapter is about similar implied pressures at lower levels. Originating in the political system – these are conveyed inwards by the boards or managements of the corporations themselves, in the form of politically-influenced appointments and promotions of broadcasting staff. Such appointments then have clear implications for the political content of programmes. For not only is it often (though not always) the case that political appointees will toe the line of their appointers or promoters, but those striving for appointments and promotions can be expected to do so as well. Officially, in all the broadcasting corporations studied, appointments and promotions are based on merit. But how do things work out in practice?

BRITAIN

In the BBC there is no overt politicisation of appointment and promotion procedures. Except for the highest and the lowest, all positions are advertised internally, and some are advertised externally as well. Appointments and promotions are made by selection boards, chaired by a member of the appointments department and comprising as a minimum the prospective superordinate of the appointee and someone representing personnel. For the top fifty to sixty positions people are invited to apply. Candidates are short listed by the board of governors. The lowest positions are advertised externally and appointments are made by selection boards.

By BBC rules and etiquette, candidates would never be asked about their political views in selection interviews, and according to several respondents, these procedures ensured the elimination of political criteria from the selection process. But clearly some covert political criteria did come through the back door, as it were.

One way in which this happened has long been the disproportionate selection of people with establishment-type – that is, public school and 'Oxbridge' type backgrounds who frequently are also the most able academically. Recently this tendency has become less pronounced, and according to some respondents, it has disappeared with respect to the recruitment of low-level positions. But respondents agreed that this change was not perceptible to the same extent on the higher rungs of the ladder; the higher one moved, the more homogeneous in their establishment-type background did position holders tend to become. As one respondent explained: 'I don't think people on selection committees would say: "let's get the public school type!" Those are just the subtle mechanisms of selection in Britain: accent, articulacy. It's just that some people seem appropriate, don't they?' Another respondent said that at the bottom people from various backgrounds were drawn in, but somehow they were selected in such a way that those with an establishment-type of background moved upwards.

According to several observers senior position holders would tend to be conservative; it would be difficult to find Labour voters amongst the BBC management. In the view of some respondents, it was quite possible that 'Oxbridge' establishment-type people who had decided to serve on the BBC would not be conservative and could even be left-wing. According to others, the selection process at senior levels none the less had political implications. For, as a respondent explained, it was a matter of 'the kind of intellectual baggage that you carry with you from this kind of background – and things follow . . . ' According to another respondent, daring people just don't get appointed'. Asked if senior people in the BBC tended to be conservative, another respondent retorted: 'Aren't they everywhere?'

An additional manner in which implicit political criteria came into the selection and promotion process was, para-doxically, through the requirements for strict balance and impartiality between the political parties in which the BBC took great pride. People who could adapt themselves to those requirements had better chances than others of obtaining positions and promotions in the BBC. If people adhered to these guidelines of impartiality in their programmes, did their own political views matter? According to several respondents, if people's political views did not show on their programmes, it did not matter 'tuppence' what these views were. Consequently, there were a lot of eccentric people with a diversity of political views on the BBC. Some respondents added, however, that people with extremist or doctrinaire political views would have problems getting promoted because they could not be relied upon to be even-handed. Other respondents concurred:

> I think it unlikely that a Trotskyite will find himself in the senior levels of the BBC . . . I mean, it just emerges that for one reason or another he appears to be disqualified.

> Any kind of pronounced political commitment would be a negative factor . . . They certainly would not take on extremists. No.

As will be seen, people with extremist views faced problems in other broadcasting corporations as well, but in the BBC these problems were more pronounced, for the BBC had taken more extreme measures than the other broadcasting corporations in this study to indentify such people. As a union representative informed me in July 1985 (shortly before the matter was widely publicised in the press) people considered as extremists had Christmas trees marked on their personal files. To make things worse, people were not allowed to see their files. In addition, selection boards were expressly forbidden to ask candidates about their political views. People thus had no means of knowing that they were suspect and no opportunity to present their side of the story. Other respondents confirmed the existence of the vetting process although they commented that people would have to be communist or 'National Front' to get those marks. All respondents who addressed the issue felt that in one way or another these procedures would be likely to influence, if not prejudice, some people's chances for appointment or promotion, although, as a union representative put it, it was all 'very subtle'. Another respondent offered: 'Obviously it is open to abuse . . . if you get people who are less than fair-minded sitting in places of authority, and yes, there will be people who are less than fair-minded sitting in places of authority.'

Following a report in *The Observer* (18 August 1985, p. 1), it was subsequently widely publicised in the press that vetting for the BBC was carried out by the Security Service, MI5, and that all current affairs appointees, and many of those involved in programme-making, were vetted. Often the word from MI5 that it regarded a person as a security risk was enough to blacklist that person and adversely affect his or her career.

Thus, A. Jacob, a BBC member of staff for over twenty years, recalled that in 1951 he was denied a position and full establishment rights because his wife was a Marxist historian. Only after her death was he rehabilitated (Jacob, 1985). Another instance was that of reporter Isobel Hilton, who, in 1976 was blacklisted from a job as a reporter in Scotland because investigators confused an academic group, for which she had been secretary, with a politically activist organisation. By chance the then controller of BBC Scotland knew her personally, took issue with the MI5 conclusion, and eventually in his words 'the facts emerged' (*Time*, 2 September 1985, p. 45). As *Time* pointed out, they emerged too late for Hilton, for by that time she had taken on another job.

The Observer (18 August 1985, pp. 1, 9) detailed the case histories of seven more individuals who were initially either prevented from obtaining a job at the BBC or were denied promotion. The report also claimed that numerous other members of staff had been blacklisted for periods of their careers for allegedly having left-wing sympathies, and that often this allegation was based on error.

In October 1985, under pressure of widespread adverse publicity, BBC management announced that it would reduce staff-vetting to an undisclosed number of posts connected with wartime broadcasting and to some posts in the external services (*The Times*, 24 October 1985, p. 2). The fact remains, however, that the previous vetting system had been in force for many years, and has had a clear influence on BBC staffing.

AUSTRALIA

In the ABC, too, selection and hiring procedures are free from a notable political slant, though covert political considerations have not been completely absent. All positions are now advertised internally and most (including senior positions) are advertised externally as well. Selection committees include at least three persons. For senior positions they include the managing director or his representative, often a board member and/or the director of human resources and someone for whom the appointee will work. The most senior appointments have to be ratified by the board. For permanent promotions there are rights of appeal to the promotions appeals board.

These appointment and promotion procedures are designed to work as objectively as possible. According to many respondents they do in fact guard against political considerations entering the selection process:

> The only philosophy that decides whether or not they get a job is whether they are or are not the best applicant for the job. I cannot [remember] – and I have sat through hundreds of interviews and have had a few myself – any questions about political philosophy, ever being asked. I mean that'll be quite outside the ball-game. I would be very surprised.
>
> I have never had instances where political views were taken into consideration.
>
> Certainly, there *are* people walking around this place convinced that they missed out on promotions because they are not politically acceptable. More often than not you will find that what has happened is . . . that they have done a programme badly.

Other respondents, however, expressed more qualified views:

> No. I haven't come across it. [But] it's possible if someone goes on a very . . . politically sensitive position, maybe a news editor or whatever. It is possible.
>
> I suppose there's a connotation of such [views being taken into account]. I mean 'we know how he thinks and we're happy with it'. It's the best answer I think I can give.

If there was a job of particularly sensitive nature, say the controller of public affairs ... whether or not the committee would discuss it ... it would be unlikely that someone who was very politically active on either side of the fence, would be appointed

A lot of people who work in the bureaucracy are politically conservative

It may be a factor in the top executive level ... They do tend to be rather, sort of a uniform Northshore set[1] ... with fairly conservative outlooks. But ... that's not to say that they are chosen because of their political views. It's more that they are chosen by people of a certain type because they themselves are of a certain type.

Interviewers find out the political views of candidates; I'm sure they do. Surprise, surprise, the rural department is very heavily oriented towards the National Country Party; the sporting department is very conservative as well. The documentary areas in radio are very Labor and left-oriented. So one way or another, they're sorting themselves out into what they want. People interested in doing programmes on social issues probably tend to be left-wing. And people interested in reporting on rural issues tend to be rural people; so you get some general societal factors coming in there. We don't have any Trotskyites or Maoists or anything like that ... The high level of news and public affairs are in the main conservative Liberal or very conservative Labor.

Also, Labor politician John Button (1982, and cited by Davis, 1985, p. 229) commented: 'The "old boy" network ... is more akin to a "safe boy" network. One of the crieria for promotion would seem to be a capacity for caution'. Similarly, Davis (1985, pp. 220–9) in his study of the ABC reached the conclusion that senior ABC management tended to be conservative, cautious or even timid.

The right of appeal may certainly be a factor in decreasing the weight of political considerations in promotions. As one member of staff put it: 'if someone's in the system it's much harder [for political factors to come into play] ... there are appeal rights, there's peer assessment. The whole thing is just much more open.' But the right of appeal does not exist for temporary appointments.[2] Hence, it is significant that more and more positions in the ABC are now temporary (on this, see also the next chapter).

In contrast to what was happening at the BBC, security-vetting did not emerge as a problem in the ABC. Lloyd (1985) pointed to releases of Commonwealth archival material showing that in the late 1940s journalists had been exposed to persistent surveillance by the security services. But no more recent data on widespread vetting, particularly of ABC journalists, could be uncovered. A staff representative on the board of management raised the matter in 1984, but in a written reply by the managing director he was told that vetting of ABC staff by the Australian Security Intelligence Organisation (ASIO) would only be carried out on request and with the knowledge of the employee concerned, that it took place only in the rare cases where people would have access to national security information, that only two members of staff had been vetted and that no one had ever been denied appointment or promotion on security grounds (Board of Management Staff Representatives Newsletter, 2 August 1984, p. 7).

ISRAEL

In Israel, until a few years ago, appointment procedures were casual. People would be brought in on the basis of their friends' recommendations, or because they were on the support staff, etc. Lately, more orderly procedures have come into effect. According to these, any new member of staff must have undergone a training-course (acceptance to which is based on an entrance examination). More senior positions are advertised and selected by a committee. Selection committees are normally made up of management representatives, representatives from the branch to which the position belongs and representatives of the staff or professional associations. For the more senior positions such as those of director of radio and television, selection committees have been made up of the board of directors, the director-general, and representatives of the journalists' association.

However, such formally correct procedures do not necessarily ensure the elimination of political considerations. Thus the claim has been frequently voiced that selection committees are subject to pressures behind the scenes so that political considerations covertly enter into appointments. A former member of the board of directors, Papo, wrote: 'The most senior staff, such as the directors of news and programme directors are "selected" on the basis of fictitious advertisements in which the results are predetermined' (Papo, 1980b, p. 13).

Former director-general Lapid, too, indirectly admitted the semi-innocuous nature of the formal selection procedures. He said that while the procedure by which senior appointments are made is complex, the director-general guides the process. He added that during the years of his term it never happened that someone he proposed was not appointed; but he had never proposed people who he knew had no chance of being politically acceptable to the board of directors.

All respondents agreed that the more senior the appointment the more important the role of political considerations in it, although professional considerations will always come in as well. All concurred that political considerations are prominent (though not exclusive) criteria in the selection of the directors of television and radio. On this a staff-member commented in 1983:

> It is well-known that anyone who sees himself as a candidate for any serious position within the broadcasting authority ... must undergo the process of lobbying with senior politicians ... For this purpose – the most important one is the minister in charge of the broadcasting authority – the minister of education and culture ... [Also] one of the most intriguing things that must be noticed is that this minister, while he is periodically criticised in the press ... is presented in an exceptionally ravourable light in the electronic media. That is not by chance.

This respondent's statement found confirmation in late 1984, when it was reported in the press that Hayim Yavin, a member of the television staff who had ambitions of becoming director of television, was lobbying with Members of Parliament and Ministers for his appointment. Consequently the chairman of the National Journalists' Association had rushed a letter to the State of Israel Attorney General and to the chairman of the Israel Broadcasting Authority, demanding that such political lobbying 'cease forthwith'.

The letter, however, could not stop the lobbying or the politicisation of appointments. At the beginning of 1985, when an advertisement for the post of director of television was published, the Minister of Education and Culture complained

Internal Pressures through Appointments and Promotions 135

of escalating political interference in the selection process (*Al-Hamishmar*, 25 January 1985). He failed to indicate whether he himself had also contributed to this escalation (see Chapter 13).

With respect to the director of radio, Gideon Lev-Ari, the general consensus amongst respondents was that his professional qualifications were outstanding. Nevertheless some respondents believed that political considerations were not entirely absent in his appointment. Since he was appointed during Lapid's term, this belief is indirectly supported by Lapid's testimony – referred to before – that he would not propose appointments that he knew would be unacceptable politically.

While the situation was eminently clear with respect to directorial appointments, there was less agreement amongst respondents as to the less senior appointments. One head of department said:

> When I was hired I was never asked about my political views, and this has never been a consideration for me – as head of department – in hiring others ... but there are differences between departments in this respect. Our department is not as important politically as the news department.

The head of another department made a similar statement with respect to her own department: 'People are not hired on the basis of their political views ... I obtained my post ... because ... they thought I was more suitable than others.'

However, it was reported by some respondents that this head of department, appointed in March 1984 under a Likud government, was known as a Likud faithful. Her professional credentials were not questioned. Nevertheless, the feeling was that her political affinities, too, had played a part in the appointment. As one respondent put it:

> I happened to participate in the discussions concerning the appointment. Political considerations were never brought up, but were in the background. But even people with differing political views conceded she was the most suitable [candidate for the position].

About heads of departments in general, one respondent said:

> The feeling [amongst the staff] is that political appointments reach

down to the level of heads of department though this is done in a most sophisticated manner ... I myself got scorched. I am not identified with any political body. Hence my chances of being appointed head of department are slim.

According to another respondent, the political factor is taken into account even in junior appointments, though another respondent seemed to feel differently saying: 'in low-level appointments – except for the usual favouritism – there are no political considerations'. The respondent refused to amplify. But another respondent filled in the gap:

> The director of radio appoints his own 'Mafia', and it is clear that many promotions are made from amongst this group of court people. Many of this group have advanced with surprising speed. They are his personal friends, his yes-people more than they are his political allies.

The tendency of the director of radio to appoint his yes-people and promote them to senior positions was also confirmed by several other key informants, radio staff and reports in the press. Many members of staff also believed that strong, independent people would not be appointed as heads of department or, if appointed, would not survive under Lev-Ari. But compliant people, his own faithful, tended to flourish. Several respondents explained the *political* significance of the appointment of the director's faithful and yes-people, as illustrated by the following statement:

> the directors' careers, their promotions, depend on their responsiveness to political pressures. Consequently they will appoint their own people to sensitive positions. Your own people are people who owe you their very position in the broadcasting authority or their promotion. And you presume that these people will not uncover things [about you]. And to those people you turn as director and you say: 'I want you to give more coverage to this or that.' And then naturally, because he owes you and belongs to your gang, he will do it without asking questions. And this then serves the [political] interests of the director.

By the testimony of some respondents, the intrusion of political criteria in appointments and promotions in Israel took the additional form of ensuring that appointees to managerial, editorial and journalists' positions would not be (right-wing or left-wing) extremists. Having been alerted to the problem of security-vetting of extremists in Britain, I tried to find out whether similar procedures were in force in Israel as well. I was told by key informants that for appointment and promotion in the Israel Broadcasting Authority – except for West Bank Arabs – there was no need to pass a formal security-vetting, but the security services were conscious of the fact that there were sensitive positions in the authority because of its close co-operation with the military in wartime. (For instance, the passwords for the mobilisation of the army reserves were stored in the authority's audiotapes. Some position-holders in the authority would know several hours before the public did that the passwords were about to be broadcast – in other words, that Israel was about to mobilise its reserve forces.) Hence the authority's security officer was in contact with the state's security services, which would caution the authority if someone was suspect as a security risk. It was then up to the authority to decide what to do. But during a five-year time-span only two such notices were received. The authority would *not* be alerted for communists or for extreme right-wingers. Only people close to the Palestine Liberation Organisation, the fringe group of people known as *Mazpen* (which has but a few hundred members), would be suspect. All in all, politically, the matter was innocuous, and no problems in this area had ever come to light.

WEST GERMANY

Here appointment and promotion procedures have been highly and overtly party-politicised. Perhaps one reason for this is that appointment and promotion procedures are less formal than in the other countries involved. Positions are customarily advertised internally and if no appropriate candidate can be found, they are advertised in the press. But there are no formal selection or promotion committees.

In the ZDF, for instance, top appointments are made by the intendant in conjunction with the (politically-appointed) administrative board. Lower-level appointments are made by superordinates; the employees' council is also consulted, but the intendant has the final say; there are no formal appeals procedures for candidates who have been passed over.

All respondents agreed that for top- and middle-ranking appointments, the candidates' party-political adherence or sympathy was an important consideration. While candidates would not be asked about their political affiliations those would be known from the candidates' previous contributions, and respondents considered it entirely 'normal' that they would be taken into account. As one respondent expressed himself: 'we don't buy a pig in a poke'. As an example, this respondent cited his own appointment as head of department. At the time, the ZDF was looking for an SPD man and settled on him. He continued: 'I was presented to the leading SPD people at the ZDF and they said: "yes, we can use this one". But nothing has come of this. The party has never been able to pressure me into anything.'

The extreme politicisation of appointments was evident from the fact that over 50 per cent of all broadcasting personnel belonged to political parties (Kutteroff and Wolf, 1985, p. 63). And as Burghart (1978) perceived the matter, broadcasting journalists, by acquiring party membership, might well signal their willingness to be useful in order to get something useful in return.

At the top and middle rungs of German broadcasting politicisation took the form of a *Proporz* principle designed to give all parties a share of the cake in proportion to their representation in parliaments and governments. Following this principle, in the ZDF in mid-1985 for instance, the intendant was considered as close to the CDU; the editor-in-chief was counted as SPD; his deputy was considered CDU; the managing director was SPD and so on down the line.

With respect to more junior appointments the *Proporz* principle would not be applied, but according to several experts politicisation was nonetheless present here as well. For here low-level position-holders would make the appointment. They would tend to select people with political affiliations close to their own as apprentices. These would then form the pool from amongst which people were selected for permanent appointments. 'In this manner the recruitment of people with like minded opinions is practically guaranteed.'

On higher levels the *Proporz* principle also signified that parties had to compromise on appointments. This had led to a tendency for appointments to gravitate into the middle: there was a tendency to prefer people who were pink and grey rather than red or black (right-wing). This also meant that people from the FDP – a small centrist party – had fairly good career chances.

As for political extremists such as communists or neo-Nazis, it was agreed amongst respondents that the house was careful not to employ too many of them. 'Greens', on the other hand, and people active in the peace movement (I was told) were not prevented from joining. Certainly, however, they were not included in the *Proporz* principle and their chances of advancing into senior key positions were minimal.

While political affiliation had a major impact on career prospects, this is not to say that qualifications and talent were immaterial, for, as one respondent explained, when someone is not talented this becomes quickly evident on the screen, and hence to millions of viewers. These would say 'Nothing much is coming out of the ZDF these days.' Hence the testimony of another respondent that careers which had their roots *only* in party affiliation and not in talent would probably come to a speedy end. He conceded, however, that if one had both professional *and* political qualifications this would be much the best for one's career.

As in Israel (and probably elsewhere as well) personal connections and political considerations were frequently intertwined. An example was recounted by a respondent who said: 'My boss is a "black" one and he is now trying to get his friends in.' Another respondent, a representative of an employee organisation, said that there were even cases in which personal favouritism outweighed political considerations, although the two often went hand in hand. He added that these were suspected cases that were difficult to prove. Another respondent testified that if someone who aspired to a certain desirable position were friends with influential politicians, his/her chances of landing the position would be enhanced, or, in the words of the respondent 'certainly it will not do him any harm'.

All this means that those people who (although talented) did not have the 'proper' political qualifications and/or personal connections, were distinctly disadvantaged and so were people who were non-partisan, or 'colourless'. As one respondent complained: 'I do not belong to any party and therefore I always fall through the grill.' In some cases, however, non-partisans might inadvertently profit from a given political constellation: when neither party was willing to concede an appointment to its rival they might sometimes settle on a compromise candidate. In such situations it was the non-partisan who – in the words of one respondent – 'might be the laughing third'.

In all this jockeying for position at the top- and middle-level appointments in German broadcasting, the CDU has recently enjoyed a distinct advantage over the SPD. This is well-documented in a study by the Mannheim Elite Study Group headed by Professors Max Kaase and Rudolf Wildenman. Included were élite position-holders and middle-level personnel in both the ARD and the ZDF in 1972 and 1981. It was established that the majority of the people studied in 1972 sympathised with the SPD. But since then a major shift had occurred: the majority of the persons studied in 1981, expressed a preference for the CDU/CSU. The shift has been noticeable especially in the ARD. In the ZDF, right-wing adherents had been in the majority even in 1972. But in the ARD there had been an overwhelming majority of left-wingers in 1972, and yet there was a clear majority of right-wingers in 1981 (Hoffmann-Lange, 1985, Kutteroff, 1984).

At the bottom layer of the broadcasting corporations, however, the situation looked different. Journalists were frequently recruited from amongst university graduates (or students) in the social sciences, and those tended to the left more frequently than to the right. They then tended to recruit people in their own images.

Accordingly, Kepplinger (1982, pp. 128–35) cited a large number of studies, all of which showed that the majority of broadcasting journalists tended to the left of the political spectrum. Some respondents maintained that this was not so much a matter of party affiliation and sympathy, but rather a matter of professional tendencies: journalists usually tended to display a negative stance to the status quo, and to favour social (though not necessarily radical) change. In practice this ammounted to the same thing: a largely critical attitude of lower-level broadcasting personnel towards the political establishment.

Despite the intense politicisation of appointments and

promotions in German broadcasting, there was one aspect in which these procedures were more free from political interference than they were in Britain for instance. By the account of key informants there was no security organisation that was in any way involved in such appointments. In the words of one respondent: 'This . . . is completely foreign to us. There is no such thing here.' Another respondent, a senior representative of the employees' council, testified that contrary to what was the case in the BBC, the employees' personal files were open for their scrutiny at any time. And his organisation had negotiated with the employer precisely what could and what could not be included in personal files. Data on security-vetting were not amongst the items that could be included. The representative added:

> Those are the official files. And in any processes concerning the employee the employer can use only those. It is, of course, impossible to prevent people from compiling their own, unofficial, personal dossiers. Nobody can prevent me from writing a note saying so-and-so is an ass, and then putting the note in a file. But such files cannot be used.

CONCLUSION

Political pressures by means of appointments and promotions were much more blatant in Israel and in West Germany than they were in Britain and Australia. In the former two countries the situation was quite straightforward: at least at top- and middle-ranking levels there was overt party-politicisation of these procedures, and in both countries political favouritism at times intermeshed with personal favouritism. Such an intrusion of party-political criteria in selection processes would have been inconceivable in Britain and Australia. In these two countries, and especially in Britain, things proceeded much more subtly, but this is not to say that political criteria in apointments and promotions were entirely absent there.

In both Britain and Australia establishment-type of people with a certain 'intellectual baggage' were more likely than others to advance into senior positions. And who is to say where intellectual baggage ends and political baggage begins? In Australia people were somehow sorted out or sorted themselves out into politically congenial programmes, with leftists gravitating into the politically-more-significant current-affairs programmes.

In all countries concerned, political extremists were selected or weeded out from responsible key positions, and sometimes from employment in broadcasting altogether. In both Britain and Israel there was some security vetting of candidates. But even though Israel has much more formidable security problems than Britain, security-vetting has been more marginal in that country, while in Britain it has had clearer political implications.

Also, since BBC boards have been expressly forbidden to discuss candidates' political views with them, and since candidates were not allowed to see their files, they never had a chance of defending themselves. It therefore transpired that the very system that was designed for scrupulous fairness and for the elimination of political bias from appointment and promotion procedures may in some instances have had precisely the opposite effect. It may well have exacerbated political bias by sweeping the whole process of political vetting under the carpet. It remains to be seen how the system will change in the future.

Notes

1. One of Sydney's wealthier areas.
2. Unless a permanent appointee obtains a contract position.

10 Internal Pressures through Dismissal, Demotion and Displacement

In addition to appointments and promotions, another channel of internal political pressure is that of dismissals and demotions of broadcasting staff. It is a device of political pressure to which staffers are particularly vulnerable personally.

DISMISSAL AND DEMOTION

Britain

BBC staff have a large measure of employment security. Only rarely would people be dismissed outright for incompetence and poor performance, because these were virtually impossible to prove. Some dismissal procedures have been negotiated with the unions, but in fact, so BBC staff informed me, dismissal occurs only in extreme cases, for instance, after a criminal offence, or gross misconduct such as theft, or sex in the office. Even in the latter case most people who chanced to come by would merely say 'So sorry' and leave, and the matter would not be heard of again.

Redundancy occurs more frequently than dismissal. In some cases redundancy would be used as a euphemism for incompetence. A related form of veiled dismissal would be that of upgrading a position. The position would then be advertised and the incumbent would not get it. But even this would happen only rarely (there might be two cases a year) and in such cases attempts would be made to absorb the people concerned elsewhere in the organisation. Another possibility is that older people could be asked to take early retirement.

There are appeals procedures for termination of employment or for downgrading. According to a union representative the National Union of Journalists would help with those appeals. Only rarely would such appeals be successful; they were nonetheless important for they could prolong the process, making dismissal difficult and thus become a deterrent.

Have people been dismissed for political reasons? According to a BBC spokesman, it was a BBC principle that if people showed their political views on programmes 'they were out'. Nonetheless, people have only very rarely been dismissed for that reason. The only cases he could recall occurred in the 1970s when two Portuguese members of staff used their posts on the BBC to make communist propaganda. He could recall no more recent cases. Certainly people would not be dismissed for being rough on politicians in their interviews or their reports. In fact, such toughness with politicans was a long-standing BBC custom. Other respondents too, said they did not know of people having been dismissed for their political views. One respondent qualified this by saying that people with extreme views would find it difficult to accommodate to the BBC. This was the case with one BBC controller who was far to the left and who eventually resigned because he realised that there was a conflict between his political views and his position.

This, however, held only for people who were on the BBC staff. Respondents agreed that for people on contract and for freelances it was a different story. Recently it was reported that the BBC would make 2000 of its 30 000 staff redundant and employ more casual people (*The Times*, 18 July 1985, p. 1). Such people tended to be more frequently in creative arts, catering, cleaning and the like, while news and political affairs people were more frequently staff members. But, according to respondents, there was nonetheless a trend for more news and public-affairs people to be on contract (although this trend did not include top people who 'sat comfortably'). And if contract-workers or freelances made programmes that were failures, they simply would not be employed again.

Would their insecurity lead contract-workers to be especially cautious politically? Respondents testified that this would not hold for the most popular current affairs people because they were paid high salaries precisely to be politically abrasive. But for contract-workers in general, caution was the rule; and since more and more people were on contract programmes had become less creative and daring. According to a union representative, there have been cases of freelances who have not been used again for political reasons. For example, there was a woman who became involved with the Greenham Common Women; after that she was no longer used on the BBC.

With respect to permanent staff, union representatives admitted that there were no cases in which they could say with certainty that people had been dismissed for their political views, and that they rarely got cases of people complaining to them about political victimisation. They added, however, that it was difficult to tell whether people had been turned away for political reasons or not: 'I mean ... how would you know? They wouldn't *say* it's for political reasons, would they?'

> **Question**: Are there cases where you suspect political reasons?
> **Answer**: Yes, there are loads of cases like that. But there is nothing that I can prove ... But I think the most serious thing is the general intimidation that's going on. I mean, the political thing is an undertone of it. But the whole system of pressures on people, frankly, lack of access to personal files; the business of people on short term contracts; the contracts not being renewed. Pressures to comply, really, with the general framework.

More recently, after the interviews had been completed, it was reported that some top BBC people including the head of radio, his deputy and a current affairs journalist were made redundant for being especially vocal on controversial issues (such as the *Real Lives* programme) and thereby provoking management's 'twitchiness' (*The Times*, May 11, 1986, p. 40 and May 12, 1986, p. 15).

Australia

Under the 1983 Broadcasting Act the previously existing nexus between the ABC and the public service board was broken and the ABC could now set its own terms of employment (Davis, 1985, p. 112). But the Act also includes provisions for redeployment of redundant (permanent) staff, whereby it is very difficult to push people out against their will. Temporary staff also gain redeployment rights after a year. But they are not permanently attached to a particular job, hence could more easily face a situation of redundancy and redeployment. People on fixed-term contracts, and casual people, could be removed even more easily.

Significantly, in the ABC, most journalists and people working on news, current affairs and other political programmes were not permanent. For instance, in May 1986, in the news and current affairs departments, two-thirds of the staff were temporary, and 13 per cent were on contract or casual. In the words of a respondent, 'most reporters, public affairs and news people are not permanent ... for a whole bewildering variety of reasons lost in mystery and I think it is a bit of a mess'. According to the *Journalist* (October 1985, p. 1), and some respondents, there was a tendency to use more and more casual staff in news and current affairs and leave permanent positions unfilled.

Asked whether impending dismissal or termination of contract had ever been used (or could be used) as an instrument of political pressure, several respondents replied in the negative. One respondent said: 'Nonsense. I'd like to see some evidence of that'. Other respondents pointed out that journalists were not timid people, and moreover, if anyone was to be sacked for political reasons this would create a furore. However, a member of staff, T. Ferguson (1982, pp. 8–9) wrote:

> The contract system had its origin in management attempts to curb its creative people. The wildest public affairs reporter, so the Broadcasting House thinking went, would be amenable to discipline when his contract came up for renewal ... I remember the occasions when errant reporters and producers were kept in the dark for weeks after their contract expired. This was done to pull them into line.

Some respondents in this study made similar comments:

> you could be victimized, couldn't you?

> People are scared because if they rock the boat their tenure is up the creek.

> It gives management power capriciously ... you run it this way or I won't renew your contract.

Most respondents felt that, so far, no overt political pressure through impending dismissal had been applied to staff, and there was no evidence that programmes had been tamed in this way and that the ABC had 'gone soft' on politicians. But most respondents also felt that the contract system had *the potential of pressure for self-censorship* built into it:

> I think that [termination of contract] can lead to, um, how shall I say, voluntary censorship in a way. A journalist could know that he's got only three months to go on his contract and maybe he doesn't want to get involved in any controversy and attack the government or attack the establishment or whatever . . . um he'll sit back a little bit for those three months. I'm sure that's a form of insidious pressure that's there. I mean, 'wink, wink, nudge, nudge, you know, you've only got three months before your contract's up, we're looking at you' sort of thing . . .

A union representative provided the following analysis: 'It is not enough that the ABC be fair. It must be *seen* to be fair. Caesar's wife must be above suspicion. This is not possible under a temporary work and contract system'. And a respondent in a senior management position said: 'because the ABC is a complex organisation, it's never clear-cut . . . In the end it's always a matter of interpretation'.

This being the case, it would seem that any trend to put more positions on contract, would place more and more people in the twilight zone, where they may see themselves as potentially vulnerable to political pressure. This is, in effect, what has recently happened at the top echelons of the ABC. In 1984 the newly created board of directors instituted a reorganisation of the institution. The top seventy managerial positions, which had previously been held permanently by tenured staff, were thrown open to external competition. They were now to be filled either by external recruits on contract, or by career staff holding those jobs on a fixed-term, temporary basis. Should it then be decided not to renew their terms they would be retained by the ABC but returned to their previous ranks. Should their previous posts have been occupied in the meantime, they would have to go on the 'unattached list' and look for new work. If they failed, they would be encouraged to retire, or might face redundancy and reployment procedures.

The reorganisation was instituted because it was felt that the ABC's rules of tenure had stifled the organisation, burdened it with non-creative people who had no incentive to perform. Its goal was therefore to cut off 'dead wood' and infuse the organisation with 'new blood'. But its immediate effect was to bring about anxiety, low morale and confusion amongst the staff, as illustrated by these statements, made by respondents in 1985:

> Everyone is unhappy and it'll be hard to find a happy person.
>
> **Question**: What has been achieved so far?
> **Answer**: Up until now, . . . a heck of a lot of confusion.
>
> Everyone's pissed off.

The staff's resentment and anxiety was also expressed by representatives of the ABC Senior Officers Association, who said the board had given senior staff the impression that they were a 'bunch of geriatric has beens' (Sheridan, 1984, p. 15) and nothing but 'rat shit'. And a board member and a personal expert admitted, that although the changes were handled humanely, none the less 'people are getting sick and people are getting heart attacks and you know, breakdowns and things like that, and it's a very messy human situation which we are responsible for'. And at the beginning of 1986 a member of staff reported that there was still 'unbelievable' antagonism amongst staff.

By mid 1986 some respondents still thought the ABC was 'a pretty rotten place to work for, full of personal struggles and vendettas'. But most respondents believed things had settled down to a certain extent and morale had improved. The people who had been made redundant were no longer there and those who were retained, mostly seemed to have adjusted to the new situation. People who were shunted sideways might still be embittered. But this was not much of a problem, because they were now peripheral in the organisation.

Respondents were divided over what the reorganisation had actually achieved. Some felt that while 'dead wood' had been cut off and 'new blood' had been brought in, some deficiencies had persisted. Some respondents thought the ABC was still stultified 'like a huge dinosaur', the bureaucracy was still highly inflated, inefficient and 'bungling', lines of authority had been confused and 'chaos' reigned, standards had remained low or deteriorated and 'everything sort of went by the board'. Others believed the organisational structure had improved, the lethargic organisation had been pushed into action, more efforts were now being put into programmes, which had generally reached higher standards.

According to some participants the contract system for top management meant that high-level staff would be more motivated to achieve. But several participants expressed the concern that contracts led managerial people to spend 'a whole lot of nervous energy' on assuring their own positions, that they spent the latter part of their contract-term (one or more years) trying to arrange new jobs for themselves, not doing their work properly. To be creative, people needed security and independence, while insecurity led to caution and 'playing it safe'. To make matters worse, people were afraid of applying for promotions for positions in which they would be on contract only, for fear of losing their present positions when their contracts were up because, as one respondent said, 'they've got families and they like to eat'. Hence, instead of encouraging flexibility, in certain respects the new system encouraged rigidity.

What is more, respondents agreed that the reorganisation may well make managerial staff open to more political pressures:

> it'll be highly dangerous to get into a situation in which the national broadcaster can be politicised through that top layer ... if you have that band across the top ... that knows ... that come a change of government they are going to be tipped out of a job ... I think you'd then get all sorts of mad things happening below.

> People might start to second guess what the government wanted and this would lead to exactly the type of organisation a lot of us would not want in Australia.

> It has to be said that the possibilities for politicisation are greater.... If you have appointments for life, the possibilities for [government influence] are substantially reduced. If, on the other hand, you have a system which involves appointments for four to five years, then clearly the possibility exists at least for influence.

Thus, the more senior people are on contract, the greater the potential for political pressures with which they (and the ABC with them) may be faced.

Israel

In Israel a case of using non-permanency as a source of political pressure was reported to have occurred in 1977. Even though that year's election had put into office a right-wing government, left-wingers were most prominently represented in the authority. Thus a person whose views did not fit Labour was harrassed by his colleagues and in effect was forced to leave.

Previous director-general Lapid, who had been appointed two years later, remarked that he had never dismissed anyone. By this, however, he meant permanent staff only. Furthermore, managerial positions are filled for three-year terms, after which if their terms are not renewed, their holders return to non-managerial positions. Lapid testified that non-renewal of such terms – in other words, demotion – was sometimes used as a subtle political weapon. He recounted that when he took up his appointment in 1979, the authority was in the hands of leftists. During the first two years of his term several leftists lost their managerial positions. This caused widespread protest from the left but satisfied the right-wing government. Lapid continued: 'Once I had removed the left-wingers from key positions, and when I reached the conclusion that television was now at the centre of national consensus, I said: no more. From then on I have been a disappointment to the government.'

As noted, none of the removals of people from key positions for political reasons were actual dismissals. Indeed, in Israel, dismissal of permanent staff from any public institution (including the broadcasting authority) was very unusual until fairly recently. By law, the authority's management had the right to dismiss anyone. In practice, however, any permanent member of staff facing dismissal would have the protection of the labour courts, the federation of labour and the employees' councils and unions; the latter would have been quick to institute industrial action.

Even so, by the beginning of 1985, the authority had greatly overstepped its budget, and drastic cut-backs became inevitable.

Internal Pressures through Dismissal, Demotion and Displacement

In July 1985, director-general Porat submitted to the board of directors a plan for such cut-backs, including the retrenchment of 258 permanent staff. By the end of July 1985 the director of radio and the acting director of television, in consultation with heads of departments, had compiled lists of the prospective retrenchees.

The question thus arose as to the criteria that had been applied in selecting the candidates for dismissal. According to one respondent, management would have pressed to effect dismissal by merit (or lack thereof); the employees' councils would have pressed for social conditions to be taken into account – particularly for sole breadwinners, widows and the like to be spared – and eventually a compromise would have been reached.

By the account of a member of radio staff, perusal of the list of those to be retrenched did not show that criteria of merit had been preponderant in their compilation. Some people known as highly successful in their work were on the lists; others, known as less than brilliant performers, were not. Some of the criteria used were clearly those of personal favouritism and vindictiveness. People who had fallen out with the director of radio were on the list; those of his own 'Mafia' were not. According to some television staff too, there were rumours that personal connections had played a role in the compilation of the lists.

The employees' councils demanded that the criteria for dismissal be announced. At the time of writing this had not yet been done. The retrenchments had not been effected as yet either, and no one knew if and when they would eventuate. But in the meantime, low morale, a murky atmosphere, mutual suspicion and animosity amongst staff had been created.

On the face of it, since the retrenchments did not involve political criteria, they are not relevant for the present analysis. But in the foregoing chapter it could be seen how personal favouritism at times has political implications: people who belonged to the director of radio's 'Mafia', who owed him their position in the authority and were personally loyal to him, would also tend to be politically compliant, to shape programmes to his political convenience. This situation was likely to be exacerbated with the fear of possible retrenchments: people who knew they were not candidates for dismissal because of their personal loyalty to the director, would most likely be even more politically compliant.

West Germany

While in Australia and Israel the trend has recently been towards more dismissals or impending dismissals, in West Germany the trend has been in the opposite direction. People in top managerial positions would serve for five-year terms only. After that, if not reappointed, they would be able to stay in the organisation but there would be psychological pressure on them to take early retirement or go elsewhere. In principle, then, those people would be in no better position than in Australia and Israel. But in practice, in the ZDF, the directors have been holding their positions for ten to fifteen years. At the level immediately below that, people would also be appointed for five-year terms only. But after that, if not reappointed, would remain in the organisation at their present salary levels. This is in contrast to Australia and Israel where such people would be demoted to their previous ranks.

At the levels below that, appointments were permanent and for all practical purposes could not be terminated. According to a legal expert at the ZDF, and other staff, there were certain legal possibilities of dismissal for persons who had transgressed the law or had stopped working entirely, but the rest of the staff were practically 'undismissable'; they certainly could not be dismissed on political grounds. According to a respondent's rather colourful description: 'It is not enough if I say to the intendant: "Mister Professor Stolte, I find your opinions are bullshit", or even if I give him a slight kick on the behind. I must have committed a weighty criminal act that has damaged the ZDF. Even when people make obvious mistakes ... they cannot be dismissed.'

There were, of course, freelances and people on contract who could be dismissed for political reasons: their contracts simply would not be renewed, but in West Germany the trend has been for more and more contract people to gain permanent employment. Since the beginning of the 1970s, many 'free contributors' had sued the broadcasting organisations before the Federal Labour Court, and the court decreed that they be given permanent employment. As a result, between 1973 and 1978, some 1300 'free contributors' gained permanent employment. Concomitantly, the court's verdicts greatly restricted the possible fields of activity for contract people (Kepplinger, 1982). Except for creative programmers, it was no longer possible to employ people for longer than three months a year, without their gaining the right to permanent employment. So greater and greater proportions of people including those in news and public affairs, were now permantly employed. Hence, as a senior representative of the staff association commented: 'Free contributors may be gotten rid of for political reasons. But for the purpose of your story you may forget about this. It's not a problem.'

DISPLACEMENT

Another channel by which management can exert political pressure on (even tenured) staff is that of displacement from specific programmes; this channel has been utilised at times in all countries concerned.

Britain

Displacement of people from positions or programmes for political or borderline political reasons was certainly not unheard of in the BBC. Thus Burns (1977, p. 185) writes that, in consequences of creating *Yesterday's Men* which drew a sizeable volume of criticism from politicians[1], one or two heads of people responsible for the broadcast did roll – in the direction of the BBC regions. Also Schlesinger (1978, p. 151) reports that people whose ideas were considered too unorthodox were relegated to less important jobs. One was 'exiled to archives – rather like Siberia'.

More recently – respondents reported – there had been cases where people were shifted around, for instance because the director-general would want to appoint his own people to key positions, because people had 'dried out', or were not considered appropriate for the positions.

Could displacements such as these have political sources or implications? According to one participant in this study, to find cases of displacement for political reasons you would have to go back to the 1970s; one would be hard put to find an example of that today. According to one participant such transferrals could not be ruled out: 'It's the British approach. As a situation arises, you consider the means of dealing with it.' The respondent added, however, that he did not know of any actual cases of people having been shifted for political reasons. Another respondent said: 'Of course people can be displaced from programmes or be moved sideways . . . But there are no cases of political victimisation.' In the view of yet another respondent, some displacements nonetheless had subtle political connotations:

> a BBC controller may be thought not to be doing a very good job. It's a management judgement; you might say it's political; he will be put somewhere else . . . things like that happen all the time. Recently the BBC had appointed a new man to be deputy director-general and he has effectively displaced the person who previously was second in control . . . the person appointed was an accountant. And the person who went out was concerned with programmes. The chairman of the board is also an accountant. The whole . . . of the BBC is being moved much more towards financial considerations rather than programme policy considerations. It's an attempt to appear to the government to be doing what the government wants them to do. Being more financially minded. Thinking in terms of economy, efficiency, rather than thinking in terms of programmes.

Australia

Displacement from specific programmes has certainly occurred in Australia in the 1960s and 1970s, the most prominent example being that of Allan Ashbolt. Ashbolt put forward a series of current affairs programmes with a left-of-centre political bent and was politically active in his private life as well. He posed a particular problem to the ABC and as Inglis (1983, chaps 5–8) reports, for many years he was constantly reprimanded, transferred from sensitive positions or demoted, but he always reappeared in equally or almost equally sensitive positions.

Once, when he had made partisan speeches during an election campaign, the general manager relieved him of any involvement in current affairs. Instead, he was put in charge of television programmes in the arts, humanities and adult education. 'There were thus two hopes invested in Ashbolt . . . that he would make imaginative television programmes . . . and that he would stop making trouble' (Inglis, 1983, p. 260). This may have worked for a time, but eventually Ashbolt reappeared in broadcasts concerned with socio-political issues.

In 1977 Ashbolt was put in charge of *Broadband* which was widely criticised in parliament and elsewhere as one-sidedly pro-communist and was dubbed 'Narrowband'. A report from the general manager to the commission concluded that it did not provide the balance that could be expected from the ABC, and the commission resolved to halve its time. In that year, Ashbolt retired for health reasons – or possibly because he had been exhausted by his political struggles.

According to respondents the situation had recently changed. One would be hard put to find an instance of displacement for political reasons today. Seen from another vantage-point, this change had not been an improvement resulting, as it did, from growing union power:

> radicals of the Staff Association now have union nominees on a whole barrage of committees and boards giving them a major, and sometimes a decisive, influence over appointments, promotions and transfers. It is virtually impossible to transfer an unwilling employee to another job within the ABC without facing the distinct probability of a procedural nightmare of tribunals and hearings (McAdam, 1983b, p. 27).

The then Chairman, Professor Dame Leonie Kramer (1983, p. 29) denied these claims without, however explaining if, for what reasons and how transfers were still being effected in the 1980s.

Israel

In Israel displacement or attempted displacement from specific programmes has been a time-honoured device of internal, political pressure. A respondent told of such a case that took place in radio in 1977. This was an attempt to harrass, and thus cause the displacement of a certain reporter, whose political views antagonised his left-wing colleagues. The attempt eventually failed 'but it caused much aggravation'.

Displacement or attempted displacement of left-wingers took place as well. One example was that of Roeh. For two years he had presented a late-night television programme: *Almost Midnight*. But he was displaced from it in November 1980, reportedly because of his unconventional slant and wry humour which made politicians uncomfortable. He subsequently became a part-time member of staff.

Another example of such displacement was that of Rafiq Halabi, who was in charge of reporting on West-Bank Affairs. According to former director-general Lapid, he publicly identified with a doveish political line 'whereas staff of the broadcasting authority have no right to pursue a political line under any circumstances'. He also began publishing newspaper articles condemning the government's policy on the territories. Thereupon he was transferred to another important though less sensitive position: deputy editor of television news. In 1985, director-general Porat made a bid to displace him from his post on the news. But the Minister of Education and Culture came to his rescue and Halabi kept his post.

One elegant way of displacing people from progammes is that of terminating or changing the latter so that staff have to be shuffled around. One case of such a displacement was that of Yaron London who came to be known as a provocative interviewer and as a left-winger. One respondent told the story of his displacements:

> In the nature of things, those to get the brunt of his treatment were members of the establishment. He got them upset, and pressures began to remove him from programmes. The board put pressure on the director-general and the director-general began to say: he is not good for this programme or that programme. Whenever programming was changed – he was not included. At that time he had already been exhausted by previous struggles. Hence, when once more management wished to displace him, he requested leave without pay. This helped those who wished to shut him up.

In January 1984, London was called back to television but, for political reasons, he was not frequently seen on the screen. In 1985 he reappeared as moderator of a literary programme. In this capacity he could utilise his provocative interviewing skills, without offending politicians.

Besides instances of displacement, attempted displacement or partial displacement, threats of displacement, too, are frequently used as a political weapon. According to one respondent, politicians or senior people within the authority might apply political pressure by letting it be known that they were unhappy with the performance of such and such a person and would be working for his/her displacement. Rumours of the displacement would then spread in the authority, making life uncomfortable for the subject of those rumours.

West Germany

Respondents reported that displacement of people from programmes for political reasons had indeed happened in the past. One case cited was that of a programme named *Panorama* in the 1960s, which did not find favour and the man in charge was transferred to another post. More recently a case cited by practically all respondents of someone who was 'put on ice', albeit temporarily, was that of Franz Alt at SWF (see Chapter 13). This, I was told, was the only recent case in which it was openly admitted that displacement had occurred for political reasons. Beyond that, respondents explained, job-rotation was in any case a normal part of the system. Therefore it was difficult to establish whether any particular transfer had been for political reasons.

I was also told that displacement occurred because mistakes had been made in the creation of a programme. Here, too, it was difficult to determine whether the mistakes were of a political nature or not. For instance, a prominent example was that of an entertainment show, one of whose instalments in 1969 was filmed at a night-club in Paris, and featured the Parisian girls entirely in the nude. The intendant at the time stopped the programme before it went on the air and the man responsible for it was transferred. This occurrence was mentioned to me as an example of transferral for non-political reasons. Yet, were they entirely non-political? One may well imagine that of the major political bodies, the Christian Democratic Union (not to mention the churches) would have been the most offended by the show.

More recent examples cited to me were those of people transferred from one department to another for personal reasons, because they no longer made significant contributions, or because there was no work in their departments. Some respondents claimed they had no political implications, others admitted that in some cases political considerations were involved as well, even though they usually occurred with the consent of the people concerned, and were not fraught with conflict. One respondent recounted:

> It happens occasionally that someone becomes [politically] inappropriate ... [sometimes] this is connected with the *Proporz* system. Sometimes when one position is newly-occupied, the entire merry-go-round is put into motion. All positions must be newly staffed. And when someone does not fit in, a new position will be created for him; usually a new department. That person will be kicked upwards.

Another respondent explained that it was in fact not easy to displace people unless they themselves consented, for then the employees' council would intervene and would not let it pass. All in all, the impression I gained was that displacement for political reasons did not pose a major problem at the present time. This, however, pertained chiefly to displacement initiated from above. There was another form of displacement, that initiated by those displaced, themselves. Just as (by the account of respondents) there was self-censorship in German broadcasting, so, too, there seemed to be cases of self-displacement. For instance, one media expert told of the case of a journalist whose contributions had frequently been cut and censored; he thereupon decided to become a foreign correspondent and asked for a transfer abroad; he never returned to Germany.

I was also told of an instance of internal self-exile which pertained to a whole group of people. There was a group of left-wingers in the ZDF who had initially been engaged to do political broadcasts. They subsequently felt that they did not enjoy the expected freedom in this domain, so they moved over into cultural programmes. Since these were watched by only a small part of the audience the boards and politicians were less concerned with them; hence (as respondents explained) left-wingers who

> could not or would not find a foothold in political journalism ... sidestepped into the domain of culture ... They have made that choice themselves. Here they continue their existence. From the social and financial viewpoints they are not badly off. But they vegetate in those niches.

All in all, however, it seems that like dismissals, displacements, and even self-displacements, were not a major factor in the politicisation of German broadcasting. As a respondent summarised: 'One must say that social conciliation is pretty strong here. People get along well with each other. The tendency to punish is minute. It is also unnecessary, because there are so many subtle means to smooth things out and to keep the people 'good'.' These subtle means are dealt with in the other chapters.

CONCLUSION

This chapter has been concerned with dismissal, demotion and displacement as forms of political pressure. Cases of displacement of people from positions and programmes as political pressure could be found in all countries studied. In Britain and Australia one had to go back to the 1970s to find them, while in West Germany and especially in Israel, there were more recent cases at hand. It is of interest, however, that in one way or another, some of the 'displaced' people eventually seemed to pop up again in equally or almost equally important positions, so displacement must be regarded as a less effective form of political pressure than dismissal and demotion.

This study produced no evidence to show that – in any of the countries studied – people permantly employed in public broadcasting have been dismissed for their political views. But in Britain people may be ousted for professional reasons with political overtones, particularly for letting their political views be evident on the air, or for being especially vocal on controversial issues. And in Israel there have been cases of people demoted from key positions for political reasons. There were also impending retrenchments where personal preferences and loyalties apparently played a role. Personal favouritism also had political implications: persons who knew they were to keep their posts despite possible retrenchments, because of their personal loyalty to the director, would be likely to become even more loyal and likely to shape programmes to the director's political convenience. Moreover, the general atmosphere of uncertainty and anxiety created by the impending retrenchments might be expected to have made staff in the authority more politically cautious than they had ever been before, at least for some time – even if the redundancies eventually did not materialise.

Non-permanent appointees, freelances and people on contract were obviously the more vulnerable to political pressures through dismissals. They were also more prone to self-pressures and to excessive caution, but there were differences between the four countries in these respects. In Israel and West Germany there was no trend over time to put more people on contract – in Britain and Australia such a trend was clearly evident. Moreover, in West Germany there was a trend in the opposite direction: more and more people on contract had gained permanent employment. In Australia, on the other hand, the trend to put more people on contract was especially pronounced. Since the people on contract now included senior management, the possibilities for politicisation through dismissals or looming dismissals, with the advent of each new government, were especially evident there.

Thus, the paradoxical situation emerged that precisely where appointment procedures are the least politicised, that is, in Britain and Australia, and especially in Australia, political pressures through possible dismissal could become the most pronounced. And precisely where appointment and promotion procedures are the most overtly politicised, that is in West Germany, people – once appointed – have the greatest immunity from political pressures.

Note

1. Even though they were Labour politicians, then out of office.

Part IV
Resistance to Pressures, Friction and Conflict

So far a variety of political pressures applied to broadcasting corporations and their staff have been analysed. These corporations and their staff are not completely powerless to resist such pressures. In this part of the book some of the sources, channels and devices of resistance to pressure are reviewed, and the resulting friction and clashes are illustrated.

11 Resistance to Pressures (I)

This chapter reviews sources of resistance to political pressures on broadcasting based on the mobilisation and activation of people – whether the public, or broadcasters themselves – in defence of broadcasting independence.

RESISTANCE THROUGH PUBLICITY

In Britain, public support for BBC independence has been a formidable factor in mitigating political interference. Respondents concurred that any attempts by government to apply 'improper' pressures on the BBC (for instance by threatening it with a cut-down of funds) would invariably be leaked to the press and would create a loud 'noise', a big 'outcry'. Such threats to the BBC had been voiced some years ago, but that would not be possible today because 'the society won't have it'. Publicity, of course, would be less effective in protecting the BBC against more subtle pressures which would be difficult to pinpoint, prove and publicise.

Participants in the study also offered the view that any tendency the BBC might have to give in to government pressure would similarly cause a big 'uproar'. This was in fact the case recently when a storm broke loose around BBC staff-vetting and the *Real Lives* programme. In these cases, public opinion turned against the BBC for giving in to government pressures – perhaps more than it turned against the government – for exerting them. Indeed, publicity (in conjunction with a staff strike) eventually aided (or constrained) the BBC to reassert its independence by announcing that it would abolish most vetting and by putting on the programme around which the storm had initially brewed.

Besides aid from the general public, aid in resisting political pressure may also come from certain groups that are natural BBC allies, as it were, in the quest for freedom of expression. These include, for instance, representatives of higher education and the arts. But as a respondent explained, these groups, no less than the BBC itself, have been weakened in recent years:

> The BBC is more isolated in public feeling than it ever was in its history. And that is due ... to the fact that this government ... has demoralised a large number of those forces which might once upon a time have been supportive to the BBC, in particular in higher education which was the BBC's natural ally. Recently *The Times* has been running a series of articles, all of which took a critical view of the BBC. Had some of these things been said ten or even six years ago, there would immediately have been a great response. The vice-chancellors would have written [to *The Times*] and [A11] the ... vice-chancellors would have lined up and marched on London. And that sort of thing does not happen because the vice-chancellors themselves are demoralised and they're too busy fighting their own battles, looking after their own backyards ... Another constituency which you could have expected to support the BBC is the arts area. Now, thanks to the current policy of the Arts Council, the arts have been fairly demoralised. And one way or another, the attack on the central liberal institutions by this government has been fairly successful and the BBC which, in a sense stood at the centre of these organisations, has suffered disproportionately.

In Australia, the fear of adverse publicity has not always deterred governments or politicians from political interference, but has several times served as a device to resist pressure once it had occurred. For instance, in 1970, the Liberal government announced funding cuts to be applied to ABC current-affairs programmes (which had irked the government because of their leftist stance). A public outcry followed: the opposition, the press, all condemned the move and the government was forced to back down.

In 1976, when the government was about to terminate the appointment of all Labor-appointed ABC commissioners (see Chapter 7) an organisation calling itself 'Auntie's Nieces and Nephews' convened a protest rally in Melbourne. About a thousand people attended; lobbying with parliamentarians took place, and once again, the government was forced to back down (Inglis, 1983, Chap. 3).

As in England, public opinion not only helps broadcasting resist political pressures but in some respects may force it to do so, as explained by an informant:

The ABC ... at times [has] not been scared to attack some of the sacred cows and some of our leading figures ... most of the people that have been making these programmes are still at the ABC.

Question: How come?
Answer: Well, if the ABC puts a controversial programme to air ... it can't very well turn around two months later and sack the persons who produced it. I mean they are going to lay themselves open to charges of political influence.

This was supplemented by another explanation as follows: 'People in the front line of broadcasting ... generally have fairly substantial public status and if someone attempts to use that sort of influence on them, they run a fair risk. The person concerned is going to have avenues of publicity and exposure [open to them].' With respect to pressure by funding another respondent said: 'It tends to become a public issue and therefore, out in the open ... and of course, that's the ultimate protection against that happening in any blatant sort of way.'

There also is a view among ABC programmers, however, that recently public support for the ABC has weakened, that 'when it comes to hearing support for the ABC there's a deafening silence ... that ... the public ... simply do not think it matters any more' (Berry, 1985, p. 54).

In Israel, publicity (via the press) serves as a device for resistance to both external and internal political pressures, as becomes clear from the following respondents' statements:

> Broadcasting journalists can free themselves from pressures by turning to the press.
>
> The press serves as an outstanding watchdog for us ... [when management pressures are publicised by the press, management] has got a problem.
>
> The reporter enjoys considerable immunity from political pressure ... through public exposure.

Nonetheless there are phenomena of broadcasting politicisation to which public opinion has simply become accustomed – or perhaps did not consider as worthy of notice in the first place. Thus, the political struggles surrounding the appointment of a director for television (Chapter 13), the attempts to force television into closure by non-ratification of the budget, for partly political reasons (Chapter 5), while widely reported in the press, have hardly raised an eyebrow. And neither has the system of political appointments and promotions as a whole which in any case is well in line with political appointments in the Israeli government bureaucracy.

In West Germany the public has only rarely been mobilised to resist political pressures on broadcasting. One such instance occurred in 1973 in Bavaria. According to Williams (1976, chap. 7) at that time the ruling CSU attempted to pass a law which would have increased the political seats on the board of the state broadcasting corporation, the BR. The opposition appealed to the constitutional court and public opinion was mobilised. A popular movement came into being; it culminated in a plebiscite which forced the ruling party to restitute the previously existing pluralistic law. Also in the 1970s, the broadcasting journalists' Statutes Movement was backed up by a general spirit of protest and reforms (see below). More recently when a journalist at SWF, Franz Alt, was – in the colourful description of a respondent – 'put on ice', widespread, mostly negative publicity ensued (see Chapter 13).

But except for this spectacular case, recently there has been little public reaction to political control of broadcasting. It must be borne in mind that direct financial political pressures on the German broadcasting system have been less formidable than in some of the other countries studied. There has not been an attempt actually to cut the income of broadcasting corporations for political reasons as in Australia. There has not been an endeavour to force broadcasting corporations into closure by not ratifying their budget, as in Israel. Hence, there seem to be few highly visible issues around which public opinion could be mobilised.

I was assured by those interviewed that if blatant cases of pressure were to occur, it would be 'hung on the big bell' (as happened in the Alt case). But the less blatant yet more frequent cases of political pressures through appointments and promotions do not attract an effective public reaction. Occasionally articles critical of the system appear in the press, but nothing much happens after that.

RESISTANCE THROUGH STAFF ASSOCIATIONS AND MOVEMENTS

Other aids for broadcasters in resisting political pressures from both outside and inside the broadcasting corporations are staff or professional associations, councils and movements. In the BBC there are at present two major unions: the National Union of Journalists (NUJ) and the Broadcasting Entertainments Trade Alliace (BETA) (in addition the BBC recognises a number of other unions) and about half the BBC staff are union members. The BBC unions negotiate with management on salaries and working conditions but have practically no involvement in appointments and promotions.

According to a union spokesman, however, the unions were involved where people felt they had been disadvantaged, where they were disciplined or threatened with redundancy. By the testimony of a BBC official, union involvement in such cases had nothing to do with defence against political pressures, simply because there was no political victimisation at the BBC. An NUJ representative agreed that there were no cases of outright political victimisation of BBC staff, but added that there were suspected or borderline cases and in such cases the union would help people with their appeals.

The NUJ also raised its voice on the issues of BBC staff-vetting and the *Real Lives* programme. It did so by negotiating with management and threatening strikes, industrial action and major confrontation unless vetting stopped and the programme was put on. It is quite possible that union action (which was also widely publicised in the press) had a substantial share in bringing this about. At the same time, union representatives in this study identified themselves as Labour persons, and it cannot be ruled out that (whether this was intended or not) the intervention they sponsored had its own political slant.

In the ABC there are currently three main relevant associations: the Staff Association (which represents all officers below the third division, class ten), the Senior Officers' Association (which represents all officers above that level) and the Australian Journalists' Association representing ABC journalists. These Associations are active not only in negotiating working conditions but in appointment and promotion procedures as well: they are represented on selection panels and boards of appeal for permanent positions whenever the candidates include permanent staff as well as others. As noted, there is no overt politicisation of appointment procedures in Australia, and it is quite possible that unions, by acting as watchdogs, have helped to prevent its development. As one respondent assured us, if security vetting of ABC staff was to occur, the Journalists' Association would 'kick up a hell of a fuss'.

The staff associations have also played a role in helping the ABC resist direct political interference. Thus, in 1978, when staff ceilings were cut by the government for apparently political reasons, there was an ABC staff strike, and a thousand or so members of staff, joined in a 'stop work' meeting called by the NSW branch of the ABC staff association. The Minister for Communications later acknowledged that these actions had had an effect on future funding arrangements. (Inglis, 1983, chap. 8).

A more recent incident in which the ABC staff association helped staff to stand up against pressure was narrated by an association official:

When Kramer apologised to the conservative [government] in Western Australia ... under pressure ... we had a stop work meeting ... We beat up Leonie Kramer quite well on that and put her back in her box. But you see, it's gotta be something of that magnitude before we get involved.

In Israel, according to Greene (1973) broadcasting employees have been covered by a variety of associations and councils – each was granted different working conditions – and this has created much chaos and conflict. This situation has not changed much since then and the authority's management is still embroiled in pervasive conflict with the employees' associations. Much of this conflict (for instance with the technicians' association) is not political, hence not relevant for the present discussion. But the broadcasters' associations also take on the role of defending staff against political pressures. As an observer commented, their role is to defend employees whose working conditions are under threat. But they argue that freedom of expression is an important element in the journalists' working conditions. Hence their activity in this area by means of strikes and programme blackouts. The effectiveness of such activity is attested by Professor Aharonson, who said: 'The journalists' association, or other country-wide associations of which the journalists are members, can call strikes that paralyse the whole country. The broadcasting authority will be wary of initiating confrontations under such conditions.' Hence in the words of another respondent: 'In many cases the employees' associations dictate what will happen.'

There have been representatives of the unions and staff councils (who frequently consist of the same people) on selection committees. By some accounts their influence was quite powerful and management would not rush to appoint someone they opposed. In some cases the associations and councils would attempt to mitigate the politicisation of the appointment process. Thus, in 1985, when television was left without a director, the associations pressured management to employ proper appointment procedures (see Chapter 13).

The associations and councils have also acted to mitigate political pressures through displacement. By the testimony of an association member:

> When management wishes to displace or remove people from programmes, for instace Rafiq Halabi or Yaron London, the associations and councils have always acted as a blocking factor. They black out news or public affairs programmes until some agreement is reached – usually a compromise.

In 1985 the employees' associations and councils were also extremely active in opposing, stalling and perhaps preventing widespread dismissals in the authority (see Chapter 10). They have thereby been instrumental in mitigating whatever political implications such dismissals may have had. All in all, however, the Israeli broadcasting associations and councils have not had a major effect in counteracting the politicisation of broadcasting particularly through appointments which by now has been firmly institutionalised.

In Israel and Australia, no less than in Britain, the possibility always exists that while the associations attempt to help staff resist political pressures, their intervention itself, may have a political slant. According to the associations' representatives employees' associations derive their power from members of staff of all political persuasions and therefore will defend all of them.

At the same time many observers, especially right-wingers, believe that people active in staff associations themselves tend to be leftists. Furthermore, the broadcasters who irk the political establishment frequently tend to be left-wingers, too. Those would be the people most likely to be displaced from sensitive programmes. Hence, the staff associations would be most frequently called upon to defend people with a leftist political stand.

In West Germany the role of representing broadcasting staff is shared by several organisations. These include the Broadcasting, Television and Film Union, the Journalists' Association and the German Employees' Union, besides some smaller unions. In addition, broadcasting employees are represented by employees' councils. Those are two distinct but related instruments of employee representation. The Employees' Council in the ZDF, for instance, is elected by the employees on the basis of lists presented by the unions.

In the ZDF, the unions' major role is to negotiate employment contracts while the employees' council deals first and foremost with working conditions and the prevention of discrimination against employees 'on whatever grounds'. Except for the most senior positions, the council has certain co-determination rights with respect to appointments. These, however, are limited by the fact that it is the intendant who makes the final decision. By the account of a senior representative it uses whatever limited powers it has to combat discrimination on political grounds. Asked whether this intervention had any impact in preventing politicisation, the representative said that it did but added: 'It is the influence of the nurse who applies the ointment, not that of the surgeon who removes the tumour.'

Here, too, it is possible that the council's intervention may introduce a political slant of its own into appointments and promotions. For the council is intertwined with the unions, which normally tend to the left. Indeed, the representative who talked to me was clearly a left-winger. He assured me that he represented all employees regardless of political affiliation. But whether he could do so with equal effectiveness for all, must remain an open question. In any event, whether or not the employees' rights were strongly supported, depended in large measure on the employees themselves. As the representative informed me, it often happened that employees preferred not to utilise the council's co-determination rights, because it could damage their career prospects or because they simply did not care enough.

Perhaps it is for that very reason that, as a representative of the ZDF informed me, there were no problems with unions and the employees' council at the corporation. Although there was much bargaining over salaries, conditions and other issues, there were no actual clashes. By the testimony of several participants the same held for other broadcasting stations as well. There might be some difficulties in one or the other of the ARD stations occasionally but by and large no major conflicts were visible.

Things had not always been like this, however. The present period of relative calm was preceded in the 1970s by strenuous resistance to political interference, with the aid of a movement of broadcasting journalists known as the Statutes Movement. As we learn from Williams (1976) and Wittich (1983) this movement's goal was to bring into force new codes of conduct or statutes designed to guarantee broadcasters' freedom of expression and to protect them against the overriding of their individual convictions. Created in 1969, the movement generated formidable opposition in particular (but not only) from intendants, who saw it as promoting the self-interest of broadcasters, and as undermining their own position.

As a result of the movement two stations, NDR and HR, issued statutes for editors and programme-makers; the rest adopted arrangements in the form of directiveness and guidelines from the intendant, in the form of regulations or in the form of modifications to existing codes of staff representation on decision-making bodies. These were but watered-down versions of what broadcasting personnel originally demanded. Nevertheless they represented some gains by setting guarantees on the rights of individual broadcasters who now would not be forced to act against their conviction, and who gained the right to speak up as part of the representative bodies in broadcasting stations.

The Statutes Movement was still vivid in the respondents'

memories. Some of them pointed out that it had emerged in the context of other similar controversies, such as the student movement and issues of freedom of the press and co-determination of employees which had been salient at the time. Even so, according to an employees' council spokesman, the movement (or organisation) had led to few dramatic successes, but it had led, for instance, to changes in the ZDF basic rules whereby no contributor could now be forced to express an opinion that contradicts his/her conviction, or to suppress or slant information. These were not major concessions 'but in the quest for success, one must bake small buns'. According to the same spokesman the most significant achievement of the movement had been the widespread participation in the discussion of principles it had elicited. 'To this day there are colleagues who say to me: "it was interesting, after all". They remember that something exciting was going on . . . continuing debate on these issues is essential in a still developing democracy.'

By all accounts, the movement had now 'fallen asleep', or died. The issues which brought it to the fore in the 1970s were no longer on the agenda today and, in the words of a respondent 'it is in the nature of high waves that they ebb eventually . . . the euphoria has vanished'. Even today there was an association rejoicing in the name of 'Journalists for Public Broadcasting', purporting to follow in the footsteps of the Statutes Movement. But apparently it was not highly significant. It came into being in 1982 and many journalists of different political colours joined. But the group could not consolidate itself and many believed it was a failure (Riese, 1984, p. 156).

According to the description of one respondent the group organised occasional gatherings of journalists from different broadcasting domains, followed by press conferences in which participants complained how terrible things were. These participants, however, were all people who had made formidable careers in their own houses – not a suppressed group by any means. By the account of another ZDF member of staff 'they usually pat each other on the shoulder but nothing ever comes out of there'.

By and large, respondents were of the opinion that since the demise of the Statutes Movement things were proceeding more peacefully in German broadcasting, and even more so at the ZDF. Perhaps one of the reasons for this was that potential conflicts were so frequently arbitrated by the Federal Constitutional Court (see Chapter 6) – which is not to say that all respondents necessarily welcomed this development. Thus a left-winger made the following comment:

> A lot has changed in the direction: silence. One may argue about whether this is a good thing . . . Peace – yes. But it may be the peace of the cemetry . . . When broadcasting has to cope with a changing world and yet there is peace, I get frightened . . . Where are the people who paint the question marks on the wall?

Another respondent, a right-winger, offered a different evaluation:

> What [the Statutes Movement] had demanded was not compatible with the public-law structure of broadcasting. No journalist may be forced to do anything that contradicts his conviction. That is obvious; it is now included in the service contracts. But it is something entirely different to argue that a journalist may have complete freedom and say whatever he wishes. That is impossible because of the principle of the general responsibility of the intendant . . . At the time, [the Statutes Movement] demanded such freedom. They have disappeared because the legal arguments [against them] were so clear cut.

CONCLUSION

The two sources of resistance to political pressure on broadcasting dealt with so far: public opinion and broadcasters' professional associations are clearly interrelated. To be truly effective staff-association activities must be anchored in issues that are on the public agenda and must be supported by public opinion. And in principle it should be easy for broadcasting associations to achieve such support for their causes since many of their ranks are also members of journalists' associations and thus have open access to the press. But by some accounts, in both Britain and Australia, public support for national broadcasting has recently weakened. And in Israel and West Germany, where politicisation of broadcasting is firmly entrenched, even publicity through the press is not always effective in counteracting political pressures. Thus, in both countries, articles critical of the politicised system which have repeatedly appeared in the press have had little impact on what actually happens. Indeed, by and large, their impact has not been greater than it would have been, had they been critical of the weather.

One obstacle which staff associations face in their attempts to make broadcasting corporations more resistant to political pressures is that the latter have little leverage over the government. While governments can hold broadcasting corporations by the purse-strings, the latter have little with which to retaliate. Their 'ultimate' weapon is the blacking-out of programmes. But, especially where public broadcasting holds no monopoly, the threat of that happening is unlikely to intimidate politicians. Thus as the *Bulletin* (23 July 1985, p. 35) reports, when the then ABC director-general Whitehead threatened that the ABC would go off the air because of budget cuts, the treasurer Paul Keating retorted: 'Now don't go making rash promises.'

12 Resistance to Pressures (II)

The foregoing chapter has been devoted to sources of resistance to pressure that need special mobilisation. In this chapter we look at sources of resistance that are 'there'. so to speak, although some of them may be enhanced by mobilisation.

RESISTANCE THROUGH THE ETHOS OF INDEPENDENCE, CREDIBILITY AND OBJECTIVITY

While public opinion in favour of broadcasting independence has to be mobilised – mostly through the press – broadcasters' own support for independence is invoked in their daily work. And despite a certain normative ambiguity in this respect (see Chapter 3) in some broadcasting corporations the ethos of broadcasting independence still afforded broadcasters some support in withstanding political pressures.

In Britain, BBC independence was viewed by staff as the major source for its credibility in the eyes of the audience. And the need to maintain that credibility was itself a source of resistance to political pressure. Thus one of the External Services staff recounted that they were subject to frequent pressures from politicians to present Britain favourably in their broadcasts, not to present views that dissented from those of the government and to play down British defeats in wartime, because this was supposedly in the national interest. The response was that if the BBC gave in to those sorts of demands it would lose its credibility for years to come – 'and BBC credibility is very much in the national interest'.

Naturally, this source of resistance is vulnerable because BBC credibility itself is fragile. Thus, in the case of the *Real Lives* programme (Chapter 4) the BBC was in fact perceived as having given in to government pressure, and to the chagrin of Bush House staff this was used by rival external services such as those of the Soviet Union to pour scorn over the BBC's credibility.

On the other hand, credibility was strengthened by politicians complaining about the BBC in public. Thus a respondent explained that when Thatcher held forth about the BBC in parliament 'this was a marvellous thing for the BBC because we could report it on our programmes. And this added to our credibility.' Public complaints by government personalities thus had a boomerang effect: they strengthened BBC credibility which then served as an additional source of resistance to pressure.

A similar boomerang effect of political pressure was reported by a respondent in Australia:

> What? Scrapping a programme because of political pressure? No, never ... in fact, usually, you'd find it's the other way around: they'd deliberately not close the programme or not alter it. The ABC is very sensitive about [that] and tends to become more determined to put it to air if there is any suggestion that there is pressure not to [do so].

Commitment to the ethos of broadcasting independence was also expressed in Israel and West Germany. In Israel one of the television staff said: 'We keep away from the issue of politics – as if it were fire.' However, particularly in West Germany, commitment to broadcasting independence was counteracted by the fact that many of the staff had already resigned themselves to its absence (see Chapter 3). In the apt words of Riese (1984, p. 158). 'The parties' domination has been internalised by most journalists and has become an ideology to legitimise their own actions.'

Closely related to the ethos of independence and credibility is the ethos of professionalism which, once again, can be invoked by broadcasters – or in their name – whenever they are subject to political pressures. The broadcaster's professional ethos, in turn, includes as one of its major components the injunction of balance, impartiality and objectivity.

This ethos has been emphasised especially in the BBC. Thus C. Curran, one-time BBC director-general wrote (1973) that it was incumbent on, and possible for, the BBC:

> to present a view of the world – or rather a series of views of the world – which, in their totality, will be regarded by most people for most of the time as reasonably balanced. That is the BBC's principal role in sustaining the democratic system.

As for the present, a BBC spokesman rounded out the picture by saying: 'of course there is no such thing as complete objectivity. But in the BBC people are expected to try. They are allowed to make mistakes. But it is expected that their mistakes will not always favour the same party.'

In Australia, too, objectivity, impartiality and balance are the established norm (or the norm of the establishment) as expressed, for instance, in the following statement by erstwhile chairman, Professor Kramer:

> In private life broadcasters have commitments to political and social philosophies ... as professionals they have an absolute responsibility not to press those commitments on their audience ... ABC staff have an obligation which derives ultimately from the trust reposed in them ... namely, to limit their own freedom of expression in order to protect the freedom of their audience to decide for themselves (*Bulletin*, 8 February, 1983, p. 29).

In West Germany, this norm found expression in the words of a respondent: 'We must be fair. We must not restrict information', and in Israel this ethos was exemplified by the statement of a respondent as follows: 'We are under an obligation to maintain political balance. When you bring the stand of one political body you must, simultaneously, bring the attitude of the rival political body as well... Every journalist defines for himself what balance is.'

This statement, however, foreshadows the problems raised by the ethos of objectivity, balance and impartiality, *namely, the difficulty of determining objectively what objectivity is* and hence of achieving it in practice. For the BBC this problem is illustrated by another former director-general, Greene, who in a public address in 1965, said that the BBC tried to treat all controversial matters with 'due impartiality' but went on to say: 'There are some respects in which it is not neutral, unbiased or impartial. That is, where there are clashes for and against the basic moral values – truthfulness, justice, freedom' (cited in Paulu, 1981, p. 212). This, of course, gives rise to the problem that political controversy is frequently focused precisely on the issue of what justice is and what type of justice society ought to have.

Thus, some ABC staff, particularly leftists, expressed the

view that 'impartiality' really means 'defence of the established view of justice and social order' (see Ashbolt, 1980). One respondent expressed this view as follows:

> The ABC likes to see itself as unbiased. That's an absurdity. Supposedly ABC journalists are to keep their attitudes out of their jobs. That's not really possible. It's better to admit one's bias than to pretend to be unbiased. So-called lack of bias is really the expression of establishment attitudes.

In addition, objectivity is hampered by selectivity. To be objective reporting in general – and broadcasting in particular – would have to mirror reality. In fact, this is impossible as the act of reporting necessarily involves selection of facts, filtering of information, interpretation of the situation, and thus value judgements. Thus, a BBC paper 'The Control of Broadcasting' (1972; cited in Briggs, 1979, p. 136) stated that the BBC had come to recognise that 'in broadcasting's claim to mirror society, the selective nature of its reflection is all-important'; and Schlesinger (1978, p. 135) wrote: 'To put a construction on the news, impose a meaning on it, is inescapable, since the production process is one that at all stages involves the making of value judgements.' Reporting thus involves construction, no less than reflection of reality. And such construction of reality cannot but be guided by explicit or implicit value judgements.

These problems and dilemmas have also been brought out in Israel where one broadcasting employee said: 'There is no such thing as objectivity ... consciously or unconsciously the reporter has his own priorities, a world view of his own ... he selects topics accordingly', and another member of staff, Roeh, made the following succinct comments in a newspaper interview:

> Objectivity is when I agree with what you say. They always say: 'Let the facts speak for themselves.' That's rubbish. After all, you select, you judge, you edit, and you decide on the priority of presentation. There is the illusion of facts and therein lies the danger (Segal, 1983, p. 5).

In West Germany similar views have been expressed as follows: 'It is impossible to present a commentary without expressing an opinion', and:

There is no such thing as unmanipulated broadcasting. The question is not whether broadcasting is manipulated, but who does the manipulating. As long as our own side is manipulating all is well. When the other side is doing it – this is clearly dangerous.

A further, related problem created by the ethos of independence, objectivity, and professionalism occurs, because broadcasting people may invoke those values in their defence, even when this is not justified. Thus, in Israel, a well-known public figure in the area of broadcasting reported:

> I am involved in many struggles on freedom of speech. But frequently I am forced to defend staffers even when they don't deserve it . . . They do a one sided, shitty report and when they are justly reprimanded they cry: freedom of the press! This is counterproductive. It undermines legitimate freedom.

According to many observers one-sidedness was a problem particularly in West Germany. For instance, an erstwhile (conservative) intendant Franz Mai (1978, p. 55) wrote that in recent years 'broadcasting journalism intent on balance has begun to be dissipitated and to be deformed into a subjective ideologically narrow-minded, missionary type of journalism', and a right-wing media expert said:

> A great many journalists make serious efforts to be objective. [But] there are many jouralists who regard themselves as . . . ambassadors of a certain idea. And these journalists change the whole scene as they frequently hold [key] symbolic positions in journalism.

In the same vein, another right-wing media expert, Dr Wolfgang Donsbach, in an interview for a local journal (Donsbach, 1984, p. 5), reported on a research project conducted jointly by the Institut für Publizistik at the University of Mainz, the Institut für Demoskopie in Allensbach and the University of Leicester in England. This study revealed that whereas the British journalists who were studied regarded it as their most important task to inform, German journalists saw it as their most important task to criticise and reveal misconduct.

Not only right-wing observers but left-wingers, too, complained of the lack of an ethos objectivity in West German journalism:

> In place of the presentation of facts and their analysis comes moral evaluation . . . the German press resorts to moral categories in its commentary on social and political processes – to a greater extent that is customary in other countries (Riese, 1984, p. 188).

The ethos of objectivity is important because (despite the problems surrounding the issue) it leads to greater objectivity in practice than would otherwise be the case. Thus, according to Burghart (1978, p. 63) while reporting can never obtain full objectivity it still makes a difference whether one makes an effort to attain objectivity or whether one surrenders to subjectivity unabashedly. According to Peleg (1981, p. 27) the ethos of objectivity, while it cannot create full objectivity creates 'para-objectivity', a term which 'expressed the intermediate situation in which there is no objectivity in the news, and yet the news is not subjective in the usual sense of intentional political slanting.'

According to Peleg (1981, p. 27) the ethos of objectivity and professionalism is also important (even if there is no full objectivity in practice) in that it 'justifies the demand for credibility' and thus serves to avert, attenuate, or aid staff in resisting political pressures. Where this commitment is strongest the defence it affords for broadcasting independence is strongest as well.

With regard to the BBC this view was also held by Schlesinger (1978), who wrote that the conception of impartiality played 'a total justificatory role' for the BBC (Schlesinger, 1978, p. 62) and that in return for being impartial in terms broadly predefined by the state, it is rewarded with the gift of independence' (Schlesinger, 1978, p. 178). Likewise, Kumar (as cited by Schlesinger, 1978, p. 201) argued that the BBC's impartiality aided it in warding off 'clutching embraces from all around'. And a BBC interviewee said, 'Since we're supposed to be impartial, if we were not, we would in fact be vulnerable to political intervention. And so we should be, because we would not be doing our job.'

In relation to Israel a practically identical view was expressed by the former director-general, Lapid:

The authority's employees have provided an opening for politicians only when they failed in observing the rules. As long as journalists were meticulous in observing professional standards it was not difficult for management to defend them and the authority's independence at one and the same time.

RESISTANCE BY DEFAULT

There is another, quite formidable source of aid to staff in resisting political pressure, namely, resistance which ensues from the failure or inability, of management to enforce its guidelines on staff. It is thus the (unintentional) result of management's ineffectivenmess in the performance of its managerial duties, or resistance through default.

This phenomenon has been documented in particular with regard to the Israel Broadcasting Authority. As the brief historical overview (in Chapter 2) has shown, fragmentation and lack of discipline have beset the authority since its inception.

This situation was perpetuated into the 1980s. This is attested for instance by a former (right-wing) member of the board, Papo who wrote (1980b, p. 13) that the relationship between broadcasters and management 'resembles an upside-down pyramid where those lower in rank and importance in fact dictate the character of the broadcasts to the editors and managers' and by a representative of the staff association who noted that:

> Administration does not flow smoothly in the correct channels. Frequently the bottom layer of the broadcasting corporation is independent. When there are complaints from the outside there is a discussion. But generally, in this administrative anarchy, you do what you want – politicially.

This view was corroborated by another respondent who noted (at the end of 1984) that although there were internal pressures they were dispelled before they reached the lower echelons 'because the pipelines through which instructions flow are clogged and ... administrative channels are blocked'. According to Professor Aharonson there was a further move in this direction recently, and under Porat as director-general there was 'total anarchy'. Porat himself, in a newspaper interview, corroborated this:

> The whole system is like a plate of spaghetti. You can never tell where a noodle starts, where it goes and where it ends ... [It's] a mad-hatter's party: By law the director-general is subordinate to the board of directors, which has seven members, each of whom sees himself as a super-director-general and the chairman as a super-super-director-general. And by the formulation of the law they are entitled to hold this view. And so we have the grotesque situation of an executive body that works under the command of eight chiefs of staff who are entited to issue commands to staff. Is it surprising then that management spends most of its time in bitter arguments, in power contests and demarcation disputes? And when management is embroiled in struggles is it surprising that staff are having a ball and each one is doing what he sees fit? Where there is no hierarchy there is anarchy (Baum, 1985, p. 4).

According to other observers and senior participants, too, the roots of this situation were to be found in the Broadcasting Authority Act which did not provide for a clear division of authority between the plenum and the board of directors and between those and the authority's professional staff. By the act, the director-general was appointed by the government but subordinate to the board of directors, while the directors of radio and television were appointed by the board, but subordinate to the director-general. The board of directors and the director-general were both appointed by the government and only the government (and not the board) could dismiss the director-general. Hence an absurd state of affairs had been created: when the board announced that it no longer had confidence in the director-general, the latter announced that he, for his part, no longer had confidence in the board of directors (*Ha'aretz*, 11 September 1985, p. 21). One respondent pointed to the fact that the director-general had referred to the board (his own directorate) as a bunch of *Shlumiels* (nincompoops) – yet both continued to coexist within the broadcasting system.

To this must be added the presence, in the authority, of a number of formidable employees' councils, each with its own interests and axes to grind. Especially powerful in television, these councils were not only countervailing management, but in the process were counteracting each other as well. Agreements reached by management with one council would frequently be obviated by another council and vice versa. This exacerbated the clogging of authority channels and thereby impeded the conveyance of instructions (and pressures) from above. The result of all this on the one hand was that the system was not functioning properly, but on the other this also meant that political pressures were frequently dissipated somewhere in between their point of departure and their point of destination and that such pressures were frequently bouncing off each other before reaching their targets.

SOME RELATED ISSUES

Resistance to pressure by default is basically a process whereby staff can resist *internal political* pressures from management because they are neutralised before they reach them. There is a kindred process whereby management can resist *external* political pressures because *they* in turn, are neutralised before they reach their target. This happens when such political pressures emanate from a variety of powerful but conflicting external sources.

This mutually counterbalancing process is prominent in West Germany where broadcasting is subject to an unusually decentralised system of political supervision: the eleven states – and marginally – the central government, all have a finger in the pie but none of them can bake the pie entirely to its own taste. The ZDF, in which all states have a share, is a special beneficiary of this system. But in some respects all broadcasting corporations are affected, for on some general matters – such as the licence fee – all states have to reach agreement before policies can be implemented. As respondents pointed out, no one state government would have sufficient power to impose its own views of such policies, and this left broadcasting stations greater political leeway.

Apart from that, the *Proporz* principle, to which there was religious adherence in West Germany, ensured that there were always opposing party representatives on the broadcasting supervisory bodies, and a variety of counterbalancing pressures (frequently resulting in political compromises) were thus practically built into the system. The same was also evident in

Israel, where the long-standing tradition of coalition governments and the party-political key of appointments to the board have also caused cross-pressures to be incorporated into the system. Besides, as a respondent informed me in 1983, pressures also emanated from a variety of other sources, including heads of government departments, diverse interest groups, the federation of labour and several professional associations.

This situation, too, was enhanced even further in 1984 because of changes in Israel's general political constellation. As the former director-general, Lapid, explained:

> In a coalition government in which both major parties participate, they neutralise each other in their ability to push the broadcasting authority into a corner, because management can always turn to the other side. What the Defence Minister doesn't like the Education Minister *does* like . . . so a kind of protective umbrella is created.

A related source of resistance to pressure is the two-party or multiple-party government-*versus*-opposition system as such, and the rotation of parties in office. With regard to the BBC this was explained by an official interviewed by Burns (1977, p. 188):

> What chiefly protects the independence of the BBC . . . is the . . . fear that something disagreeable done by one party when it's in power would lead to the Opposition, when it was in power, doing something even more disagreeable. It's as though the independence of the BBC was maintained by mutual agreement between the two, because of the common interest they have in the kind of neutrality, objectivity or impartiality of the BBC as such.

In the same vein a BBC official interviewed by me explained: 'The opposition is keen for the BBC [independence] to be preserved because [an independent BBC] is like a watchdog, picking up things about politicians of the government.'

The rotation of parties in office serves to keep broadcasting corporations more independent than would otherwise be the case because it means that management must keep in mind the possibility that it will have to work under a government of a different political colour in the future. Also, the director-general must take account of the possibility that the question of his reappointment will be decided under a new government with a different political constellation from the one under which he might be working at the time. This is relevant in all countries, but especially in Israel, where the director-general is appointed directly by the government.

This can best be illustrated by the following example. There was wide agreement amongst respondents that former director-general Lapid, though a Likud-government appointee, had not toed the Likud line. According to Lapid himself, this was because of his commitment to broadcasting independence. A different interpretation, offered by another respondent, was that Lapid wished to open the door for his reappointment under a possible, subsequent, Labour government. Hence, it was particularly before the 1981 election that Lapid saw to it that broadcasts were 'from balanced to pro-Labour'. Whether or not this interpretation is correct in this particular case, it does, in any event, alert us to the fact that the democratic processes themselves may help to protect broadcasting against political pressures.

Yet another source of resistance to political pressure is the fact that chairmen of boards, directors-general and other senior broadcasting personalities are frequently people with well-established careers. This means that they have to consider their reputations and cannot readily turn into government lap-dogs. These people frequently also have prestigious positions to which to return should their terms not be renewed. Thus, chairman Kramer had a position as a Professor of English at one of Australia's top universities waiting for her and director-general Lapid returned to a position as a journalist and editor at one of Israel's major newspapers upon the termination of his appointment.

This counter-weapon to political pressures has some limitations built into it: not all chairmen and directors-general are in the same happy state of having prominent positions on which to fall back. Moreover, even in the most favourable cases, the posts to which these persons can return, are not as much in the public limelight and do not carry as much power as the ones they may be called upon to vacate. Nonetheless, those top-position-holders who have prominent posts to which to return, are certainly better placed to resist political pressures than those who do not.

Some senior broadcasting people had gained the ability to resist political pressure through their personal stature. In West Germany, at least one senior broadcasting personality seemed to have had a unique basis for this stature. As recounted by an admirer:

> When someone has been thrown into prison by the Nazis and survived all that, and then comes a little party-politician and threatens him, then he will say: 'get lost' . . . politicians noted after a short while that for people like that they were totally uninteresting.

Another senior broadcasting personality, Bausch, seemed to have gained such special stature simply by the fact that he has been a very successful intendant for a great length of time. Similarly, ZDF intendant Stolte seemed to have gained such stature, and a measure of political independence, by his adeptness in political manoeuvring and in satisfying all political sides in the past. For this reason he had amassed widespread support and it would now be difficult for politicians to dislodge him. In the words of one of his subordinates: 'They will not get him out in a hundred years.'

CONCLUSION

This and the previous chapter have reviewed various sources and devices that aid broadcasters in resisting political pressures. All of these are beset by certain limitations and problems. Public support for broadcasting is volatile, in some countries has recently decreased, and is not always effective. The intervention of staff associations and unions may (though not necessarily) introduce a political bias of its own into the broadcasting system. The ethos of broadcasting credibility as a shield against political pressure faces the problem that credibility itself is rather fragile. It can be damaged by even one instance of succumbing to political pressure – whereupon its shielding effect is also impaired. With respect to the ethos of objectivity as defence against political pressure the problem is that – like beauty – objectivity is at least partly in the eyes of the beholder: what seems objective to some broadcasters may well seem biased to other broadcasters – or to politicians. 'The facts speak for themselves' – but broadcasters select the facts to which they wish the public to listen. With regard to resistance by default the problem is that liberty has to be bought at the price of anarchy. The balance between political parties increases tolerance to balance in broadcasting – but only as long as this balance is within the brackets of the existing party system.

None of the aids to countering political pressures are thus all-pervasive or foolproof – any more than are the political pressures themselves. But neither are they innocuous. And what actually happens on the ground is the result of pressures, resistance and counter-pressures all being pitted against each other, and the emerging conflict and/or balance at any given time. This is the topic of the next chapter.

13 Friction and Conflict: Some Case-Studies

This book's main thesis is that ambiguities of rules and norms have made it possible for politicians to promote their interests by applying pressures on broadcasting, that these ambiguities have also enabled some broadcasters to promote their interests by resisting pressures, and that this has resulted in friction and conflict. Ambiguities, pressures and resistance, have been documented before, but friction and conflict have only been alluded to intermittently. In this chapter four cases of conflict are described and analysed.

THE CASE OF THE VANISHING CHRISTMAS TREE (BRITAIN)

On 18 August 1985 *The Observer* (p. 1) informed its readers that the security service MI5 'secretly controls' the hiring of BBC staff:

> Senior executives in the corporation have revealed to us a series of cases in which the careers of journalists, directors and broadcasters have been affected by MI5 blacklisting ... The most disturbing aspect of the vetting system, which can make or mar the careers of BBC ... staff, is that often the blacklisting is quite misguided or based on simple errors of fact ...

The Observer then went on to explain that candidates for appointment or promotion considered as subversives had their files stamped with a Christmas tree. This meant that a second file, with security details, was being held. If such a candidate was short-listed, the file was given to the appropriate head of department for perusal. Neither staff nor candidates had access to their files and hence did not know that anything was being held against them and could not appeal. Finally, the newspaper detailed the case histories of eight people who initially had been denied appointment or promotion in the BBC on the basis of this vetting; it claimed that many others had been affected and showed that in several cases blacklisting was based on an error.

Union representatives and BBC staff had not been entirely ignorant of the vetting system; the former had alerted me to it and the latter had confirmed its existence (see Chapter 9). But before it was publicised in *The Observer* the phenomenon had passed largely unnoticed. Following the publication, a brief but intense public storm broke loose. The vetting system was attacked in parliament. David Steel, leader of the Liberal party, said that the BBC was under the control of the Home Office. Foulkes, Labour front-bencher, said that the affair showed the 'illusion' of BBC independence (*Guardian*, 13 August 1985, p. 1).

Thus senior BBC representatives who had been staunchly defending the BBC from government interference over the *Real Lives* programme, found themselves having to explain how they had allowed government interference in this respect. Some ex-BBC governors said the disclosure had caught them by surprise. Some senior BBC executives and former executives conceded embarrassment and one of them claimed that they had not realised the extent of MI5 activities, but BBC management admitted that vetting had been going on since 1937, although the director-general, Alisdair Milne dismissed the matter as 'greatly over-dramatised' (*The Times*, 19 August, p. 1).

BBC management claimed that only a few people on sensitive positions were being vetted (*Guardian*, 24 August, p. 1). This claim by management was contrary to the information I had been given by union representatives and by other respondents. It was also contrary to the revelation in *The Observer* which told of people in less than sensitive positions who had been blacklisted.

A further revelation in *The Observer* (25 August 1985, p. 1) was that MI5 regularly provided senior BBC people with 'background briefs' on industrial disputes and the alleged involvement of 'subversives' in trade-union activity. Senior BBC executives admitted that the briefs could have coloured some stories although they insisted that the system had now been scrapped.

The NUJ warned the BBC that if the vetting of its members

was not terminated within seven weeks there would be a 'head-on collision' which 'would be as fundamental a battle as this union has ever undertaken' (*Sunday Times*, 25 August 1985, p. 1).

The vetting system was also attacked at the tenth Edinburgh International Television Festival. As Cox (1985) described it: 'The *Observer* scoop exploded into the event, adding the combustible ingredient "MI5" to the already potent mix of "Peacock" and *Real Lives*. By the end of the festival it was hard to believe the BBC could recover from the battering it had received during the previous four days.'

Towards the end of October it was reported in the press that BBC management had backed down and announced that MI5 vetting of staff in domestic services would be reduced to employees occupying key positions in case of a national emergency, although vetting of some external services staff would continue. The elusive Christmas tree would thus vanish from at least a major part of BBC personnel files, but staff would still be refused access to their files. The BBC unions announced immediately that they deemed this offer unacceptable. Later on staff were also promised access to their files.

Was vetting of BBC staff justifiable for reasons of security? On this, respondents' views were divided. One said: 'I mean, it's a perfectly proper precaution . . . Sometimes it is necessary for [people] to know things . . . particularly in the intelligence field. Also [some] people . . . become privy to financial information which then could be abused.' Others expressed different views:

> It would not be a matter of people getting hold of secret information and passing it on the Soviet Union and Albania. It would be a matter of the BBC worrying that these people's ideologies would influence their programmes and . . . that they would get into influential positions and bring people like themselves into the organisation.
>
> I think this is unjustified. Because being on BBC staff cannot involve a security risk. After all there are no security installations here and as far as programmes are concerned they go on the air so they are out in public.

In a similar vein, *The Times* editorial (20 August 1985, p. 13) argued that the point of guarding secret information would have only very limited application for the BBC. Vetting must therefore serve another purpose: to preserve the BBC from penetration by extremists. But *The Times* continued:

> journalists . . . who are committed to values that contradict those of the organisation . . . betray themselves not in their affiliations but in what they produce . . . If distortion or subversion is not . . . offered for public consumption, then where's the harm? It no more needs MI5 to spot it than it needs the Spanish Inquisition.

According to the *Guardian* (20 August 1985, p. 20) vetting was the result of the Home Secretary's self-contradictory position. He was responsible for the BBC, and constitutionally, the protective guardian of its independence, but he was also responsible for the security services whose intrusion into the BBC jeopardised the very independence he was supposed to protect. A few days later, *The Observer* (25 August 1985, p. 8) again raised its voice against vetting: '"security" . . . is there to detect foreign spies, not to exclude journalists from BBC jobs because they may (or may not as it turns out) hold views . . . that fall outside a narrowly defined official orthodoxy.'

Interpretation

This case shows how political pressures (translated into internal pressures) were applied to BBC staff and candidates. These pressures were at times based on error and thus misfired (indeed jesters referred to MI5 as an acronym for *M*ission *I*mpossible). But they did create an intrusion of criteria with political overtones into appointment and promotion procedures. These pressures also took the form of a generally close (one would be tempted to say incestuously close) relationship between the BBC and the security service. This was expressed also in the security service passing secret information on 'subversives' to the BBC, and in the fact that the minister in charge of safeguarding BBC independence was also in charge of the secret service.

The incident also demonstrated the ambiguity of rules and norms as to the propriety of vetting and its justifiability on security grounds. This ambiguity was well exemplified by the management's reaction to the disclosure. It first attempted to play down the matter but eventually announced that vetting for staff on domestic services would cease. This raises a question: if vetting was essential on security grounds, why did management buckle down under pressure and abolish it? If, on the other hand, vetting was not essential for security reasons why had it been part of the BBC system for so many years?

The same ambiguity of rules and norms also explains why some of those involved defended vetting while others expressed embarrassment at the disclosure or condemned the process. All this created a noisy controversy which was instrumental in counteracting the pressures and led to a partial abolition of vetting. But the controversy also put BBC management in the embarrassing position of having to back down from the practice under the glare of publicity.

All this coming on top of the *Real Lives* mishap, put an additional question-mark on the hitherto-renowned BBC independence, exacerbating and highlighting its current crisis, and it did nothing to enhance the BBC stature in the eyes of the public. On this, Hetherington, former Controller of BBC Scotland and a media research professor at the University of Stirling, had the following comment to offer:

> At present, unhappily, the BBC is going through both a crisis of confidence and an internal constitutional crisis. Neither the governors nor the top management have come well out of recent events . . . Because of its superb contribution to British broadcasting and British life in the past, the Corporation deserves public support and a secure future. But it will have to convince itself and the rest of us that it still knows how to conduct its own affairs (Hetherington, 1985, p. 13).

THE CASE OF THE MYSTERIOUS TELEPHONE CALL (AUSTRALIA)

This case unfolded and hit the headlines of the Australian media in April–May 1983, shortly after a Labor government had come to office. The state of New South Wales also had a Labor government headed by the premier, Neville Wran, who became the central mystery figure of the present case.

On 30 April 1983 an ABC current-affairs programme, *Four Corners*, examined the administration of Rugby League in New South Wales and, in particular, the hearing in 1977 of fraud charges against the secretary manager of a league's club. In the programme the allegation was made that the magistrate hearing the case had dismissed the charges upon instructions from the chief stipendary magistrate following a telephone call which – the chief stipendary magistrate claimed – came from premier Wran.

Premier Wran subsequently denied the report, and accused the ABC of 'trial by media'. The NSW leader of the opposition called for a judicial inquiry as the allegations were of conspiracy to pervert the course of justice and thus of a very serious nature. Premier Wran stated, however, that he did not intend to let the ABC make false allegations and then expect an inquiry to establish the facts.

In a subsequent interview on the ABC the then chairman Professor Kramer, said she did not believe the ABC chairman should act as a censor, that she had never rejected any story referred to her, and when consulted, had had no doubts about putting this one on. She also stated that the ABC acted 'without fear or favour'. On this a respondent commented:

> the managing director should have made that decision and . . . didn't . . . He referred it to Kramer and Kramer quite rightly said that isn't for me, so she acted correctly . . . you know politically, but organisationally she should have given the managing director a kick-in-the-bum and said 'it's your decision, buster'.

For his part, the leader of the government in the Australian Senate, Senator Button, made the following remarks:

> The chairman of the ABC [stated] that the ABC acted in these matters 'without fear or favour'. This is an appropriate position for the chairman of a body such as the ABC to adopt. My only regret is that the chairman of the ABC did not, in my view, always adopt this attitude in the past (*Canberra Times*, 5 May 1983, p. 1).

The then deputy leader of the federal opposition, John Howard, declared that Senator Button's comments were 'extraordinary' and criticised him for failing to make any public explanation (*Canberra Times*, 6 May 1985, p. 1). Senator Button then revealed that he had cast doubt on the impartiality of the ABC because an ABC journalist had been unfairly reprimanded by a senior officer, for making an 'aside comment' in an interview with the then Liberal Prime Minister Fraser before the recent election (*Canberra Times*, 12 May 1983, p. 10). He subsequently revealed than an allegation detrimental to Prime Minister Hawke had also been part of the quarrel. Hawke later confirmed to parliament that he had made a strong protest to the ABC chairman over a radio programme which, he said, had impugned his integrity by suggesting that there existed in a safe somewhere some incriminating evidence that concerned him. He added that he was surprised that an allegation like this had been allowed to go unchallenged while there had been concern about a minor interjection by a staff-member (*Canberra Times*, 13 May 1983, p. 8).

As pressures for the appointment of a commission of inquiry mounted Premier Wran had to back down from his initial refusal to contemplate such a move; on 10 May 1983 a Royal Commission was established. Wran stepped aside as Premier for the duration of the investigation. Soon afterwards the Australian Broadcasting Commission was replaced by the Australian Broadcasting Corporation, headed by a board of directors, and chairman Kramer was replaced.

The Royal Commission of inquiry into the *Four Corners* allegations eventually exonerated Premier Wran – but recommended that the chief stipendary magistrate and the magistrate in the case be charged with perverting the course of justice (they were eventually tried and found guilty). The telephone call which started the whole furore had apparently been made, but there was no evidence that it had come from Premier Wran.

In the meantime Wran initiated defamatory action against the ABC. At a subsequent news conference he also accused an ABC journalist of being blatantly biased against him. This resulted in industrial action by ABC journalists. The journalist, for his part, brought defamation action against the Premier. An out-of-court settlement on the Premier's action was eventually reached; it included the broadcast of an apology to Mr Wran by the ABC.

Interpretation

This case gives an apt illustration of the various pressures which politicians in Australia apply in their attempts to influence the ABC. There were complaints, both privately and in public, thus adding publicity to displeasure as a source of pressure. Legal action against the ABC (a type of pressure that is prevalent particularly in Australia) was also taken. Although – like complaints – this is pressure after the fact, it may well be efficacious in preventing (or decreasing the chance) of similar occurrences in the future.

In addition, it is probable that staffing was also used as a sanction. By some accounts, even before the controversial item had appeared on *Four Corners*, the Hawke government had decided that most members of the commission would not be appointed to the new board of directors which was being established at the time (Walsh, 1983), but shortly before the membership of the new board was announced, Communications Minister Duffy publicly stated that he would be surprised if chairman Kramer was not a serious candidate for reappointment. Apparently, then, her candidature was seriously considered and rejected. It would be inconceivable that the *Four Corners* case had nothing to do with that rejection.

The case also illustrates some of the sources for the ABC's ability to withstand political pressures. These include staff industrial action, court action by an ABC journalist against a politician, and last but not least, the independent career and position of the ABC chairman, the fact that she could return to being 'only' a full professor at one of Australia's major universities and that she was thus not greatly dependent on the ABC chairmanship (and thus on the government) for her status and livelihood.

Finally, the case illustrated how political pressures which by the existing (ambiguous) legislation, convention and norms are not entirely legitimate, and the resistance to such pressures, lead to confrontation. Such confrontations, while not actually detrimental to either the ABC or the government, nonetheless caused embarrassment all around. In Semmler's words: 'The *Four-Corners*–Wran imbroglio, leading ... to the Senator Button–Kramer confrontation, was but another example of the problems always besetting the ABC *vis-à-vis* governments and of the floundering once everyone lands in the inevitable mess' (Semmler, 1983, p. 32).

THE CASE OF THE MISSING DIRECTOR (ISRAEL)

This case unfolded in Israel chiefly in 1985, under a broadly-based coalition government in which Labour was now the senior partner, but the Likud was a formidable partner as well. Much that happened in connection with this case is explicable through this peculiar political constellation.

In December 1984, the term of the director of television was about to run out, and the position was advertised. The advertisement stipulated that candidates must have a minimum of nine years' broadcasting experience and that external candidates must be holders of an academic degree. Several candidates applied but only three were considered to have realistic chances of being selected:

- Hayim Yavin, a long-time senior television journalist and editor – considered to have some left-wing sympathies but not closely identified with any political party.
- Dan Shilon, also a long-time senior television journalist and editor (who had previously left the authority to found his own, private, television productions enterprise) – closely identified with the Labour Party.
- Yossi Zemach, a long-time television programme director and producer – not closely identified with any political party, but considered to be sympathetic to the Likud.

The Likud members of the board supported Zemach but were willing to settle for Yavin. They furiously opposed Shilon and were willing to go to any lengths to prevent his appointment. The Labour members of the board supported Shilon, and opposed Zemach. Director-general Porat, also a Likud person, supported both Yavin and Shilon, but opposed Zemach, whom he considered insufficiently qualified.

As Likud politicians were therefore unable to achieve the appointment of their own candidate they now invested their main efforts in working against the appointment of Shilon, whom they considered as the most objectionable of the candidates. Thus it came to pass that Yavin, previously considered a left-winger, suddenly enjoyed the support of senior Likud politicians who were now lobbying for him all around, while looking for ways and means to torpedo Shilon's appointment.

The selection committee which consisted of the board, the director-general and two representatives of the journalists' association was to make the appointment on 21 January 1985. On that same day Israel's Attorney-General announced that Shilon's candidacy was to be disallowed, as he did not meet the advertisement's requirements of possessing an academic degree. A storm broke out as Labour activists accused Likud activists of having engineered Shilon's downfall, by having the authority's chairman consult the Attorney-General.

When the committee met, the Likud members of the board announced that it was business as usual. They proposed to go through with the selection process - with Shilon now no longer a candidate. The Labour members of the board disagreed, proposing instead to alter the terms of the advertisement retrospectively so that Shilon could be considered as well. The Likud people flatly rejected this proposal. A heated controversy ensued and shouts emanated from the meeting room. After several hours of futile altercations the Labour members of the board stalked out of the meeting, followed by the director-general. Thereupon Yavin announced that he was no longer a candidate. For the time being the appointment was thus aborted.

A day later, the television journalists and producers called a meeting in which they denounced the politicisation of the appointment and demanded that it be made solely on the basis of professional criteria. This demand was ignored as accusations and counter-accusations amongst politicians abounded, and frenzied activity began in an attempt to settle on new selection procedures. Labour demanded that a new advertisement be published deleting the requirement of an academic degree. The Likud demanded that the position be readvertised on the old terms. Thus the confrontation was escalating and the appointment continued to be stalemated.

As the term of the previous director of television in the meantime expired an acting director was appointed as an interim measure. In September, when his term expired, the director-general announced that he would temporarily fill the void himself, but he was rebuffed by the journalists' council which announced that it would not co-operate with anyone but a properly-appointed director.

Meanwhile, Israeli television was without a director – the reason as Paz-Melamed (1985a) aptly put it, was the difficulty of locating someone with the proper qualifications; the main qualification being that of having the support of both Likud and Labour. For in the meantime Labour policians continued to support Shilon and Likud politicians supported Yavin. But when it became clear that Shilon did not have the support of senior government ministers (who by now had become directly involved in the appointmet) Labour decided to support Yavin. Precisely at this time, however, the Likud decided to oppose Yavin and announced that it now, once again, supported Zemach.

As the stalemate continued some Likud politicians announced that they were willing to compromise by accepting Yavin as director of television, provided that their own candidate, Zemach, be made deputy director and that the main television news programme, *Mabat*, with which the Likud had been unhappy, be run on a principle of rotating editorship. Thereupon *Ma'ariv* (23 October 1985, p. 10) commented (tongue in cheek) that this was a brilliant proposal which, however, could be improved upon even further by having the news edited by the faithfuls of a different minister each evening. Only thus could all politicians rest assured that their interests were properly safeguarded on television.

However, just as the agreement on the Likud proposal was about to be reached, the employees' councils announced that they opposed it, on the ground that it involved the creation of a new position of 'deputy director' and that this could not be done without prior consultation with themselves. Thereupon the Likud politicians reverted to their previous position, announced that they stuck to Zemach as their candidate, and the matter was further stalemated.

In November it was reported that the director-general, Porat, candidate Yavin and the head of the journalists' council, Halabi, were all visiting the USA. This led jesters to comment that after Israel's politicians had failed to effect an appointment, the matter was now to be laid before Congress or even a higher American authority (*Ha'aretz*, 19 November 1985, p. 10).

Back in Israel, the stalemate, coming on top of broadcasting's financial crisis led pundits to predict televisions' imminent collapse. But in the event, this did not happen. In December 1985, as if to mark the stalemate's anniversy, a non-political director of television – Yair Aloni – was quietly appointed by the director-general with the consent of the board. He soon resigned and in April 1986 Yavin was appointed to the post. But this is no longer part of the present case study.

Interpretation

In this case the political pressures on broadcasting took the form of political intervention in a senior broadcasting appointment. There were some attempts on the part of the employees' councils to resist political pressures, but they were largely ineffective. Voices from the press protesting or ridiculing these pressures were intermittently heard – but not heeded.

Thus, the year-long deadlock did not come about through resistance to political pressures. Rather, it was the result of countervailing pressures, whereby the major political parties continually blocked each other's moves. However, in a way, this mutual blocking had a mitigating effect on politicisation. It made it impossible for any one political party to dominate the appointment process and eventually it led (if only through the exhaustion of all concerned) to a compromise appointment.

Until this point of exhaustion was reached, political pressures and counterpressures had led to the most embittered struggle that had ever beset broadcasting in Israel. This row, together with the financial problems it was facing, led Israel television to the brink of collapse.

Eventually this did not occur. After all, (as respondents explained) the public was ever hungry for news and politicians were ever eager to produce it – as far as possible in front of the cameras. For several months, however, the best that could be said was that television was still there. For Israeli television (as for the famous aristocrat who managed to dodge the guillotine during the French Revolution) merely surviving was thus a major achievement.

THE CASE OF THE BROADCASTER WHO WAS PUT ON ICE (WEST GERMANY)

In October 1983 something rather unusual on the German broadcasting scene happened: the intendant's office at SWF in Baden Baden notified Franz Alt, the head of the editorial board of the current-affairs programme, *Report*, that he would be temporarily relieved from moderating the programme. SWF intendant, Willibald Hilf, gave as the reason for his decision Alt's strong engagement in favour of the peace movement and against NATO, and the fact that this engagement had become clearly noticeable in his work. In the words of a respondent, this act 'raised a lot of dust' in West Germany.

The conflict surrounding Alt's displacement took place on several levels. First, it occurred on the normative level. For as Mathes (1985) explains, the controversy was over the rules that were to govern broadcasting journalism. Intendant Hilf justified his action on the basis of the moderator's political bent which made it impossible to meet the requirement of offering balanced programmes on SWF. Alt justified his conduct by the principle of freedom of speech and emphasised the illegitimacy of political interference in broadcasts.

The conflict was also political: Alt's suspension had been preceded by an extended controversy, for, according to the *Proporz* principle, his programme had been 'counted' as conservative and Alt himself (despite his commitment to the peace movement) had been counted as a CDU man. Hence Alt's suspension was instigated by CDU politicians. Since intendant Hilf was himself a CDU man who had climbed to the position of SWF intendant from the position of head of Chancellor Kohl's bureau in Mainz (Riese, 1984, p. 122) it is not surprising that SPD sympathisers opposed the suspension.

A further level on which the conflict was waged was that of the media, where it gained extensive coverage and was widely disputed. Mathes (1985) who conducted a content analysis of media coverage of the case, found that in the five weeks in which the issue was on the public agenda, seven major publications had brought no fewer than 677 statements relating to it. Of these, 511 contained value judgements – 76 per cent in support of Alt and 24 per cent in favour of Hilf. The press was thus generally more sympathetic to the displaced moderator than to the displacing intendant.

Finally the conflict took place on the legal level. On 19 October 1983, Alt brought the matter before the labour court, arguing that his suspension from the programme countervened his employment contract. The Solomonic verdict brought down by the court was that on 1 November Alt would be reinstated as moderator of the programme but that, until the end of the year, topics connected with peace would be dealt with by other colleagues.

Even though Alt was kept 'on ice' for re-use by the same programme later on, his case was frequently mentioned by respondents as an – admittedly rare – example of displacement for political reasons. However, respondents diverged in their views: not surprisingly, right-wing media experts gave the following account of the case:

> Franz Alt . . . was active politically within broadcasting . . . and so there was a role conflict there: between the role of a journalist who must be independent and the role of a politically active man. There was danger there that he would no longer be able to see things objectively.
>
> Franz Alt . . . is not entitled to abuse his role as journalist in order to propagate his political views . . . so Hilf excluded him from moderating the programme for a certain timespan. I find it was his damned duty to do so . . .

At the same time respondents sympathetic to the left saw this case as specially important because, unlike other cases where political motives could be suspected but not proved, in this case the political grounds for the displacement had been freely admitted. Also of interest were the comments of other respondents that the question of whether Alt should lose his post had never been open for discussion: 'He has a contract that cannot be transgressed. They can't get rid of him . . . He keeps his post.'

Interpretation

While the case of a broadcaster being 'put on ice' was an unusual occurrence in West Germany in recent years, it nevertheless highlighted some features that are rather typical of German broadcasting. First, the case highlighted the importance of the *Proporz* principle, in broadcasting. What irked right-wing politicians was not so much the fact that left-wing views had been expressed on a programme for, after all, political magazines with leftist affinities could be found in many broadcasting stations where they coexisted peacefully with right-wing-oriented programmes (as well as with the consciences of the respective intendants and politicians). Rather, what irritated CDU politicians in this case was the fact that a programme which 'belonged' to their side, had defected to the other side, and that the *Proporz* principle had thereby been transgressed.

It is also clear that in the conflict surrounding the Alt case, ambiguities in norms played an important part. Because in the allocation of programmes the *Proporz* principle ruled *de facto* but not *de jure* it was not clear, and indeed was widely disputed, whether Alt's conduct had or had not been ethical and whether Hilf's reaction had or had not been within the bounds of propriety.

The case is also instructive because in the final analysis it is a testimony not only to the political pressures pervading West German broadcasting, but also to the limits of such pressures, and to the resources German broadcasters have in resisting them. Alt's being 'put on ice', was temporary. Even so, it instantly became the focus of widespread (mostly negative) attention in the press. Perhaps partly for that reason, but also because of German broadcasters' tenure in office, the possibility of Alt being permanently frozen out never became a real possibility.

CONCLUSION

The cases presented in this chapter have illustrated a variety of political pressures brought to bear on broadcasting by actors on the political scene, sometimes transmitted inwards and downwards by the governing authorities or the management of the broadcasting corporations themselves. Because of the ambiguity of broadcasting norms it was not clear whether or not such pressures were legitimate within the respective normative frameworks of the countries concerned. Indeed, the chapter showed that these pressures were usually controversial, calling forth support, justification, but also, and more frequently, condemnation and protest. The latter usually came from rival politicians, from broadcasting staff, union representatives and some of the press. These actors may well have had their own political axes to grind. Nonetheless they were instrumental (albeit to various degrees) in helping broadcasting to resist political pressures.

Most importantly, the chapter demonstrated how each case of pressure and resistance (or counter-pressure) resulted in a public political row, and in some cases (especially in Britain and West Germany) the dispute and the publicity surrounding it, were themselves instrumental in furthering the resistance to political pressures.

Some observers have argued that such struggles may be seen as a normal and healthy part of broadcasting and democracy. This chapter has shown that once political pressures had been applied, counter-pressures, controversy, publicity and 'bringing the thing out into the open' all played a role in curbing such pressures. Inasmuch as the power of incumbent politicians was thereby countervailed by rival politicians, broadcasters, other élites and public opinion, this may in fact be considered as 'healthy' for democracy. Inasmuch as this prevented government politicians from using broadcasting as an instrument of manipulation, it may also be considered as 'healthy' for broadcasting. The chapter also documented, however, that in Britain and in Israel, and to a lesser degree in Australia, all this has exacted a heavy price in terms of an impairment in the functioning of the broadcasting corporation, a weakening of self-confidence, a lowering of morale, and a diminution of its stature in the eyes of the public.

Conclusion

The main conclusion reached on the basis of this study is that by and large the general theses presented at the outset have found empirical support in all the countries studied, but the hypothesis that was meant to differentiate among the countries is supported only in part. In line with the general theses, there is, in all four countries, legal and normative ambiguity with regard to the independence and impartiality of broadcasting; in all four countries, considerable political pressures bear down from politicians on broadcasting corporations and from those corporation's top echelons on their staff; in all four countries this calls forth resistance and, at least intermittent, tension and conflict.

In line with the hypothesis presented at the beginning Israel and West Germany – which have party-politicised bureaucracies – also have party-politicised broadcasting systems, while Britain and Australia do not. *But, contrary to the hypothesis, the British and Australian Broadcasting Corporations and their staff have been facing political pressures that were no less and sometimes more severe than those faced by their Israeli and West German counterparts, and they have been no less and sometimes more vulnerable to such pressures.*

Pressures from politicians on broadcasting corporations (external pressures) have taken the form of attempts at direct interference in policies and programmes, financial pressures through the control of funding and through the threat of privatisation, and pressures through politically congenial appointments at the broadcasting corporations' most senior levels. While each of these types of pressure is formidable in its own right, their power really lies in their combination.

This is most clearly evident with regard to the combination of pressures through funding and through impending privatisation. Some people argue that the fate of broadcasting will be determined not by political pressures but by the upcoming technological revolution. In fact, however, technological developments, privatisation and political pressures are all inextricable interlinked. With the advent of more private competition (especially through cable and satellite broadcasting) the audience of national public broadcasting may be expected to shrink. This in itself must necessarily detract from the importance of national broadcasting. In addition, the public may be expected to be more reluctant to pay for public broadcasting (either through the licence fee or through taxes) and the government may become more reluctant to impose such payments. Thus the budget for public broadcasting may well decrease in real terms and this may increase the likelihood of commercial advertising or a pay-as-you-go- system being imposed on public broadcasting (where this has not been done already). Public broadcasters may thus have to face a manifold competition with private ones: over the audience (to convince the government to maintain public funding) and over subscriptions and/or the advertising market.

Importantly, the combination of these pressures puts broadcasting on the spot *now*, irrespective of whether this scenario is ever fully realised. The mere prospect, or implied threat that it may be, is already having a major effect on public broadcasting. It is already forcing public broadcasting to make its programmes more palatable to the mass audience. It is also forcing it to be 'on best behaviour' so as not to antagonise the government which has it in its power to tighten the combined loop of private competition and the budget. Thereby current affairs programmes, which in most countries (with the exception of Israel) are not highly attractive to the mass audience and at the same time tend to irk the government, are usually the main sufferers. They tend to be 'softened', deleted, shortened or as an observer put it 'shunted out to the margins'. So it is the hard-hitting current affairs programmes which are on the way to be most hardly-hit. But it is precisely these programmes which form national broadcasting's most important contribution to democracy.

Some say: competition enlivens the business and there is no harm in public broadcasters having some of their fat trimmed off. But here, as elsewhere, Miles's Laws applies 'where one stands depends on where one sits'. 'Trimming off fat' takes place when programmes one does not like are deleted, when organisations other than one's own are cut down and when people other than oneself become superfluous. As soon as oneself is adversely affected, this is no longer the trimming-off of fat but a stab into the living flesh. Thus, looking at the matter from the perspective of national public broadcasters themselves, the combined threat of impending budget-cuts and privatisation (even if never actually put into effect) are already having adverse effects on their operations.

Pressures by politicians on broadcasting corporations (external pressures) are reflected in pressures *on behalf of politicians* by broadcasting corporations on their staff (internal pressures). These take the form of 'guidance' from above and from peers, frequently translated into self-guidance ('osmosis', 'scissors in the head' or 'pre-emptive buckles'). They also take the form of politically-congenial appointments and promotions at the less senior levels of broadcasting organisations and (when this proves insufficient) of politically-motivated demotions, displacements and dismissals. While broadcasting corporations as entities are the most vulnerable to external pressures, members of staff as individuals are the more vulnerable to internal pressures, particularly to the threat of dismissal because (as one respondent somewhat bluntly put it) 'they like to eat'.

In the exertion of pressures politicians (and those who apply pressure on their behalf) rely on the power of office, on the control of resources and on the control of posts. In the resistance to such pressures broadcasters rely on (rather volatile) public opinion, on their own associations (which sometimes have political axes of their own to grind), on norms of impartiality and objectivity (which, however, are not always clear-cut), on their own personal stature (wherever possible), on blocked authority channels and on pressures from various sources counteracting each other.

The results of all this (in combination with other clashes of interest) are frequently tension, friction and conflict. This is the case for the BBC which, as the *Sunday Times* (29 December 1985, p. 7) put it, has recently been the subject of an 'unseemly row'. It is also the case for the ABC which, according to respondents, is surrounded by a frequently recurring 'hullaballoo' and which according to Simper (1983) 'is a seething mass ... of ego, rumour, argument and conflict'. And it most certainly goes for the Israel Broadcasting Authority which, according to a widely reported observation by director-general Porat 'resembles Lebanon: everybody shoots at everybody else'. Only the West German broadcasting system, which has been the subject of extensive conflicts in the 1970s, seems to have experienced few major conflicts in recent years. Perhaps this is because political pressures (but also their limits) have been institutionalised there to a greater extent than elsewhere and because, more than elsewhere, potential controversy is handled through litigation.

The result of all this is also that national broadcasting corporations have effectively been put under siege. For instance, in Britain a (conservative) observer has asserted that having defeated Argentina over the Falklands and the miners at home, Prime Minister Thatcher was now set to inflict a similar defeat of the BBC. And the *Economist* (5 July, 1986, p. 13) wrote that in future the BBC might no longer be necessary. About the ABC some observers have claimed that it was virtually in danger of extinction and others have likened it to the *Titanic* (Crisp, 1985, p. 24). With regard to the Israel Broadcasting Authority some observers have expressed the view that part of the political establishment was intent on choking it into temporary closure if not into compliance. With regard to the West German broadcasting system, observers have noted that it is subject to a 'rapidly growing political paralysis' (*Der Spiegel*, 13 February 1984, p. 41), and about national broadcasting in general, a respondent has observed that it is becoming an 'anachronism'.

Even if these claims are greatly exaggerated, this study has shown that the combined external, internal and technological pressures bearing down on public, national broadcasting corporations have been leading to a vicious circle: to an impairment of their self-confidence, a diminution of their assertiveness and a shrinking of their stature in the eyes of the public, which in turn has led to a further lowering of their self-confidence. From the viewpoint of democracy there can be no doubt that through the combination of these pressures the role of public broadcasting as observers and critics of the political establishment is being visibly eroded.

A comparison of the four broadcasting systems under study highlights the special stature of the BBC; in one way or another the other broadcasting systems have set out to emulate it, but only in Australia which (with some variations) follows the British political tradition – including that of a non-partisan bureaucracy – has the BBC tradition of non-partisanship caught roots. In both Israel and West Germany the broadcasting system was set up under British rule and influence, but the British tradition could not be transplanted into these countries (even though in West Germany there was an attempt to do so) because the existing political patterns (including those of the bureaucracy) differed so substantially from the British ones.

In both countries the leaders at the time – Ben Gurion in Israel and Adenauer in West Germany – held the belief that broadcasting ought to be under state control. In both countries the patterns actually adopted partly followed but partly deviated from this idea. As broadcasting was put under the control of political parties, this gave the ruling party – as proxy for the state – a large measure of control over broadcasting. But it gave representation to other parties and groups as well.

Contrary to expectation, the fact that the British and Australian broadcasting corporations are not party-politicised and the Israeli and West German broadcasting authorities are, does not mean that the former are subject to less severe political pressures than the latter. This study has shown that the BBC and the ABC are subject to pressures through direct intervention and funding, and the BBC is subject to pressures through privatisation, no less than the Israeli and West German broadcasting systems. In addition the BBC was seen to be subject to subtle pressures through 'incestuously' close relations with the establishment: top BBC personnel have close, informal relations with politicians, two chairmen of the board have been relatives of government ministers; the BBC is privy to inside information from government services; the very minister who is in charge of safeguarding BBC independence is also in charge of the service which for many years has been encroaching on that independence.

Indeed, at this particular point in time, the combination of these pressures bears down with particular vehemence on the BBC, and, despite its long-standing reputation for independence, the BBC has proved strangely vulnerable to such pressures. This vulnerability has found expression not in the introduction of pro-government bias into BBC programmes but in the decline of BBC assertiveness, in growing timidity. As far back as 1977, the Annan Report noted that the BBC's weakest parts were its current affairs and (to a lesser extent) its news programmes and that those programmes were characterised by excessive caution. The report went on to say: 'By and large we subscribe to the generally held view that ITV has the edge over the BBC news and that ITV current affairs is more adventurous and interesting' (Annan 1977, p. 92). And according to practically all respondents this trend has been exacerbated even further in recent years.

Political pressures at the behest of politicians by means of appointments and promotions were much more blatant in Israel and West Germany than they were in Britain and Australia. In both Israel and West Germany appointments and promotions by political criteria at top and middle levels were quite strightforward, although in West Germany they were institutionalised to an even greater extent than in Israel via the *Proporz* principle. Such an overt intrusion of party-political criteria into selection processes would have been inconceivable in Britain and in Australia, but this is not to say that political criteria in appointments and promotions were entirely absent there.

In both Britain and Australia senior positions were likely to be occupied by establishment-type people, with a certain 'intellectual baggage' most likely of a conservative nature. And in Australia people tended to 'select themselves out' into politically congenial programmes, with the (politically important) current-affairs programmes – the most likely to attract leftists. In Britain and Australia, as in the other countries concerned, all people outside a certain broad, but well-defined, political spectrum – that is, political extremists – were weeded out from responsible key positions and sometimes from broadcasting altogether. In the British as in the Israeli Broadcasting Corporations some security-vetting was going on, but in Israel only people suspected of tangible ties with the enemy, and in Britain larger groups of political extremists, have been affected. So security-vetting has had clearer political implications there.

Moreover, because in Israel and West Germany politicisation in appointments and promotions has been more overt, the system has enabled all political parties to monitor the process as well as to secure a chunk of the cake for themselves. In Britain and Australia, on the other hand, because the process is subtle and covert, it does not provide for party or public scrutiny as the chance revelation of vetting in the BBC has so clearly demonstrated.

This study has produced no evidence to show that in any of the countries studied people permanently employed in broadcasting have been dismissed for their political views. But in Britain there were some cases in which people were ousted for letting their political views show on programmes, in Israel there were cases where people have been demoted from key positions for political reasons, and in all countries there have been cases where people have been displaced, side-tracked or shifted around for political or borderline-political or professional reasons.

Non-permanent appointees – freelances and people on contract were obviously the more vulnerable to political pressures through possible dismissal. The possibility that this would lead people to self-censorship was mentioned in various countries, but there were differences among the countries in these respects. In Israel and West Germany there was no trend to put more people on contract (although in Israel even permanent staff may now face retrenchment); in West Germany there was also a trend whereby more and more non-permanent people had gained permanent employment. By contrast, in Britain and especially in Australia, a trend to put more and more people on contract was clearly evident. Since in Australia the people on contract now included senior management, the possibility of politicisation through the implied threat of dismissal has become especially pronounced there. Thus, the paradoxical and rather surprising situation emerged that it is precisely in Britain and Australia, where appointments are generally less politicised, and especially in Australia, that the potential for pressures through dismissal is the most pronounced and that broadcasters are the most vulnerable to this sort of pressure; and precisely in West Germany, where appointments are the most overtly politicised, people – once appointed – have the greatest personal immunity to such pressures.

Dye and Zeigler, in their book, *The Irony of Democracy* (1975), make the point that democracy which preserves the rights of the masses is itself preserved not by the masses but by the élites in their commitment to democratic rules. In this connection my reading has been that Israeli democracy is based to a lesser extent than several other Western democracies on the élites' meticulous adherence to democratic rules, and to a greater extent on the struggle between various élites and the balance of power thus created. This study has shown that this is certainly the case with regard to broadcasting. To the extent that Israeli broadcasters have been able to snatch any independence out of the jaws of the system, this has been much less the result of mutually-accepted guidelines for action, much more the result of mutually contervailing pressures. Such pressures have come from the two large, rival, governing parties, from various interest groups, and from different echelons within the broadcasting corporation itself: from various factions in the board, from management and from employees' associations – which are all at loggerheads with each other. All this has resulted in a mutually limiting perpetual conflict but also in a balance of forces.

In conclusion, there has clearly been some similarity between the British and the Australian broadcasting corporations on the one hand and between the Israeli and the West German broadcasting corporations on the other. Surprisingly, this has not been expressed in the latter corporations' greater vulnerability to political pressures, but rather the reverse: in their greater immunity in some respects. In West Germany the greater proportion of people with tenure in office, and in Israel the balance of multiple countervailing pressures – whatever negative implications they may otherwise have had for broadcasting – have proved to be rather effective sources of immunity to pressure.

By contrast the BBC and the ABC have been beset by greater vulnerability to political pressures than could have been expected. Although with regard to the BBC the *institution* has proved more vulnerable to pressure while in the ABC broadcasting personnel (including senior personnel) as *individuals* have become more vulnerable, vulnerability is evident in both; but vulnerability to pressure is not the same as totally succumbing to it, and so far both the BBC and the ABC have been able to sustain and perpetuate their tradition of non-partisanship.

This analysis includes no attempts to 'forecast' the future of national broadcasting on the assumption that the best time to predict what will happen is when it has already happened. As for development so far, this study has documented pervasive pressures on national broadcasting and vulnerability to such pressures, but also resistance. It has documented a state of siege that threatens to diminish public broadcasting's stature, its role and significance in democratic society, but it has also shown that national public broadcasting has not become as insignificant as its optimistic enemies and its pessimistic friends might have wished to believe.

References

Aharonson, S. (ed.) (1974) *The Broadcasting Authority and the Political System* (Jerusalem: Mif'al Hashihpul (Hebrew)).
Aharonson, S. (1983) 'Television: the Queen of Counter Reaction', *Ha'aretz*, 6 December (Hebrew).
Annan (Lord) (1977) *Report of the Committee on the Future of Broadcasting* (The Annan Report) Cmnd 6753.
ARD (1983, 1984) *ARD Jahrbuch* (an ARD publication).
Aron, R. (1968) *Progress and Disillusion* (London: Pall Mall Press).
Aron, R. (1978) *Politics and History* (translated and edited by M. Bernheim-Conant) (New York: Free Press).
Ashbolt, A. (1980) 'The Role of the ABC', in O'Dwyer, B. (ed.) *Broadcasting in Australia*, Proceedings of the National Conference at the Australian National University, Canberra, July, pp. 153–60.
Barnett, D. (1985) 'Mandarins Feel the Squeeze', *Bulletin*, 5 February, pp. 32–3.
Baum, I. (1985) 'In the Clutches of the Electronic Octopus'. *Ma'ariv*, 26 April pp. 4–5 (Hebrew).
Bausch, H. (1980) *Rundfunk in Deutschland* (München: Deutscher Taschenbuch Verlag, GMBH & Co.) vol. 4.
Bausch, H. (1983) 'Ein Neues Medium Wird 60 Jahre Alt', *ARD Jahrbuch* (an ARD publication).
BBC (1972) 'The Control of Broadcasting', Paper IV, 28 (a BBC publication).
BBC (1980) *News and Current Affairs Index* (a BBC publication).
BBC (1982) *Voice for the World*. External Services Publicity Unit (a BBC publication).
BBC (1985) *BBC Annual Report and Handbook 1985* (a BBC publication).
Berry, M. (1985) 'Why ABC Program Makers Seethe', *Bulletin*, 25 June, pp. 54–6.
Briggs, A. (1961, 1965 and 1970) *The History of Broadcasting in the United Kingdom* (Oxford: Oxford University Press) vols. 1, 2 and 3.
Briggs, A. (1979) *Governing the BBC* (London: BBC).
Broder, H. M. (ed.) (1976a) *Die Schere im Kopf* (Köln: Bundverlag).
Broder, H. M. (1976b) 'Intendant Gegen den Rest der Firma', in Broder (ed.) *Die Schere im Kopf*, pp. 94–111.
Brooks, R. (1985) 'Ready, Willing and . . . Cable: Britain', *Sunday Times*, 25 August, p. 47.
Burghart, H. (1978), 'Journalismus in Bedrängnis', in Geiger *et al.*, *Der Öffentlich-Rechtliche Rundfunk*, pp. 60–82.
Burns, T. (1977) *The BBC* (London: Macmillan).
Burton, M. G. and Higley, J. (1984) 'Elite Theory: the Basic Contentions', paper presented to the Annual American Sociological Association Conference, San Antonio, August.

Button, J. (1982), *The ABC* (Canberra: Office of the ALP spokesman on Communications, Parliament House).
CDU (1976), 'Ausgewogenheitspapier' in *Epd Kirche und Rundfunk* 42, 2.6 (a CDU publication).
Conrad, H. W. n.d. 'Radio and Television in the Federal Republic of Germany', *Internationes*.
Coombs, H. C. *et al.* (1977) *Report of the Royal Commission on Australian Government Administration* (Canberra: The Commonwealth Government Printer).
Cox, B. (1985) 'Broadcasting Discontent in Edinburgh', *Guardian*, 26 August, p. 6.
Crawford (Lord) (1926) *Report of the Broadcasting Committee* (the Crawford Report) Cmnd 2599.
Crisp, L. (1985) 'The ABC's Fight for the Future. *National Times*, July 19-25, pp. 24–5.
Curran, C. (1973), 'A Maturing Democracy'. Speech to the National Liberal Club, 14 March (a BBC publication).
Davis, G. (1984) 'Government Decision Making and the ABC: the 2JJ Case', *Politics*, 19 November, pp. 34–42.
Davis, G. (1985) 'The Political Independence of the Australian Broadcasting Corporation', Ph.D. thesis, the Australian National University, Canberra.
Deamer, A. (1981) 'Self Censorship', in Windschuttle, K. and E. (eds) *Fixing the News* Sydney: Cassell Australia) pp. 41–7.
Dix, A. T. (1981) *The ABC in Review* (the Dix Report) Canberra: Australian Government Publishing Service).
Dogan, M. (1975) 'The Political Power of the Western Mandarins: Introduction', in Dogan, M. (ed.) *The Mandarins of Western Europe* (New York: Wiley) pp. 3–24.
Donsbach, W. (1984) Öffentlich-Rechtlicher Rundfunk', *Medien Kritik*, 6/6, p. 5.
Dye, T. R. and Zeigler, L. H. (1975) *The Irony of Democracy*, (3rd edn) (North Scituate, Massachusetts: Duxbury Press).
Ellul, J. (1965) *The Technological Society* (translated by J. Wilkinson) (London: Cape).
Etzioni-Halevy, E. (1979) *Political Manipulation and Administrative Power* (London: Routledge & Kegan Paul).
Etzioni-Halevy, E. (1985) *Bureaucracy and Democracy: A Political Dilemma* (London: Routledge & Kegan Paul) revised edn.
Ezard, J. (1985) 'How the BBC Escaped from its Minders', *Guardian*, 22 August, p. 17.
Ferguson, T. (1982) 'Semmler', *New Journalist*, no. 38, pp. 8–9.
Francis, R. (1977) 'Broadcasting to a Community in Conflict', lecture at the Royal Institute of International Affairs, 22 February (a BBC publication).
Geiger, W. (1978) 'Sicherung der Informations Freiheit des Bürgers als Verfassungsproblem', in Geiger *et al.*, *Der Öffentlich-Rechtliche Rundfunk*, pp. 11–43.
Geiger, W., May, F. and Burghart, H. (1978) *Der Öffentlich-Rechtliche Rundfunk* (Zürich: Edition Interfrom AG).
Gotliffe, H. L. (1981) 'Israeli General Television' doctoral dissertation,

Wayne State University, Detroit, Michigan.
Grattan, M. (1984) 'ABC Leaves a Lot to be Desired: P.M.', *The Age*, 14 September, p. 6.
Green, F. J. (1976) *Australian Broadcasting* (The Green Report) (Canberra: Australian Government Printing Service).
Greene, H. (1973) 'Report on the Israel Broadcasting Authority' in Aharonson, S. (ed.) *Broadcasting and the Political System*, pp. 100–6 (Hebrew).
Greulich, H. (1976) 'Die Schere nicht nur im Kopf' in Broder (ed.) *Die Schere im Kopf* pp. 15–22.
Haagen, B-U (1985) 'Die Verpackungskünstler', *Neue Medien*, no. 3, 1 January, pp. 58–63.
Harding, R. (1979) *Outside Interference* (Melbourne, Sun Books).
Henderson, B. (1985) 'The Case for Two Systems', *The Observer*, 1 September, p. 8.
Hetherington, A. (1985) 'The Empire that won't Strike Back', *Guardian*, 2 September, p. 13.
Hill (Lord) (1974) *Behind the Screen* (London: Sidgwick & Jackson).
Hoffmann-Lange, U. (1985) 'Eliten Zwischen Alter und Neuer Politik', Manuskript für: Klingeman, H. D. and Kaase, M. (eds) *Wahlen und Politischer Prozess* (Opladen: Westdeutscher Verlag).
Howard, G. (1982) 'Broadcasting and Politics', speech given at Hull College, 26 April (a BBC publication).
Humphrey, S. (1984) 'At Grassroots the View is Choked with Weeds', *Weekend Australian*, 18–19 August, pp. 15, 17.
Inglis, K. S. (1983) *This is the ABC* (Melbourne: Melbourne University Press).
Israel Broadcasting Authority (1983) *Guidelines for News and Public Affairs* (an internal Israel Broadcasting Authority publication) (Hebrew).
Jacob, A. (1985) 'How I Got Padlocked by MI5 in Auntie's Bosom', *The Observer*, 25 August, p. 8.
Johnson, N. (1973) *Government in the Federal Republic of Germany* (Oxford: Pergamon Press).
Kaltefleiter, W. (1985) 'The New Media – A Chance for Pluralism?', paper presented at the International Political Science Association Congress, Paris, July.
Keller, S. (1963) *Beyond the Ruling Class* (New York: Random House).
Kellner, P. (1985) 'In Defence of Brittan', *The Times*, 28 August, p. 10.
Kepplinger, H. M. (1982) *Massenkommunikation* (Stuttgart: Teubner).
Kepplinger, H. M. (1983) 'Political Parties: Communications Policy in the FRG', *Gazette*, 32, pp. 169–78.
Kepplinger, H. M. (1985) *Die Aktuelle Berichterstattung des Hörfunks* (Freiburg: Verlag Karl Alber).
Kramer, L. (1983) 'Leonie Kramer Replies to Takeover Charge', *Bulletin*, 8 February, pp. 29–30.
Krüger, U. M. (1985) 'Soft News', *Media Perspektiven*, no. 6, pp. 479–91 (German).
Kutteroff, A. (1984) 'Politische Macht und Massenmedien', in Kalter, J. W., Fenner, C. and Greuen M. T. (eds) *Politische Willensbildung und Interessenvermittlung* (Opladen: Westdeutscher Verlag).

Kutteroff, A. and Wolf, G. (1985) 'Moderne Massenmedien' (unpublished).
Lipset, S. M. (1965) *Sociology of Democracy* (Neuwied: Luchterland).
Lipski, S. (1981) 'The Dix Report Still Lives', *Bulletin*, 8 December, p. 39.
Lloyd, C. (1985) *Profession: Journalist* (Sydney: Hale & Iremonger).
McAdam, A. (1983a) 'A Red Scare on Radio', *Bulletin*, 25 January, pp. 25–7.
McAdam, A. (1983b) 'Critic Replies to Letter by Kramer', *Bulletin* 15 February, p. 31.
McQueen, H. (1977) *Australia's Media Monopolies* (Melbourne: Visa).
Mandel, E. (1975 *Late Capitalism* (translated by J. de Bres) (London: New Left Books) revised edn.
Mathes, R. (1985) 'Der Publizistiche Konflikt um das Moderationsverbot für Franz Alt' (Mainz: Institut für publizistik) (unpublished).
May, F. (1978) 'Zwei Dezennien der Etnwicklung des Öffentlich-Rechtlichen Rundfuntsystems', in Geiger *et al.*, *Der Öffentlich-Rechtliche Rundfunk*, pp. 44–59.
Meynaud, J. (1964) *Technocracy*, (translated by P. Barnes) (London: Faber & Faber).
Miliband, R. (1973) *The State in Capitalist Society* (London: Quartet Books).
Mills, C. W. (1959) *The Power Elite* (New York: Oxford University Press).
Minutes of BBC News and Current Affairs Meetings (1985) (unpublished)
Mish'al, N. (1978) 'Israel Broadcasting Authority – Political Dynamics', MA thesis, (Ramat Gan: Bar Ilan University) (Hebrew).
Mosca, G. (1939) *The Ruling Class* (translated by H. D. Kahn) (New York: McGraw Hill).
Noelle-Neumann, E. (1980) *Die Schweige Spirale* (München: Riper Verlag).
Norgard, J. D. (1981) 'The Future of National Broadcasting in Australia', the C. G. Lewis Memorial Lecture, delivered at the Australian Institute of Public Administration, Adelaide, 14 October, *Scan*, October–November.
O'Brien, C. C. (1985) 'Terror and Television', *Time and Tide*, Autumn, pp. 21–3.
O'Connor, J. (1978) 'The Democratic Movement in the United States', *Kapitalistate*, 7, pp. 15–26.
Pal, M. (1980) 'Public Pressure Groups in Broadcasting', in Dwyer, D. (ed.) *Broadcasting in Australia*, pp. 137–43.
Papo, A. (1980a) 'Television and the PLO', *Ha'aretz*, 13 May, p. 14 (Hebrew).
Papo, A. (1980b) 'The Government and Television', *Ha'aretz*, 24 June, p. 13 (Hebrew).
Paulu, B. (1981) *Television and Radio in the United Kingdom*, (London: Macmillan).
Paz-Melamed, Y. (1985a) 'Israeli Television Needs no Director', *Ma'ariv*, 13 September, p. 18 (Hebrew).
Paz-Melamed, Y. (1985b) ' "Wolf" on the Second Channel', *Ma'ariv*, 18 October, p. 20 (Hebrew).
Peleg, I. (1981) 'Objectivity in Television News', Ph.D. dissertation (Jerusalem: Hebrew University) (Hebrew).
Peters, B. G. (1978) *The Politics of Bureaucracy* (New York: Longman).
Poulantzas, N. (1978) *State, Power, Socialism* (translated by P. Camiller) (London: New Left Books).

References

Riese, H. P. (1984) *Der Griff Nach der Vierten Gewalt* (Köln: Bundverlag).
Ron'el, I. and Cohen, A. (1985) 'The Race over the Second Channel', *Al Hamishmar*, 20 September, pp. 5–7 (Hebrew).
Rowat, D. C. (1985) 'Bureaucracy and Policy Making in Developed Democracies', paper presented at the International Political Science Association Congress, Paris, July.
Salpeter, E. and Elizur, Y. (1973) *The Establishment* (Tel-Aviv: Levin-Epstein) (Hebrew).
Samuel, E. (1970) *A Lifetime in Jerusalem* (London: Valentine Mitchell).
Schlesinger, P. (1978) *Putting Reality Together* (London: Constable).
Schumpeter, J. A. (1976) *Capitalism, Socialism and Democracy* (London: Allen & Unwin) 5th edn.
Seeman, K. (1980) 'Die Politisierung der Ministerial-Bürokatie in der Parteiendemokratie als Problem der Regierbarkeit', *Die Verwaltung* no, 13, pp. 137–56.
Seeman, K. (1981) 'Gewaltenteilung und Parteipolitische Ämterpatronage' *Die Verwaltung*, no. 2, pp. 133–56.
Segal, M. (1983) 'Objectivity is When I Agree with What You Say'. *Jerusalem Post*, 3 March, p. 5.
Semmler, C (1981) *The ABC: Aunt Sally and the Sacred Cow*, (Carlton, Victoria: Melbourne University Press).
Semmler, C. (1983) 'As Difficult as ABC', *Bulletin*, 24 May, p. 32.
Sheridan, G. (1984) 'The ABC's Crisis of Confidence', *Weekend Australian*, 18–19 August, p. 15.
Simper, E. (1983), 'To Stir the Devil's Brew . . . ' *Australian*, November 5–6, p. 12.
Spranger, C-D (1985) 'Die Persönliche Meinung' *Münchener Merkur*, 22 June, p. 4.
Summers, S. (1985) 'Mr Cool in the Hot Seat', *Sunday Times*, 25 August, p. 7.
Swann, M. (1978a) 'BBC and IBA' 20 February (a BBC publication).
Swann, M. (1978b) 'On Disliking the Media', lecture at the University of Salford, 7 November (a BBC publication).
Therborn, G. (1977) 'The Rule of Capitalism and the Rise of Democracy', *New Left Review*, 103, pp. 3–41.
Therborn, G. (1978) *What Does the Ruling Class Do When it Rules?* (London: New Left Books).
Thomas, A. (1980) *Broadcast and Be Damned* (Melbourne: Melbourne University Press).
Tracey, M. (1983) *A Variety of Lives* (London: Bodley Head).
Tunstall, J. (1977) *The Media Are American* (London: Constable).
Tunstall, J. (1983) *The Media in Britain* (New York: Columbia University Press).
Ullswater (Lord) (1936) *Report of the Broadcasting Committee*, (the Ullswater Report) Cmnd 2599.
Von Beyme, K. (1983) *The Political System of the Federal Republic of Germany* (New York: St Martin's Press).
Walsh, M. (1983) 'New Focus on ABC Bill', *Bulletin*, 10 May, p. 24.
Ward, P. (1985) 'Can Aunty be Saved?' *Australian Weekend* 12–13 January, pp. 1, 14.

Wass, D. (1985) 'The Civil Service at the Crossroads', *Political Quarterly*, July–September, 56, pp. 227–41.
Watt, D. (1985) 'Peacock's Mid-Term Blues', *The Times*, 6 December, p. 16.
Wilfert, O. (1976) 'Gewerkschaftsarbeit im Rundfunk', in Kotterheinrich, M., Neveling, U., Paetzold, U. and Schmidt, H. (eds) *Rundfunkpolitische Kontroversen* (Frankfurt: Europäische Verlaganstalt).
Wilfert, O. (1984) 'Referat des Personalratsvorsitzenden zur Ausserondentlichen Personalversammlung am 8.2.84' (unpublished).
Williams, A. (1976) *Broadcasting and Democracy in West Germany* (London: Bradford University Press).
Williams, R. (1982) 'Starving Auntie', *New Journalist*, no. 38, May, pp. 6–7.
Wittich, E. (1983) 'Communication Policy in the Federal Republic of Germany', in Edgar, P. and Rahim, S. A. (eds) *Communication Policy in Developed Countries* (London: Routledge & Kegan Paul) pp. 167–216.
Yefet, Z. (1985) 'All Moonlighting Leads to London', *Ha'aretz*, 1 November, p. 15 (Hebrew).
ZDF (1963) 'Richtlinien für Sendungen des Zweiten Deutschen Fernsehens', 11 July.
ZDF (1976) 'Grundregeln für die Zusammenarbeit im ZDF' (Leitordnung) 1 December (a ZDF publication).
ZDF (1984) *ZDF Jahrbuch* (a ZDF publication).
Zedaka, S. (1985) 'Facelift for Britain's Government', *Ha'aretz*, 29 September, p. 14 (Hebrew).
Zimmer, V. (1982) 'Politisierung oder Professionalisierung?' (unpublished).

Index

Notes: (1) Most references are to both radio and television. (2) References to political parties in the countries concerned may be found within the country entries themselves.

ABC (Australian Broadcasting Commission), *see* Australia
abortion, programme on, 125
Adenauer, K., 21, 23, 34, 35–6, 208
advertising
  committee of review on, *see* Peacock
  private, *see* privatisation
  revenue of, 65, 67, 69
  see also commercial
Aharonson, S., 19, 27, 118, 169, 181
Al-Hamishmar (Israel), 135
Almog, S., 33, 101
Almost Midnight (programme, Israel), 156
Aloni, Y., 199
Alt, F., 157, 166, 200–1
ambiguities, 7–8, 24–37, 204
  legal, 24–9
  normative, 30–6
  in rules and regulations, 29–30
  see also dilemmas; friction and conflict; internal pressures
analysis, framework of, 3–10
  theoretical background, 3–6
  theses and hypotheses, 7–10
  see also dilemmas
Annan, Lord and Report (Britain, 1977), 45, 59, 89, 90, 208–9
appointments and promotions
  external pressures through, 89–106, 209: Australia, 91–2, 96–8, 100–1, 105; Britain, 89–91, 94, 95–6, 99–100, 105; directors-general, 99–104; Israel, 92–3, 98, 101–2, 105; West Germany, 93–5, 98–9, 102–4, 105
  internal pressures through, 127–42:

Australia, 131–3, 141; Britain, 127–30, 141–2; Israel, 133–7, 141–2; West Germany, 137–41
see also boards
Arabs, 119
ARD (Arbeitsgemeinschaft der öffentlich-rechtlichen, etc.), 21, 22, 54, 55, 81–3, 84, 140, 171
Aron, R., 4
Ashbolt, A., 114, 154–5, 178
ASIO, *see* Australian Security, etc.
associations and movements, resistance through, 167–73, 174
'Auntie's Nieces and Nephews' (Australia), 164
Australia (ABC), 9–10, 204, 207–11 *passim*
  ambiguities: legal, regulatory and normative, 25–6, 29–30, 31–3
  appointments, 91–2, 96–8, 100–1, 105
  external pressures: direct intervention, 47–51, 56; funding, 61–4, 69, 164; privatisation, 76–8, 87; *see also* appointments *above*
  friction and conflict: *Four Corners* case, 192–6, 203
  historical setting, 14–16
  internal pressures: boards, management and peers, 112–16, 126; dismissal and demotion, 145–50 160; displacement, 154–5, 159; *see also* appointments *above*
  legislation/legal status/regulations, 15, 25–6, 29–30, 31–3, 145
  resistance to pressures, 164–5,

219

167–9, 173–4, 176–8, 185
Australian, The, 9, 49
Australian Broadcasting Commission, *see* Australia
Australian Financial Review, 112
Australian Journalists' Association, 167–8
Australian Labor Party, 59
Australian Security Intelligence Organisation, 133
Austria: satellite television, 82

Barnett, Lord, 10, 106
Baum, I., 182
Bausch, H.
 on external pressures, 54, 67–8, 85
 on independence, 35, 104, 186
 on internal pressures, 103, 121
Bayrischer Rundfunk, 20, 93, 166
BBC (British Broadcasting Corporation), *see* Britain
Begin, M., 52, 102
Ben Gurion, D., 17–18, 23, 208
Berry, M., 165
BETA, *see* Broadcasting Entertainments, etc.
Bland, Sir H., 97
boards
 external pressures through, 89–95: chairmen of, 95–9
 management and peers, internal pressures from, 109–26: Australia, 112–16, 126; Britain, 109–12, 125–6; Israel, 116–21, 126; West Germany, 121–5, 126; *see also* appointments; management
Bond, T., 97, 113
Bowers, P., 113
BR, *see* Bayrischer Rundfunk
Briggs, A.
 on conventions, 25
 on external pressures, 12–14, 41, 43, 89, 178
 on internal pressures, 108, 110
Britain (BBC), 8, 9–10, 204, 206–11 *passim*
 ambiguities: legal, regulatory and normative, 24–5, 29, 30–1

appointments, 89–91, 94, 95–6, 99–100, 105
external pressures: direct intervention, 41–7, 57; funding, 58–60, 69; privatisation, 71–6, 87–8; *see also* appointments *above*
friction and conflict: Christmas tree case, 129, 188–92, 203
historical setting, 11–14
influence on and comparison with other systems, 11, 207–8; Australia, 14–16, 22, 26–7, 115, 132, 207; Israel, 16–18, 23, 27, 51, 53, 208; West Germany, 20, 23, 28, 34, 141, 208
internal pressures: boards, management and peers, 109–12, 125–6; dismissal and demotion, 143–5, 160; displacement, 153–4, 159; *see also* appointments *above*
legislation/legal status/regulations, 24–5, 29, 30–1, 91
resistance to pressures, 163–4, 167, 173, 175–8, 180, 184
British Broadcasting Corporation, *see* Britain
Brittan, L., 45–6
Broadband (programme, Australia), 155
Broadcasting Entertainments Trade Alliance (Britain), 167
Broadcasting, Television and Film Union (West Germany), 170
broadcasting, national, *see* ambiguities; analysis; external political pressures; friction and conflict; historical; internal political pressures; resistance
Broder, H.M., 124
Brooks, R., 72
Bulletin (Australia), 174, 177
bureaucracies, 5
 non-partisan, 9: *see also* Australia; Britain
 party-politicised, 5, 9–10: *see also* Israel; West Germany
Burghart, H., 138, 180
Burns, T., 12, 13, 41, 109, 110, 153, 184

Index

Button, J., 32, 97, 132, 193–4, 195

cable television, 71, 72, 76, 80, 81, 82
Canberra Times, 32, 193–4
casual, *see* temporary workers
caution, excessive (BBC), 43, 99, 208–9
chairmen of boards, 95–9
Cohen, A., 80
commercial broadcasting, beginning of, 11, 14, 21
  see also advertising; privatisation
commissions, *see* boards
competition, *see* privatisation
complaints and threats, *see* external pressures
Conder, W., 15
conflict, *see* friction
Conrad, H.W., 21
contract workers, 144–5, 146, 149, 152, 160, 210
contradictions, *see* dilemmas
Coombs, H.C. and Commission (Australia), 26, 32
co-operative, working, *see* ARD
countervailing power, 4–5
Cox, B. 190
Crawford Lord and Report (1926), 12, 31
credibility ethos and resistance, 175–81
Crisp, L., 63, 207
Curran, Sir C., 109, 176
Curtin, J., 32

Daily Telegraph, The (Britain), 91
Davis, G., 14–15, 62, 113, 116, 132, 145
Deamer, A., 116
decentralised system, *see* West Germany
default, resistance by, 181–3
democratic-élitist perspective, 3–5
Department of Broadcasting (Israel), 17
Department of Communications (Australia), 16
Department of Interior (West Germany), 55

Department of Media (Australia), 16
Departments of Posts and Telephones
  Australia, 16
  Israel, 17
Deutsche Welle, 20, 67, 93
Deutschlandfunk, 20, 67, 93
dilemmas
  of broadcasting, 6–7
  of bureaucracy, 5–6
  of democracy, 4
  see also ambiguities
direct intervention, external pressures through, 41–57, 204
  Australia, 47–51, 56
  Britain, 41–7, 57
  Israel, 51–3, 56
  West Germany, 53–6
directorship case in Israel, 196–9, 203
dismissal and demotion, internal pressures through, 143–53, 159–60, 206, 210
  Australia, 145–50, 160
  Britain, 143–5, 160
  Israel, 150–1, 160, 169
  West Germany, 152–3, 160
  see also displacement
displacement, internal pressures through, 153–60, 206
  Australia, 154–5, 159
  Britain, 153–4, 159
  Israel, 155–7, 159, 169
  West Germany, 157–9, 200–1, 203
  see also dismissal
Dix, A.T. and Report (Australia, 1981), 14, 25–6, 32–3, 62, 77, 91
DLF, *see* Deutschlandfunk
Dogan, M., 5
Donsbach, W., 179
Duckmanton, Sir T., 100
Duffy (Australian communications minister), 195
Duffy, M., 48, 49
duopoly, *see* West Germany
DW, *see* Deutsche Welle
Dye, T.R., 210

Economist, The (Britain), 58, 207

Eden, A., 14
Edinburgh Conference (1985), 31, 190
educational representation and resistance, 163–4
élites, 3–5, 89, 91, 210–11
Elizur, Y., 19, 102
Ellul, J., 5
Eshkol, L., 18
ethos, conforming with, *see* self-censorship
Etzioni-Halevy, E., 9–10
External Services (Britain), 47, 175
external political pressures, *see* appointments; direct intervention; funding; privatisation
Ezard, J., 13

Falklands War, 43–4, 96, 207
Ferguson, T., 146
files, secret, Christmas tree symbol on, 129, 188–92, 203
finances, *see* funding
Focus (programme, Israel), 120
Foreign Office (Britain), 47
Foster, Judge A.W., 15
Foulkes (British politician), 189
Four Corners (programme, Australia), 98, 193–5
France: satellite television, 71
Francis, R., 110
Fraser (Australian prime minister), 61, 63, 97, 194
freelances, *see* temporary workers
Frenkel, S., 117
Freundeskreise ('circles of friends'), 95
friction and confict: case-studies, 188–203, 206–7
 Australia: *Four Corners* case, 192–6, 203
 Britain: Christmas tree case, 129, 188–92, 203
 Israel: directorship case, 196–9, 203
 West Germany: displacement case, 200–2, 203
Fuchs, Y., 98
funding, external pressures through, 58–70, 204, 205
 Australia, 61–4, 69, 164
 Britain, 58–60, 69
 Israel, 65–6, 69
 West Germany, 67–9
 see also advertising

Geiger, W., 35
German Employees' Union, 170
Germany, *see* West Germany
Givton, H. 18
Glasgow University Media Group, 44
Gotliffe, H.L., 17, 18, 19
governors, *see* boards
grants, *see* funding
Grattan, M., 49
Green, F.J., 32
Greene, H. (later Sir)
 and external pressures, 8, 14, 43, 45, 91
 and independence/impartiality, 99, 100, 177
 and internal pressures, 116
 and Israel, 27, 51, 168
Gremien (supervisory organs), 93
Greulich, H., 122, 124
Guardian (Britain), 44, 45, 47, 72, 73, 90–1, 112, 189, 191
guidance from above, *see* internal pressures
Guidelines for News and Current Affairs (Israel), 30

Ha'aretz (Israel), 199
Haagen, B.-U., 82
Halabi, R., 156, 169
Harding, R., 48
Hawke, R., 48, 49, 50, 62–3, 97, 194, 195
Hayden, W., 49
Hessischer Rundfunk, 20, 93, 171
Hilf, W., 200
Hill, D. 98, 101
Hill, Lord, 59, 95, 99, 110
Hilton, I., 130
historical setting, 11–23
 Australia, 14–16
 Britain, 11–14

Index

Israel, 16–19
    West Germany, 19–22
Hoffmann-Lange, U., 140
Holzammer, K., 103
Home Office/Home Secretary
    (Britain), 11, 16, 45, 59, 181,
    191
Howard, G., 12, 24, 44
Howard, J., 193
HR, *see* Hessischer Rundfunk
Humphrey, S., 64
Hussein, King, 80
Hussey, M. 96

IBA, *see* Independent Broadcasting
    Authority
impartiality, 29–30
    see also independence
implied pressures, *see* internal
    pressures
inconsistencies, *see* ambiguities
independence of broadcasting, 7–9,
    12
    ambiguities with respect to, 24–9,
    30–6
    ethos and resistance, 175–81
    myth of, 111
    see also pressures
Independent Broadcasting Authority
    (Britain), 71, 73, 75, 209
informal relations and contacts, 41,
    46–7, 50–1, 53, 56–7
Inglis, K.
    on independence, 31
    on internal pressures, 154–5
    on resistance, 164, 168
    on external pressures, 15, 16, 48,
    62, 97
intendant, *see* directors-general
interference, *see* pressures
internal guidelines, 29–30
internal political pressures, *see*
    appointments; board; dismissal;
    displacement
intervention, *see* pressures
IRA, *see* Northern Ireland
Israel, 9–10, 204, 206–11 *passim*
    ambiguities: legal, regulatory and
    normative, 27, 30, 33–4

appointments, 92–3, 98, 101–2,
    105
external pressures: direct
    intervention, 51–3, 56; funding,
    65–6, 69; privatisation, 78–81,
    87; *see also* appointments *above*
friction and conflict: directorship
    case, 196–9, 203
historical setting, 16–19
internal pressures: boards,
    management and peers, 116–21,
    126; dismissal and demotion,
    150–1, 160, 169; displacement,
    155–7, 159, 169; *see also*
    appointments *above*
legislation/legal status/regulations,
    18, 27, 30, 33–4, 66, 79, 80, 92,
    118, 182
resistance to pressures: 165–6,
    168–9, 173, 176, 179, 181–2,
    184–5
Israeli Broadcasting Service, *see*
    Israel
ITV, *see* Independent Broadcasting
    Authority

Jacob, A., 130
Jennings (general manager,
    Australia), 100
Journalist, The (Australia), 30, 74, 146
Journalists' Association (West
    Germany), 170

Kaase, M., 140
Kaltefleiter, W., 82
Keating, P., 174
Keller, S., 4, 8
Kellner, P., 45, 57
Kepplinger, H.M., 35, 72, 93, 140,
    152–3
Kohl, Chancellor, 200
Kramer, Dame L.
    and external pressures, 61, 63, 97
    and internal pressures, 113, 155
    and resistance to pressures, 177,
    185, 195
    and unions, 168
Krüger, U.M., 86
Kutteroff, A., 56, 138, 140

Lapid, Y.
    on external pressures, 52, 65
    on independence, 27, 33–4, 180–1, 184–5
    on internal pressures, 116, 117, 118, 134, 135, 150, 156
law, *see* legislation
legislation/legal status/regulations
    Australia, 15, 25–6, 29–30, 31–3, 145
    Britain, 24–5, 29, 30–1, 91
    Israel, 18, 27, 30, 33–4, 66, 79, 80, 92, 118, 182
    West Germany, 20, 21, 27–8, 30, 34–6, 81, 83, 93, 152, 166, 173
Lev-Ari, G., 135, 136
licence fees, 58–61, 65, 67, 68–9, 75–6
Lipset, S.M., 4
Lipski, S., 114
Livni, Y., 101
Lloyd, G., 133
London, Y., 156, 169

Ma'ariv (Israel), 198
Mabat (programme, Israel), 198
McAdam, A., 114, 155
Mai, F., 104, 179
Maier, R., 35
management, 209
    ineffectiveness, resistance through, 181–3, 185
    intervention, *see* internal pressures
    see also board; chairmen; directors-general
managing director, *see* directors-general
Mandel, E., 5
Mannheim Elite Study Group (West Germany), 56, 140
Marxism, 3
Mathes, R., 200
Mazpen (group), 137
Menzies, R., 14
Meynaud, J., 6
MI5 (Britain), *see under* security vetting
Milne, A., 44, 99–100, 189
Ministries of Communications
    Australia, 48, 62, 168

Israel, 79
Ministry of Education and Culture (Israel), 18, 79, 134
Ministry of Information (Britain), 13
Mish'al, N., 17–18
monopoly, threatened, *see* privatisation
Mosca, G., 4
Moses, Sir C., 100
Myer, K., 97–8

Nathan, A., 78
National, The (programme, Australia), 88n
national conflicts (Britain), 43
    see also Falklands; *Real Lives*
National Union of Journalists (Britain), 144, 167, 189
National Viewers' and Listeners' Association (Britain), 45
Nazis, viii, 19, 35
NDR, *see* Norddeutscher Rundfunk
News and Current Affairs Index (Britain), 29
newspapers/journals
    Australia: external pressures as reported in, 9, 30, 32, 42, 49, 78; friction and conflict as reported in, 193–4; internal pressures, 112–13, 156, 174; resistance to pressures, 177
    Britain: accountability, 31; external pressures, 44–7, 58–9, 71, 72–4, 76, 90–1, 130, 207; friction and conflict, 188–91; internal pressures, 112, 144–5, 206; resistance to pressures, 164
    Israel, 198, 199
    West Germany, 55, 104, 135, 207
    see also individual names
Noelle-Neumann, E., 53–4
non-elected elite, 5, 7
non-partisan bureaucracies, 9
    see also Australia; Britain
Norddeutscher Rundfunk, 20, 93, 121, 171
Norgard, J.D., 97
normative ambiguities, 30–6

Index

Northern Ireland, 59
  see also Real Lives
NUJ, see National Union of
  Journalists

objective ethos and resistance, 175–81
Observer, The (Britain), 47, 130, 188–91
O'Connor, J., 5
Ogilvie, F., 13
One Plus (programme, West Germany), 82

Palestine Broadcasting Service, 16
Palestine Liberation Organisation, 137
Panorama (programme, West Germany), 157
Papo, A., 34, 133–4, 181
Papua New Guinea: complaint from, 98, 114
party-politicised bureaucracies, 5, 9–10
  see also Israel; political; West Germany
Paulu, B., 14, 41, 59, 89, 90, 95, 177
pay-as-you-view system, 76
Paz-Melamed, Y., 80, 120, 198
Peacock, A. and Report (Britain, 1986), 72–6, 190
Peleg, I., 180
Peters, B.G., 6
pluralist theory of democracy, 4
political parties and politicians: influence
  ambiguities and, 35–6
  by, see external pressures
  for, see internal pressures
  historical, 12–1, 16, 17–18, 21
  popularisation, 87–8
  see also privatisation
Porat, U., 65, 102, 117, 151, 156, 181–2, 196, 198, 206
Postmasters-General
  Australia, 16
  Britain, 11–12
Poulantzas, N., 5
power struggles, 4–6
  see also pressures
press, see newspapers
pressures, see external; internal; resistance
privatisation, external pressures through, 71–88, 204–5
  Australia, 76–8, 87
  Britain, 71–6, 87–8
  Israel, 78–81, 87
  West Germany, 81–6, 87
  see also commercial
professionalism, see objectivity
programmes, specific
  Australia, 47, 77, 88n, 155: conflict over, 98, 192–6, 203
  Britain, 41, 74, 99, 110, 153: see also Real Lives
  Israel, 120, 156, 198
  removal of staff from, see displacement
  West Germany, 82, 157, 200
  see also named programmes
promotions, see appointments
Propaganda Ministry (West Germany), 19
Proporz principle (West Germany), 138–9, 183, 202, 209
public representation, see boards
publicity, 6–7, 47
  directorship and (Israel), 196–9, 203
  displacement and (West Germany), 200–2, 203
  Four Corners and (Israel), 192–6, 203
  resistance through, 163–7, 173, 175
  security vetting and (Britain), 129, 188–92, 203
  see also newspapers

Question of Ulster, The (programme, Britain), 41

Radio Bremen, 20, 93
Radio One and Two (Britain), 76
Radio Stuttgart, 35
radio, see preliminary note
RB (Radio Bremen), 20, 93
Real Lives (programme, Britain),

44–6, 90, 96, 100, 110, 145, 163, 167, 175, 189–90, 192
redeployment, 145–6
redundancy, 143, 144, 145–6, 148
regulations, *see* legislation
Reith, J., 12, 13, 110
reorganization (Australia), 147–9
Report (programme, West Germany), 200
resistance to pressures, 7–8, 163–87, 204
  by default, 181–3
  through independence, credibility and objectivity ethos, 175–81
  through publicity, 163–7, 173, 175
  related issues, 183–6
  through staff associations, 167–73, 174
retirement, early, 143
retrenchment (Israel), 150–1
revenue, *see* funding
Riese, H.P., 35, 172, 176, 180, 200
Roeh, Y., 120, 155–6
Ron'el, I., 80
Rowat, D.C., 10
Royal Charter (Britain), 11, 14, 24, 31
Royal Commissions (Australia), 26, 32, 194
Rubinstein, A., 79, 80
Rugby League, *see* Four Corners
rules and regulations, ambiguities in, 29–30
  see also legislation

Saarländischer Rundfunk, 20, 93
Salpeter, E., 19, 102
Samuel, E., 16–17
SAT 1 & 3 Sat (satellite television), 82, 85
satellite television, 71–2, 76, 77, 78, 81, 82
Scan, 59, 71, 78
Schlesinger, P., 95, 110–12, 153, 178, 180
Schumpeter, J.A., 4
SDR, *see* Süddeutscher Rundfunk
secret files, *see* files

security vetting
  in Australia, 133
  in Britain, 13, 100, 129–30, 189–91, 203
  in Israel, 137, 142
  in West Germany (lack of), 141
Seeman, K., 10
Segal, M., 120, 178
selection, *see* appointments
selectivity, 178
self-censorship, 111–12, 115–16, 120, 124, 126, 147, 158, 210
self-displacement, 158
Semmler, C., 48, 91, 110, 195–6
Sender Freies Berlin, 20, 93
Senior Officers Association (Australia), 148, 167
SFB, *see* Sender Freies Berlin
Sheridan, G., 148
Shilon, D., 196–8
Shinui (Israel), 79
Simper, E., 61, 206
Singer, A., 90
Sixty Minutes programmes
  Australia, 77
  Britain, 74
Special Broadcasting Service (Australia), 63
Spiegel, Der (West Germany), 55, 104, 207
Spranger, C.-D., 55–6
SR, *see* Saarländischer Rundfunk
staff associations, resistance through, 167–73, 174
  see also internal pressures
Staley, T., 62
Statutes Movement (West Germany), 171–3
Steel, D., 45, 73, 189
Stolte, D., 85, 103, 104, 125, 152, 186
Süddeutscher Rundfunk, 20, 93
Südwestfunk, 20, 157, 166, 200
Suez Crisis (1956), 14, 41–2
Summers, S., 100
Sunday Times (Britain), 31, 45, 190
supervisory organs in West Germany (*Gremien*), 93
Swann, M., 109, 110
SWF, *see* Südwestfunk

Index

Switzerland: satellite television, 82
Sydney Morning Herald, 42, 113

television
  establishment of, ix, 19, 21–2
  limited in Israel, 52
  see also cable; satellite *and preliminary note*
temporary workers (casual and freelancers), 144–5, 146, 152–3, 160, 210
That Was The Week That Was (programme, Britain), 41, 99
Thatcher, M., 9, 42, 44–6, 73, 75, 89, 90, 207
This Day Tonight (programme, Australia), 47
Thomas, A., 15
threats, *see* complaints
3ZZ (station, Australia), 62
Time, 130
Times, The (Britain), 45, 46–7, 72, 76, 91, 130, 144–5, 164, 190–1
Tracey, M., 99
Trethowan, I., 99
TV SAT (satellite television), 82
2JJ (station, Australia), 62

Ullswater Report (Britain, 1936), 12
unions
  and dismissals and displacements, 144, 145, 147, 155
  and resistance, 167, 170, 171
  satellites and, 78
United States, viii, 198–9

values, conforming with, *see* self-censorship
vetting, *see* security
Vogel, B., 98
'Voice of Israel', 17–18
  see also Israel
'Voice of Peace' (Israel, pirate radio), 78
von Beyme, K., 10
von Hase, K.G., 103, 125

Wallenreiter, C., 104
Walsh, M., 195
War, Second World, effect of, 13, 19–20, 94
Wass, D., 9
WDR, *see* Westdeutscher Rundfunk
Wedgewood Benn, A., 37
Week, The (programme, Israel), 120
Wells, H.G., 15
West Germany (mainly ZDF), 9–10, 204, 206–11 *passim*
  ambiguities: legal, regulatory and normative, 27–8, 30, 34–6
  appointments, 93–5, 98–9, 102–4, 105
  external pressures: direct intervention, 53–6; funding, 67–9; privatisation, 81–6, 87; *see also* appointments *above*
  friction and conflict: displacement case, 200–2, 203
  historical setting, 19–22
  internal pressures: boards, management and peers, 121–5, 126; dismissal and demotion, 152–3, 160; displacement, 157–9, 200–2, 203; *see also* appointments *above*
  legislation/legal status/regulations, 20, 21, 27–28, 30, 34–6, 81, 83, 93, 152, 166, 173
  resistance to pressures, 166, 170–3, 176–7, 179–80, 183–4, 186
Westdeutscher Rundfunk, 20, 93
Whitehead, G., 100–1, 174
Whitehouse, M., 45
Wildenman, R., 140
Wilfert, O., 81
Williams, A.
  on external pressures, 20–2, 35, 94–5
  on internal pressures, 121, 122, 171
  on resistance, 166
Williams, R., 62, 63
Wilson, H., 41, 59, 95, 99, 110
Wittich, E., 20, 35, 104, 171
Wolf, G., 138
Wran, N., 192–4

Yaron, R., 98

Yavin, H., 134, 196–9
Yesterday's Men (programme, Britain), 41, 110, 155
Yinon, M., 98
Young, S., 73, 95–6

ZDF, *see* Zweites Deutches Fernsehen

Zedaka, S., 46
Zeigler, L.H., 210
Zemach, Y., 196, 198
Zweites Deutches Fernsehen, ix, 22, 93
  see also West Germany

HE 8689 .6 .E89 1987

DATE DUE